THE THEATRE OF ENDA WALSH

THE THEATRE OF ENDA WALSH

edited by

Mary P. Caulfield and Ian R. Walsh

Carysfort Press

A Carysfort Press Book

The Theatre of Enda Walsh
Edited by Mary P. Caulfield and Ian R. Walsh

First published in Ireland in 2015 as a paperback original by
Carysfort Press, 58 Woodfield, Scholarstown Road
Dublin 16, Ireland

ISBN 978-1-909325-77-7
©2015 Copyright remains with the authors

Typeset by Carysfort Press
Cover design by eprint limited
Printed and bound by eprint limited
Unit 35
Coolmine Industrial Estate
Dublin 15
Ireland

This book is published with the financial assistance of
The Arts Council (An Chomhairle Ealaíon) Dublin, Ireland

Table of Contents

Acknowledgements

We are grateful for the editorial guidance and patience of Eamonn Jordan and the staff at Carysfort Press who were tremendously supportive throughout the project. The editors would also like to thank the Arts Council of Ireland whose Title by Title Grant supports this project.

Many of the essays in this book result from the relationships that blossomed at the annual conferences hosted by the Irish Society for Theatre Research. The editors would like to offer their deep gratitude to the Society.

This book would not have been possible without the outstanding work from our contributors, whose passionate knowledge of Irish theatre was commensurate with their tireless commitment to the project. The editors would like to extend our sincere thanks to all who contributed to this book.

Ian R. Walsh would like to thank the staff, students, and faculty of Drama, Theatre and Performance at NUI Galway and Drama Studies at UCD, in particular Cathy Leeney for reading many of the articles; James and Esther Walsh, Anne and Conor O'Kelly, Niamh Walsh, Vivienne, Denis and Gavin O'Kelly.

Mary P. Caulfield would also like to thank the staff, students, and faculty of the Department of Drama at Trinity College Dublin and of the English Department at the State University of New York at Farmingdale; Dolores and Jack Caulfield, Scott and John Caulfield; B, M, and M Caulfield-DiBlasi; Nancy and Joseph DiBlasi; Christopher Collins, Michael Jaros, Marcia Littenberg, Holly Maples, Brian Singleton, and Melissa Sihra.

Finally, the editors would like to thank Matthew DiBlasi and Antonia, William and Isabelle Walsh to whom this book is dedicated.

Introduction

For director and actor Mikel Murfi, writing in this collection, Enda Walsh "is a theatre-maker like no other. He is radical in his approach to form, technique and text. With Walsh there are no limitations". Walsh is one of Ireland's most internationally successful, award winning and critically regarded playwrights, but yet his work has been neglected by theatre scholarship. This publication is the first collection of essays on Walsh's work and as such is an important intervention that seeks to address this concern. In a wide range of essays, this book explores Walsh's radical theatrical imagination, its development, its contexts and its ability to flourish across genres from theatre to film to musical.

Although born in Dublin, Walsh first came to prominence in Cork. His first play was for children, *Fishy Tales* and was produced by Graffiti theatre company at Pope's Quay for ACTIVATE '93 and then later produced at the Dublin Theatre Festival. But it was his work in the mid-1990s with the Cork-based Corcadorca theatre company, of which he was a founding member, that was to establish Walsh's reputation. His first work as a playwright for the company was a radical adaptation of Dickens's *A Christmas Carol* and interestingly adaptation is something that he has continued to do successfully throughout his career. This was followed by his first breakout piece *The Ginger Ale Boy* that toured to Dublin and Limerick with his flair for language and theatrical inventiveness noted in the national press. But it was his next play with the company, *Disco Pigs* (1997) starring young actors Cillian Murphy and Eileen Walsh, that was to bring his greatest early success with a host of accolades including the Stewart Parker Award, George Divine Award and The Scotland on Sunday Critics Award when presented at the Edinburgh Festival. Walsh has credited his early success with

Corcadorca to his collaboration with the director Pat Kiernan whose imaginative staging of these plays aided their success.

Disco Pigs toured internationally in 1998-1999 throughout Australia, Canada, Denmark, Hungary, the UK and Germany where it seems to have struck a particular chord. Werner Huber writing in an article on Irish plays produced in Germany writes that this play has "undoubtedly been the darling of German-speaking theatre directors and dramaturgs, with forty-two different productions between 1998 and 2001" (84). Walsh has been particularly successful in continental Europe and unlike many of his contemporaries that have seen premieres of their plays exclusively in Dublin, London or New York Walsh has instead enjoyed commissions and first productions from theatres in Munich, Lisbon and Zurich. Lisa Fitzpatrick explains the popularity of Walsh's work on the continent as due to its tendency "towards expressionism, rather than the broadly naturalistic performance style of most Irish Theatre" (451).

Sucking Dublin (1997) the play that immediately followed *Disco Pigs* was an Irish commission from the Abbey Theatre's Youth Outreach. This play, which won Walsh a second George Devine award, developed from workshops in deprived areas of Dublin and was performed at the Samuel Beckett Theatre. Walsh returned to work with Pat Kiernan in Corcadorca in 1999 writing and starring in his own monologue piece *Misterman*. This production was to be his last for the Cork-based company as he began to accept more independent commissions from festivals and theatres at home and abroad. He premiered *bedbound* (2000) as part of the Dublin Theatre Festival and this went on to the Traverse Theatre as part of 2001 Edinburgh Festival Fringe and then to The Royal Court Upstairs. Just like *Disco Pigs* before it, *bedbound* proved a hit in non-English speaking countries and has been translated into eighteen different languages.

A series of thematic commissions and adaptations from international theatres guided the work over the next few years. Walsh contributed the short play *Lynddie's Gotta Gun* at the Teatro Nacional D. Maria II, Lisbon, as part of the Conferencia de Imprensa e Outras Aldrabices that saw a group of playwrights pen sketches inspired by the work of Harold Pinter. In 2005, Walsh returned to Cork to collaborate with co-producers Asylum Productions. The result was *Pondlife Angels*, a play that takes its audience through the day-in-the-life of a Cork-city shop girl. This work was commissioned for the Cork Midsummer festival—a festival that started in 1997 as a mechanism for Cork-based artists to find a creative platform to showcase their work.

These commissioned works encouraged international collaboration and adaptation. *The Small Things* (2005) was performed by Paines Plough as part of "The Other England" Festival at the Menier Chocolate Factory. *Chatroom* (2006) was written for the National Theatre in London, as part of its NT Connections season which aimed to create a space for teenagers to debate social issues. In 2007 The Abbey Theatre and London's Barbican Theatre issued a joint commission to Walsh and the London-based theatre company Theatre O. What resulted was the collaborative effort *Delirium*. This devised and interdisciplinary piece revisited Dostoevsky's *The Brother's Karamazov* and premiered at Dublin's Peacock Theatre in 2008. Like many of Walsh's plays, most recently *Ballyturk*, *Delirium* employs music, dance, sound effects, puppetry and projected visuals, to create a multi-media theatre of the dysfunctional and dysmorphic.

Walsh's collaboration with the Galway-based Druid Theatre Company brought many of his most successful plays to life including *Penelope*, which first premiered in Ireland at the 2008 Galway International Arts Festival. In 2008 Druid would also bring *The New Electric Ballroom* (2004)—directed by Stephan Kimmig—from the Kammerspiele Theatre in Munich, to both the Galway International Arts Festival, and the Edinburgh Festival Fringe where it won an Edinburgh Fringe First Award. Drawing his inspiration from another iconic literary rendering, Walsh wrote *Penelope* (dir. by Mikel Murfi and produced by the Druid Theatre Company) as part of a special series of commissions by the Oberhausen Theatre where several international playwrights were asked to adapt a play in response to episodes from Homer's Odyssey. Based on Homer's final episode, *Penelope* met great success in its American premiere in New York City's St. Ann's Warehouse. *Penelope* would mark the third collaboration between Walsh, the Druid Theatre Company, and St. Ann's Warehouse. *The Walworth Farce*, *The New Electric Ballroom*, and *Misterman* (which initially premiered with Cork-based company Corcadorca in 1999), also held their American debuts in this Brooklyn-based theatre, which continues to champion Walsh's work.

Much like Corcadorca, the Galway International Arts Festival hosted many of Walsh's plays in their early stages of development. This was also the case with Walsh's *Ballyturk*. Similarly to his earlier *Delirium*, this 2014 collaboration with Landmark Productions and founder Anne Clarke also blended various media and techniques to bring a carnival of the grotesque to the theatre space.

Walsh says of growing up in 1980s Ireland that he and his father would often watch "The Three Stooges" films on RTÉ. It is no wonder then how his initial creative impulses were either to "form a music band or to be a filmmaker" (Billington). Walsh explored his passion for film during a very different kind of collaborative project with filmmaker Steve McQueen, which led to the creation of the film *Hunger* in 2008. The specific subject of Katarzyna Ojrzyńska's chapter, *Hunger* directed by McQueen, dramatized Irish republican Bobby Sands' controversial leadership of the hunger strikes in the Northern Irish HM MazePrison. This film premiered at the 2008 Cannes Film Festival and received the Camera d'Or award for first-time filmmakers. Additionally, *Hunger* won the Sydney Film Prize, The Grand Prix of the Belgian Syndicate of Cinema Critics, and the best picture from the Evening Standard British Film awards. Hunger would also receive two BAFTA nominations (winning one) and six IFTA awards in 2009 (having been nominated for eight). *Hunger* is the second of three cinematic renderings that Walsh would accomplish having also adapted his own original plays *Disco Pigs* (2001) *and Chatroom* (2010) into full-length feature films.

Once, Walsh's musical book adaptation of John Carney's 2007 film, would present an unusual challenge for Walsh yet earn him the Tony Award for Best Book of a Musical in 2012. This musical adaptation, discussed in greater length in Mary Caulfield's chapter on *Once*, was Walsh's first film-to-theatre adaptation—a challenge that he initially saw as a "potentially disastrous project" (Walsh). This first attempt at a musical production adds another genre to Walsh's repertoire. Under the direction of John Tiffany, *Once* saw its evolution through workshop and cabaret. It began with the American Repertory Theatre in Massachusetts in 2011 then travelled to the New York Theatre Workshop where it debuted in New York before a successful four year run in the Bernard B. Jacobs Theatre on Broadway.

The breadth of Walsh's repertoire—from play, to musical, radio to film, and most recently, an operetta—is wide-ranging and multi-faceted. As a result, this collection cannot claim to be a comprehensive critical investigation of all of Walsh's works yet seeks to integrate and engage Walsh's work within and against the canon of Irish theatre. And, as his international presence continues to grow, his work is considered within the shifting landscapes of the theatre community worldwide. This collection's title suggests a focus on Walsh's theatre. However, much like Walsh whose work travels across mediums and employs a variety of techniques, this collection relies on different approaches and lenses to explore his dynamic work.

In an analysis of the treatment of space in two plays developed while he was working with Corcadorca Theatre Company, *Disco Pigs* and *Misterman*, as a point of departure, Jesse Weaver situates Walsh's theatre practice within the changing landscape of theatre practice in the 1990s. He identifies such shifts in approach at this time as, "an ensemble-led mode of production that favours group devising over a pre-written text and a focus on the body and movement with an emphasis on the interdisciplinary use of dance, music, and visual art." For Weaver this collaborative and visual approach to storytelling "sought actively to disrupt the textual basis of traditional theatre production". The essay then argues that, on examination of how space functions in these early plays compared to later work, an evolution can be charted in Walsh's work after he breaks from his collaboration with Corcadorca and seeks to "determine his own specific theatrical vision".

Popular variety entertainments are ubiquitous in Enda Walsh's work according to Ian Walsh. In his essay he specifically locates how the popular theatre traditions of the ventriloquist and music hall double act are fundamental to an understanding of the dramaturgy of Enda Walsh's plays. He does this through an analysis of Walsh's early breakout play *The Ginger Ale Boy* that concerns the breakdown of a ventriloquist. The essay contends that in using variety entertainment as theme and structuring device Walsh discovered in this early play an adaptable dramaturgical model that can be identified in his subsequent works. It goes on to then confront how "The escapism offered by performance as entertainment is presented repeatedly as a deadly pursuit by Walsh in his dramas" but "yet in the skill and exuberance that is demanded of actors in the enactment of his plays he cultivates a feeling of utopia in the audience." Drawing on the theories of Richard Dyer and Jill Dolan it is argued in this chapter that Enda Walsh uses these popular entertainments as a dialectical device that enables him to interrogate the efficacy of performance in relation to its contradictory dystopian and utopian effects.

Questions of gender and identity, according to Kevin McCluskey, are at the core of Walsh's 2001 screen adaptation of his play *Disco Pigs* (1996). McCluskey's chapter argues that in this cinematic revisiting of the original play Walsh, with director Kirsten Sheridan, spotlights Runt's struggles to find her own developing identity within the constraints of her co-dependent relationship with male best friend Pig. Sheridan's *mise-en-scène* in tandem with Walsh's screenplay is closely read, raising questions of the effects of medium and processes of adaptation. McCluskey suggests that in Walsh's cinematic re-exploration he more radically confronts issues of male violence, sex, and society's strains on counter-normative behaviour in the younger population of twenty-first century Ireland.

Lisa Fitzpatrick analyses two minor plays from different times in Walsh's career: the early *Sucking Dublin* that depicts the rape of a teenager at a party and the later *Lynddie's Gotta Gun* that sees the interrogation of a prisoner by a character loosely based on Lynndie England, the American soldier charged with abusing prisoners in Abu Ghraib prison in Baghdad. Fitzpatrick uses these two plays to explore a recurring concern she identifies in all of Walsh's work with human vulnerability and responses to that vulnerability. The performance of violence in the plays is found to explore vulnerability of both victim and perpetrator alike. Interrogating how this concern is represented and performed in the plays, specifically in relation to gender and sexual violence, Fitzpatrick draws on the work of theorists Judith Butler, Adriana Cavarero, Erinn Gilson and Ann Murphy to support her arguments. The essay charts a change in Walsh's treatment of this issue in the early plays that "represent violent characters and their victimization of others" to the later plays where "characters repeatedly create performances and stories that make sense of their experiences of hurt or threat."

In her essay Kay Martinovich examines abjection in Walsh's dark expressionistic play *bedbound*. She tells us that "Abjection is Julia Kristeva's term for the horror and disgust that humans experience when faced with filth, bodily excretions, or the dead." Martinovich argues that the characters of Dad and Daughter "represent the homicidal compulsion on the one hand and the traumatized abject body on the other." She does this through a sensitive and considered analysis of the language and representation of the "abject" body in the drama. Interestingly, despite its savage brutality Martinovich finally contends that by the close of the play a space is created through the performance in its re-construction and revision of past traumatic events for a type of reconciliation for these characters "to each other and to society."

In his essay on *Chatroom* Kevin Wallace examines how Walsh treats the complex issues of teenage identity and cyber-bullying. As in other chapters, Wallace finds Walsh's dramaturgy to pursue ambiguity in its conclusions rather than simple resolution as well as introducing "empathy in a space devoid of it." *Chatroom* is considered a political play in this essay in confronting an audience with an important social issue: the impact of Internet bullying. Wallace writes of how the play exploits the medium of theatre, an art form reliant on representation and embodiment, to defy the anonymity of the Internet and depict the "person on the other side of a username." The essay situates *Chatroom* historically in a ten-year period (1996-2006) that saw concern and direct engagement with issues of suicide in the work of Irish and British playwrights, but it also sees the piece in terms of the medieval morality play tradition and in relation to Walsh's earlier works discovering it to have a particular "resonance" with *Disco Pigs*.

Finian O'Gorman wishes to place *The Small Things* within the wider context of contemporary European theatre practice by considering how the play adheres to German theatre scholar, Hans-Thies Lehmann's concept of postdramatic theatre: "an interrogation of the fundamental structures of representation inherent in the dramatic tradition". In the play two older characters share a stage and the telling of a terrifying story but never acknowledge or interact with one another. O'Gorman identifies how, through their speech, these characters "construct a musical dynamic that provides a sonic structure to the action of the play. This structure can only be realized and recognized through the co-presence of the audience and the actors in the moment of performance". Thus dramatic coherence and imminence is not created here in the visual representation of a knowable reality but through the sound of the delivered speeches. Further to this O'Gorman explores how Walsh, through the device of ringing alarm clocks and the sounds of timpani drums, plays with temporal dramatic structures making time an active agent in the piece interrupting and controlling proceedings. It is the contention of this essay that a postdramatic analysis of this play "emphasizes the importance of performance in meaning-making and reveals a broader, more fluid range of possible experiences and interpretations of Walsh's plays".

Nelson Barre writing about *How These Desperate Men Talk* (2014) discusses Walsh's characters (John and Dave) and their struggles with locating objective and subjective memories of the past. In an effort to define purpose and meaning in their lives, Walsh's characters are forced under threat of death to *accurately* remember "what really happened". The challenges they face with recalling their own narrative process raises questions as to whether or not verity in recounting the past is ever achieved. Barre suggests that Walsh's *Desperate Men* mimics the human tendency to create and invest in a "preferred history" thus making us "masters" of our own lives' narratives, in an attempt to mask and revise an undesirable past. Walsh's performative strategies expose a universal human anxiety that links the search for truth in remembering our pasts with "survival". Barre argues that

Walsh's play explores the impossible task of a truly objective remembering and rendering of the past.

Katarzyna Ojrzyńska's chapter explores the 2008 film *Hunger* co-written by Walsh and British visual artist/director Steve McQueen. *Hunger* recalls the events in the Maze Prison leading up to the 1981 hunger strikes and the death of twenty-seven year old protest leader and MP, Bobby Sands. Ojrzyńska contends that Walsh and McQueen are likely collaborators because they share a tendency to write about and dramatize "claustrophobic situations" (Walsh, interview by Gompertz) in which their characters are wardens in their own self-constructed prisons. *Hunger*, according to Ojrzyńska, relies less on a devoutly historical narrative and more on a focus of the material and the body—what Ojrzyńska calls the "visceral dimension" of Sands's struggle. Ojrzyńska problematizes the filmmakers" treatment of the universally human issues at the core of this iconic and politicized event. By placing Sands somewhere between republican warrior and Christian martyr, Walsh and McQueen's "historical" drama challenges ideas of politically purposed self-sacrifice.

Audrey McNamara confronts the notion that Walsh's plays "do not comment on or reflect Irish society" (Fitzpatrick 451) by examining *Penelope,* in the context of the recent economic collapse in Ireland. She identifies how Walsh adapts the suitors episode from the Odyssey with its condemnation of "excessive behaviour" to comment on the same "excessive behaviour" of the business and banking elite during Ireland's prosperous Celtic Tiger era. Walsh does not do this in any heavy-handed direct manner but instead through allusion in naming the suitors after key figures that contributed to Ireland's downfall and through the form of the play. McNamara identifies how the drama follows Aristotelian form in terms of prophecy of doom, impending crisis and catastrophe and how appropriate this form is to capturing the experience of an economic crash. She contends at the end of her article how Walsh's play in its final image of a burning barbeque (a synecdoche for the destruction of the suitors on Odysseus's return) provides a cathartic image of finality but that such closure has yet to be delivered to the Irish people with the many agents of the crash still to be financially burned.

It has long been known, yet perhaps underestimated, that "music and musicality have always been important if not essential for Irish plays" (Lonergan). Why then were audiences so surprised when film-turned-musical *Once* set Broadway and the West End ablaze in its 2011 stage adaptation? Walsh admits that he "was a very peculiar choice"

(Walsh) to work on this uncharacteristically light-hearted script. However, the rake of awards that *Once* received reveal his appropriate candidacy for such an "odd" task. Mary Caulfield's chapter examines Walsh's book, alongside a careful consideration of the musical's *mise-en-scène*, to locate how Walsh renegotiates the themes and representations of Ireland's theatrical past to reflect and shape a more international community in Ireland's present. By privileging the story of Girl—a young Czech émigré—and her influence on the "stopped" career of a young Irish man, Caulfield suggests that Walsh evokes shared images of female inspiration in both Ireland and the Czech Republic's political repertoires thus presenting newly revised theatrical traditions for an increasingly global community in Ireland, post European Union enlargement, in the first decade of the twenty-first century.

Ballyturk, the most recent of Walsh's plays discussed in this collection, was performed at the Galway International Arts festival in 2014, and is the specific concern of Michelle Paull's chapter. Paull sees Walsh's use of the comical and physical (Paull points out co-lead actor Mikel Murfi's training within the Jacques Lecoq and Phillip Gaullier's school of theatre) as a performative means to subversively confront the serious questions of human emotions, identity (crisis) and, ultimately, death. At the first level of performance we are faced with what Paull describes as "playful comedy" however, what lies beneath is an encounter with life's larger questions. In this way, Paull locates the Beckettian resonances in Walsh's *Ballyturk*. Rather than a violent confrontation with such sombre subjects, Paull describes *Ballyturk* as a "theatrical spectacle" structured much like a musical composition. The play negotiates its narrative between reflexive moments of dialogue and circus-like acts of entertainment. Paull suggests that this strategy affects the audience both intellectually and viscerally thus providing for a more engaging and intense assertion of and interrogation into life's deeper meanings and intentions.

In a short perceptive essay written while he was rehearsing *Ballyturk* Mikel Murfi reflects on his own collaboration with Enda Walsh as both actor and director. Interestingly, he echoes the voice of many of the contributors to this volume in viewing Walsh's work as "uplifting and life-enhancing" rather than dark and bleak. He identifies how the work appeals to the performer writing:

> No matter how much energy you expend, the play's muscularity, the speed with which it asks you to think, the types of energies it asks you to put at its disposal become all consuming. You give it all

you have—it will demand, nay, roar for more. It's a thrilling experience.

The essay offers us a unique insight into Walsh's process telling us how he shifts seamlessly from playwright to director and uses rehearsals to explore and discover more about the text, often changing and tweaking the script as a result. Murfi stresses the immediacy of Walsh's theatre and how it must be experienced in performance and asks that academics resist fixing meaning to the work, which offers new insights each time it is performed.

Nursen Gömceli offers a fascinating study on the processes of cultural exchange and adaptation in producing theatre work in translation for a foreign audience. Her essay examines the production and reception of *The Walworth Farce* in Turkey translated into Turkish under the intriguing title, *We Laugh A Lot When Mum's Away* by the theatre company Tiyatro Gerçek in 2011. She analyses how the reception of the work was shaped by the company through an examination of promotional "paratexts" such as poster, flyers and the theatre programme. The madcap antics of the characters and metatheatricality of *The Walworth Farce* runs counter to the dominant naturalistic form of plays staged in Turkey. With this in mind, we learn from Gömceli that in order to generate an audience for Walsh's play Tiyatro Gerçek stressed the comedy and the storytelling aspects of the piece knowing these elements would make it more appealing. Gomceli then analyses how the work was received through the many comments left on several online forums and websites. These comments all register alarm at how the play differed from their expectations but how they enjoyed the play's surprising form.

In Siobhan O'Gorman's conversation with the French scenographer Sabine Dargent we are treated to a rare insight into the scenographic process, that most neglected area of theatre scholarship. Dargent has been working in Ireland since the late 1990s and has brought a fresh perspective to Irish theatre design drawing on her enthusiasm and experience of physical theatre in France. It was this interest in physical theatre that led Dargent to work with Mikel Murfi and to design Druid's productions of Walsh's *The Walworth Farce* (2006), *The New Electric Ballroom* (2008) and *Penelope* (2010). Her design of *The Walworth Farce* won her an ESB/Irish Times Theatre Award in 2006. The interview reveals "the collaborative ways in which Dargent, Walsh and Murfi sculpted the spaces of Walsh's theatre". For Dargent, Walsh's plays are not wordy but visual and prompt her to paint associated images and search out artists' work that speaks to the pictures conjured by the script. These gathered visuals, (such as the paintings of Yves Klein when designing *Penelope*), led her to the development of a coherent and consistent look for the production, not only for the set but also for the props and costumes.

This collection does not cover all of Walsh's work and contains many gaps due to issues pertaining to unpublished scripts, the timing of the publication and issues of space. Whilst this publication was being written Walsh premiered an adaptation of Roald Dahl's *The Twits* at the Royal Court, London; his first opera, *The Last Hotel* is to be staged at the Edinburgh International Festival 2015 and it was announced that he is to collaborate with David Bowie on a new musical. It was impossible to include all these exciting new pieces but it is hoped this collection proves a starting point to further research on Walsh and that other scholars and practitioners will write about those works that were not addressed in this publication.

As is evident from the essays in this collection Walsh is deeply invested in the power of performance across the varied media of theatre, film, radio, musicals and now opera. Throughout his work he challenges us to re-evaluate our assumptions of what we understand as identity, memory and history. His body of work dwells in a messy complex world of intense contradiction. He presents to us philosophical conundrums balanced by silly gags and incompetent characters who deliver marvels of great skill. His uneasy theatre beguiles, entertains and delights as it confronts pain, fear and uncertainty. It is thus almost impossible not to be affected by Walsh's work and to want to talk about it after the event. Here we offer some discussions that we hope will inspire a continued conversation that will, in similar fashion to the work itself, lead to repeated revision, re-enactment and wonder.

Works Cited

Billington, Michael. "Enda Walsh: 'Pure theatre animal'" explores solitude and the void below." *The Guardian* 18 Sept. 2014: n.pag. Web. 6 Dec. 2014.

Fitzpatrick, Lisa. "Enda Walsh." *The Methuen Drama Guide to Contemporary Irish Playwrights*. Ed. Martin Middeke and Peter Paul Schnierer. London: Bloomsbury, 2010. Print.

Huber, Werner. "Contemporary Irish Theatre in German-Speaking Countries." *Irish Drama: Local and Global Perspectives*. Eds. Nicholas Grene and Patrick Lonergan. Dublin: Carysfort. 2012. Print.

"'Taking on Once The Musical Was Potentially Disastrous'—Enda Walsh Interview." *The Irish Post*. N.p., 10 Apr. 2013. Web. 02 May 2015.

Walsh, Enda. "Tony Nominee Enda Walsh on How Writing Once Lightened His Soul." *Broadway.com*. N.p., 22 May 2012. Web. 22 Jan. 2015.

1 | Enda Walsh and Space: The Evolution of a Playwright and Practitioner

Jesse Weaver

Confinement is a significant theme in the work of Enda Walsh. Characters are confined by the hellish compulsion to perform the past over and over again, by the repetitions and revisions of a language fuelled by that compulsion and by the material reality of the enclosed worlds they're forced to inhabit. These confined worlds that Walsh creates find particular expression in the ways Walsh circumscribes space both imaginatively and as a physical reality of performance. In plays like *bedbound* (2001), *The Walworth Farce* (2006) and *Penelope* (2009), Walsh situates his characters in stifling, deteriorating physical spaces that echo both the constricted world-view of the play's inhabitants and that serve as objects of resistance from which performers can build and shape their performance. The spaces in which the action of these plays occurs (a child's bed, a dilapidated council flat, an empty swimming pool) are specifically prescribed by stage directions within the text. While it's acknowledged that these prescriptive descriptions of space the performers are meant to inhabit allow some room for interpretation by directors and designers, they still are meant to serve as a primary component in how the play is received both on the page and in production.

It wasn't always this way, though. The text of two of Walsh's early plays are relatively devoid of stage directions that offer a definitive description of the space that performers are meant to inhabit and that spectators are meant to engage with visually: *Disco Pigs* (1996) and *Misterman* (1999, revised 2011). The lack in the text of explicit stage directions that describe and demarcate the space within which the play's action occurs puts less emphasis on an authorial determination of "scenic space", which Christopher B. Balme terms as the space that "designates where the actors perform, including set design" and which he describes as the "narrow realm where the performer acts and therefore transforms his or her surroundings" (48, 54). Instead, emphasis is placed on a performative representation, primarily through the expressive power of the body and voice, of "dramatic space", which Balme defines as "the spatial coordinates fixed in and evoked by the theatrical text", or the imagined, fictional space within which the world of the play resides (49). Therefore, without specific authorial directions determining scenic space to be found within these two texts, it could be suggested that scenic space in the case of *Disco Pigs* and *Misterman* is a provisional element created and determined by the interrelated use of Walsh's language, the performers' physicality, and the collaborative input of the ensemble in attempting to represent the dramatic space of both plays. Scenic space and dramatic space become then deeply interwoven elements, the expression of which depends on the creative relationship that exists between the members of the producing ensemble.

Using his treatment of both scenic and dramatic space in *Disco Pigs* and *Misterman* as a point of departure, this essay will investigate how Walsh incorporated significant shifts in theatre practice in Ireland during the 1990s into his playwriting, particularly in terms of his stint as a member of Corcadorca Theatre Company. Such shifts included, but were not limited to, an ensemble-led mode of production that favours group devising over a prewritten text and a focus on the body and movement with an emphasis on the interdisciplinary use of dance, music, and visual art. These approaches to theatre making sought actively to disrupt the textual basis of traditional theatre production, placing visual storytelling and the body at the centre of the process. Taking such shifts in theatre practice into account, this essay will first interrogate Walsh's collaborations with director Pat Kiernan and Corcadorca Theatre Company in the mid-nineties. It's during this time that the practical context of working closely with actors and a director in an ensemble context may have negated the need for Walsh to dictate prescriptive authorial directions in the texts of *Disco Pigs* and *Misterman* that circumscribe time and space, making those texts more open to how they were to be interpreted in performance by a collaborative ensemble of theatre practitioners. It will be argued that Walsh's eventual break from Corcadorca, coupled with his own development as an independent writer, significantly altered the way he deals with both scenic and dramatic space, as well as how he has ultimately sought to determine his own specific theatrical vision.

Corcadorca Theatre Company was founded by director Pat Kiernan in 1991 and experimented aggressively with a range of approaches to theatre-making within the specific context of Cork city. These included ensemble-led devising, staging new writing, and site-specific productions. Enda Walsh first came in contact with Corcadorca in 1993 after moving to Cork to act for the theatre-in-education company Graffiti Theatre, and shortly thereafter he began working with Corcadorca and Kiernan to devise work with space secured through Cork's Triskel Arts Centre (Weaver 132). Kiernan, Walsh and sound designer Cormac O'Connor worked closely together during the 1990s in defining Corcadorca's aesthetic, which for Walsh "was like an apprenticeship. It felt like we didn't know what we were doing, but we loved the work and loved putting it on. I was the only one interested in writing and Pat Kiernan was a good director—probably a much better director than I was writer (2008)." Johnny Hanrahan, founder of Cork's Meridian Theatre Company, notes that Walsh and Kiernan's close collaboration determined Corcadorca's artistic direction in the 1990s. "During that phase Enda's writing combined with Pat's direction to embody Corcadorca's stated artistic policy," says Hanrahan, "to electrify audiences and to represent the city authentically (97)." It would appear then that the boundaries between the roles of writer and director were somewhat porous, and that a more collaborative approach towards making new work was favoured. "I was very close to the direction process without actually directing anything in there," says Walsh, "so [Kiernan's] direction really influenced my writing" (2008). This close collaboration found its specific articulation in the production of Walsh's play *The Ginger Ale Boy* in 1995, about a fame-seeking ventriloquist. Kiernan's direction attempted to match the ambitious, absurd, and epic narrative Walsh had crafted by incorporating a host of performance elements including live music, dance, and video. For Walsh the play was "pretty makeshift stuff. I had no idea what I was doing. [...] The production was fantastic though, and that was all Pat." For their next collaboration, Walsh says, "I knew I had to write a proper play for Pat, and something cheap also. We were broke" (vii). The next two plays Walsh wrote for Corcadorca, *Disco Pigs* and *Misterman*, could indeed be produced inexpensively given their small cast sizes and lack of specific, prescribed scenic spaces. What they would require, as is suggested by the texts of both plays, would be a more stripped-back, performer-centric approach.

Disco Pigs is a two-hander that concerns the insulated relationship of two Cork teenagers, the male Pig and female Runt. Born within a minute of each other, Pig and Runt share the same birthday, the same housing estate, and the same invented baby-talk language between them. The one-man show *Misterman*, staged a few years later, was also directed by Pat Kiernan with Walsh playing the role of Thomas, the self-appointed moral judge of the Irish Midlands town of Inishfree. Though both plays share a great deal in terms of their treatment of space and language, they would follow very different paths in terms of production. *Disco Pigs* became an international success that quickly propelled the careers of its performers, writer, and director. The original production of *Misterman* would signal a break between Walsh and Kiernan, with Walsh leaving Corcadorca and going solo as a writer and director of his own work. Walsh would ultimately revise *Misterman* and restage it twelve years later at the 2011 Galway Arts Festival.

In discussing how both plays use and construct scenic and dramatic space both textually and performatively, and what that means in terms of Walsh's own development as a writer, it should first be noted that *Disco Pigs* and *Misterman* were written at a time when the monologue play as a form was permeating the Irish stage. Playwrights such as Conor McPherson and Mark O'Rowe made names for themselves both in Ireland and abroad writing single or multi-character monologue plays. The late 1990s saw the production of McPherson's *This Lime Tree Bower* (1995), *St. Nicholas* (1997), and O'Rowe's *Howie the Rookie* (1999), all of which utilize the form. The cast sizes of all three plays are small, all the speaking characters are male and the actions of the play are reported to the audience rather than enacted in their entirety. Without the need for direct character interaction, and the delivery of narrative rather than its mimetic enactment, it's possible to foreground the writer's language in production without it necessarily being overtly mediated by a director's conceptual intention. Writing in 2001, Brian Singleton suggests that such an approach to playwriting "points to an attempt to turn theatre into a purely literary medium; since relatively little happens on the stage, the focus is on the writer's storytelling abilities, and the actor's ability to serve the writing" (12). And with the necessary components for the text's delivery being simply an actor, a stage, and an audience, such an approach can foreground the material actuality of the theatre space rather than necessarily masking it in a set design that communicates to the spectator a particular setting within which the dramatic action is meant to take place. The space the dramatic action takes place in is then ultimately a construct of the audience's imagination mediated by the writer's language and the actor's delivery, not necessarily by a physical set. The prescription of scenic space then can be left, in many ways, in the mind of the audience as mediated through the direct delivery of a dramatic narrative by the performer.

While not constructed as a monologue play in its totality, there are elements of monologue in *Disco Pigs*, as when Runt and Pig report narrative directly to the audience. But the performative nature of the language, which has the characters living out, in the present tense, the story they're telling points to an active denial of the literary sensibilities that Singleton talks about. Runt and Pig also directly engage with each other, using the other's dialogue to build upon the narrative drive of the play, as when they take a taxi out of Cork to the sea:

> **RUNT.** An off we do!
> **PIG.** Now das reel class!
> **RUNT.** Look how da scummy wet grey a Pork City spindown da plughole.
> **PIG.** as da two speed on, an on we speed! Sa so long to dat sad song, hey Runt!!
> **RUNT.** Up an out ova da valley, Pig!! An da black a da country like a big snuggly doovey it cuddle us up reel good yeah!!
> **PIG.** Snuggle down outta town!
> **RUNT.** Hey da fresh air, pal!!
> **PIG.** Wine down da windy an drink it all in, Runt! (16)

The dialogue is at once based in the reported narrative of the characters' ride out of the city, similarly to the way monologue behaves, and is also emblematic of the close rapport shared between them. And because the events being reported and discussed are described in the present tense rather than in the past tense, it offers the actors and director the opportunity to create performatively the moment of discovery the characters make as they work to describe to each other and the audience what they're seeing and experiencing. The language also places the performers in multiple dramatic spaces at once: they simultaneously inhabit the space of the play's imagined Cork, the world of Pig and Runt's private language, and the past and present of both characters' existence. The same is true for the 1999 version of *Misterman*. Thomas's story is told within three overlapping dramatic spaces: through monologue delivered to the audience, through dialogues he holds with the edited cassette recordings of the voices of his mother and of Edel, the object of his deluded affections, and through dialogues in which he jumps between playing himself and the person he's supposedly speaking with:

(*He adopts a suitable voice for Mrs. O'Leary.*) "Oh, the cold,
Thomas?'
Are you full of it, Mrs. O'Leary?
"Sure, once I get it into my body it's very difficult to get the thing
out, Thomas." (39)

Also, just as in *Disco Pigs*, Thomas both experiences and narrates
his story as it unfolds, such as when he describes walking out of his
house into the streets of Inishfree: "I feel the front door's gentle shove
behind me as I step out into Inishfree. Thoughts of the Universe and the
phlegmy basin that sits under Mammy's bed, belting about my head
with a mad swishy swish. The Lord God at my side, the day open and
big" (39). Here he is paradoxically at once removed from and embedded
in the act of stepping out into the street, allowing for the multiple co-
existence of spaces both physical and imagined, scenic and dramatic.

The form that Walsh's writing takes in both plays, with its energetic
use of language, limited use of stage directions, the use of the
performer's body to channel a host of characters, and an
unconventional approach to narrative structure, demands a close
collaboration between director and actors, and points to a process that
centralizes the actor's body as the prime carrier of meaning. The lack of
parenthetical directions within the published texts of *Disco Pigs* and
the 1999 version of *Misterman* also points to the close collaboration
between director, actor, designers, and writer in staging the play. Given
the close working relationship within the company, and between Walsh
and Kiernan, approaches to staging could be communicated directly in
workshops and rehearsals rather than remotely through the written
text. The lack of a prescribed scenic space in the playscript suggests that
the shape and function of the scenic space is rendered through a
collaborative dialogue that includes actors, designers, a director and a
writer. Scenic space is therefore a provisional element of performance
determined ultimately by the imaginative input of a creative ensemble
of theatre practitioners. The written text is only one material element
determining the shape of a production, and is not necessarily the
determinant element in defining how scenic space is to be made
manifest in performance.

However, the role that language plays in determining the shape and
function of both scenic and dramatic space in *Disco Pigs* and
Misterman should not be overlooked. In particular, a great deal of the
performative potential in *Disco Pigs* stems from the heightened, private
language that Runt and Pig share, a language that draws from a
rhythmic lyricism that demands a heightened physicalization in its

consistent monosyllabic structure. Combined with the uniqueness of a Cork accent, the language is at once theatrically muscular and utterly baffling, drawing an audience or a reader relentlessly into the private and suffocating dramatic space that the characters inhabit. But this language's relentlessness also serves as a key to understanding that space. As actor Cillian Murphy, who originated the role of Pig, notes in a 1996 radio interview, the invented language of Pig and Runt is "like any language or like any slang. The more used to it you are, the more sense it makes" (Leach). For Walsh, confronting the audience with a language that is at first alienating is part of a dramaturgical strategy of almost entirely immersing the audience in the world of the play. No matter where the play was produced, whether in Cork, Dublin, or further afield, the audience "still had to learn about the play as they watched it", says Walsh (Weaver 134). The language also evokes potential scenic spaces of the play in performance, carving out through sharp plosives and guttural utterance specific locations contained in the drama. This is apparent when Pig breaks out onto the dance floor of a nightclub:

> Jus me jus me jus me jus me jus me!! Oh yes!! Dis da one!! Real soun set Pig swimmin an swimmin in da on-off off-beat dat is dance! Beat beat beat beat beat thru da veins full a drink! An pig he wee wee full of drink! (11)

The constant rhythmic repetitions ("Jus me jus me jus me jus me...") mimics the rapid techno beat one would hear in a club, as well as suggesting an unbridled physical performance generated through an embodiment of a language barely hindered by standard grammar or punctuation. The play's language also points to a performative physicality that's made all the more apparent by the fact that the two actors are meant to perform all the other players in Runt and Pig's life, suggesting then a tightly contained scenic space evoked by and shared between two performing bodies that in turn mediate, through voice and physicality, the dramatic space of the play.

Having discussed in some detail how scenic and dramatic space operates in *Disco Pigs* and *Misterman*, it is now worth analyzing the ways in which "theatrical space" may have dictated the production and reception of both plays. As Balme notes, "theatrical space" broadly refers to "the architectural conditions of theatre, usually a building, and encompasses performance and spectator space" (48). An analysis of the function of theatrical space, and the dialogic relationship between performer and audience encompassed within that space, is particularly useful in determining how the original productions of both plays were shaped by the venues they were first staged in, as well as how the aesthetic considerations of writer, director, and ensemble helped determine the plays' receptions. Discussing his general attitude towards staging a play, director Pat Kiernan describes the performance of *Disco Pigs* as an experience rather than merely staging a straightforward narrative: "There isn't a fourth wall there for starters [...] they [Pig and Runt] enter through the audience [...] Any production is attempting to create a whole experience, whether it's in a theatre or a site other than a theatre" (175). The physical proximity of the play's action to the audience in a number of the venues where it played appears to bear out the claim of staging intensely intimate, highly performative experiences: the play originated in the relatively small (at the time) Triskel Arts Centre, and then moved to the International Bar for the Dublin Fringe Festival, a cramped space atop a pub. Walsh states that "everyone says the *best* it played was in the International Bar [...] as opposed to the West End where it was crap" (473). When the production played at the Bush in London, itself a small theatrical space atop a pub, the audience was placed on either side of the performance area. Margaret Jones Llewellyn found that

> the actors' close proximity, sweat and breathing contributed to the sense of the abject body conjured up by sound uttered. Miming births to the sound of a heavy heartbeat started the show, and the sense of bodily presence developed from pig-grunts while eating amid speech, to scatterings of scatological words and heavy use of plosives throughout. (42)

The guttural manner in which language was treated in performance and the physical fact of the actors' bodily presence was foregrounded in the biological act of sweating and laboured breathing. The fractured, non-linear treatment of language also suggests a staging that is performative and extremely physical in approach and, in the case of the original production, the proximity of the audience and the emphasis on staging an "event" rather than a mere representation of written text suggests a strategy to actively engage the spectator as almost a participant in the action. As Walsh describes it, the elements of the production all coalesced extremely well and resulted in the play's runaway success. "Pat's direction and my writing came together," says Walsh, "and Cormac O'Connor's sound design was immense. I wrote it for Eileen Walsh, who played the character Runt, and we were fortunate enough to get Cillian Murphy...he and Eileen just gelled" (Weaver 133). The play earned Walsh and Corcadorca an international reputation, winning critical praise with productions at the Dublin Fringe Festival, the Edinburgh Fringe Festival, and the Bush Theatre in London.

Misterman saw Walsh returning to the stage as a performer and attempting to replicate, as a writer, a stripped-down aesthetic similar to *Disco Pigs*. Also directed by Pat Kiernan, *Misterman* tells the story of Thomas, whose religious dogmatism and priggish, neurotic attitudes towards sex ultimately lead him to murder a young woman he becomes obsessed with. *Misterman* is in essence a monologue play, performed by one actor and utilizing direct address in order to relate the play's narrative, creating a dramatic space through language, and arguably focusing the audience on the craft and skill of the writer. According to Walsh, the success of *Disco Pigs* had helped define a kind of dramaturgical strategy in his writing, which ultimately features characters constrained by the limits of language and extreme emotional and psychological circumstances. Walsh states that he "didn't have a voice for ages until *Disco Pigs*, and I thought that was sort of a notion of a play that I wanted to write" (2008). While *Misterman* adheres even more strictly to the formal structure of a monologue play, Thomas self-consciously performs his own narrative through his playing of all of Inishfree's inhabitants, and is at once present and removed from the play's action. Armed only with a small notebook and a single tape recorder, Thomas performs the act of recording and cataloguing the sins of his fellow townsfolk, sins he simultaneously engages in and begs off through the embodied performance of those very townsfolk. The scenography, at least in terms of how it's articulated in the 1999 text, is minimal, with lighting and sound serving as the primary technical elements that mark out space and time in the story. The reliance on sound and lighting in setting the scene is more than likely a necessity for production: the scenes shift quickly from a host of locales. Thomas's pilgrimage through Inishfree leads him quickly from his mother's kitchen, to a garage, to a cemetery, and into more ethereal realms: Thomas ascends to heaven several times during the story. The demands made by the play's dramatic space, as articulated for the most part in Thomas's dialogue, specifically require a collaborative negotiation between designers, the director, and in this case, the actor/writer in terms of the creation of the scenic space. How the scenic space is marked, delineated, and shifted over the course of the play is left open by the text. The text, by absenting a specific description of scenic space, is in fact cueing those embarking on staging a production that a focused, creative approach to the construction of space is needed. Despite the range of settings indicated in the narrative, by limiting the description of scenic space, Walsh ultimately was looking for a production aesthetic that was minimalist in its aims. For Walsh this minimalist strategy "was a direction I wanted it to go in. I wanted [this production] to be really poor—I wanted to stop all the big presentation [that Corcadorca is now known for] and I just wanted it to be a poor presentation, and instead it became this massive thing" (2008). It could be argued that Walsh's movement towards a minimalist aesthetic supports Brian Singleton's assertion that the nature of the monologue play pushes out the role of the director, turning the production process into, as Singleton says, a "writing-and-acting exercise" (12). Walsh's decision to perform in the piece seems to bear this out: his presence as performer would allow him some directorial control over the delivery of his text, and his close working relationship with Kiernan and others would mean that Thomas's Inishfree would be made manifest through a negotiation during the course of development, rehearsal, and performance of the piece. However, when Walsh decided to appear in the first version of *Misterman*, he had not been a stranger to performing. Walsh had appeared in his own work before, performing the role of Bobby in the 1995 production of Corcadorca's *The Ginger Ale Boy*. He had also performed earlier in Dublin Youth Theatre, and had worked as a performer in the Cork-based theatre-in-education company Graffiti. Indeed, it could very well be his experience as a performer, as someone who is intimately familiar with the creative power that can be generated by the act of performing that makes his approach to language and character so unique.

In retrospect, though, Walsh is fairly critical of his decision to cast himself as Thomas in the 1999 Corcadorca production of *Misterman*. Speaking in 2008, Walsh cites his overarching concerns over the play as a writer bleeding into his work as an actor in the piece. "I want every sort of detail to be right in my writing," he says, "and I brought that into the performance. You can't do that as an actor" (2000). Walsh's process of writing is one that is initially fast, furious, and completely committed to inhabiting the world of the characters. He produces a first draft in a matter of weeks. "I've got a much stronger relationship with the characters [than the actors]," says Walsh, "because I live with them in my head for days and weeks. An actor has only a four week rehearsal period; I live with the characters in a much, much stronger way" (2008). This suggests that Walsh's insistence on inhabiting the characters as completely as possible within the process of writing may have affected his ability to establish a suitable aesthetic distance between himself and the character of Thomas. This lack of distance possibly clouded his interpretation and muddied a connection that could have been forged between performer and audience. Says Walsh, "I suppose I sort of became the character in terms of wanting to inhabit this man's life. I completely ran myself into the ground; I lost loads of weight and became this skeletal creature. The performance was strong but I really wasn't telling the story of the play. I was really just locking the audience out" (2008).

Misterman was the last time Kiernan and Walsh would work together, and Walsh left the company to pursue his own writing outside of a company context. As mentioned above, Walsh claims that he was interested in a more minimalist aesthetic, or "poor" aesthetic as he termed it, and felt that Kiernan's vision and his own were proving incompatible with each other. Since then Corcadorca's artistic trademark has, in large part, been its pursuit of producing site-specific work that engaged with significant locales in Cork city itself. By doing so Corcadorca upends the traditional notion of locating municipal theatre in a purpose-built building. In the case of Corcadorca, the municipality *is* the theatre, and by grafting theatrical work on historically and culturally resonant spaces throughout the city the company offers a double-sighted staging that includes the theatrical event and the resonances evoked by the site's social, political, or historical significance. Corcadorca's mission to stage work in non-traditional spaces that highlight both the play's thematic and the local cultural significance of the site, point to an active attempt to build a community-based audience deeply invested in the company's artistic output. It is perhaps because of the specificity of Corcadorca's mission, which requires such a sustained relationship with a specific, urban space in order to determine, at least in part, the meanings of the work the company stages that Walsh opted to develop his own writing outside of those prescribed strictures. Without necessarily being tied geographically to a specific location, Walsh would be free to explore his own writing free of both a specific company and city helping to determine its outcome. Having broken from Corcadorca, Walsh would direct his next play *bedbound* for the Dublin Theatre Festival in 2001, and would articulate within the text a more descriptive and prescriptive vision of the play's scenic space, a "small child's bed inside of a box" within which nearly the entire action of the play would take place.

Following a trajectory of exerting more authorial control over how scenic space is determined in the staging of his plays, Walsh revised and directed *Misterman* in 2011, casting Cillian Murphy in the role of Thomas and significantly defining, both within the text and on the stage, the scenic space in which Thomas enacts and embodies the citizens of Inishfree. Whereas the text of the 1999 version makes no mention of the kind of scenic space Thomas inhabits as he performs the people of his town, the 2011 version very specifically lays out the parameters of an abandoned industrial space:

> Pre-show and we're looking at an abandoned depot/ dilapidated factory. The space immediately feels inhabitable and dangerous with electrical cables everywhere. And yet dotted about it are small tiny "stages", pristine in comparison to the surrounding debris. It suggests that someone is trying to live and has lived here for some time. (7)

There is a concreteness ascribed to the playing space, a material reality that Thomas will exist in that is, despite its dilapidation, a recognizable, real-world setting rather than the more liquid playing space suggested in the text for the 1999 version. This later version of the play has also been populated by far more characters than its predecessor, and as a result more voices have been added to the recordings Thomas plays as a means of creating the context of scenes he attempts to play out. How these voices manifest has also been altered. No longer do the sounds and voices of Inishfree live on a single cassette recorder, compressed within a singular archival object carried by Thomas. As the script designates, and as the production at Galway's Black Box bore out, the "small tiny stages" are demarcated and anchored with a reel-to-reel tape recorder placed in them. Rather than being able to directly control the output of the recordings, as he would have been with a single recorder on his person, Thomas is forced at times to traverse the scenic space in great leaps and bounds, a servant to malfunctioning machines that play of their own accord and the ferocious howling of a dog that is heard from outside the depot/factory. Rather than Thomas exerting control over both the scenic and dramatic spaces of the 1999 version, as when he mediates sound cues and recorded exchanges with his mother via his portable tape player, the scenic and dramatic spaces of the 2011 version appear to control and create the world within which Thomas functions. Thomas is run mad attempting to negotiate an expanding, increasingly chaotic universe created by the seemingly autonomous reel-to-reel tape recorders that may or may not obey his command.

It is also interesting to note, in reference to Corcadorca's past staging of expansive, site-specific performance in Cork city, the sheer vastness of the play's set as it was staged in the Black Box performance space in Galway. The stage directions indicating the scenic space as an abandoned depot/factory were taken quite literally, with massive concrete pillars and rusted iron rails and stairs demarcating the playing area. If an audience member were not familiar with the Black Box as a purpose-built performance venue, he or she could be forgiven for assuming that the production was an example of "site-generic" performance, meaning theatrical performances that require "a specific *category* of space, but are not tied to one place" (Balme 61). It is interesting then that Corcadorca's offering in the 2011 Galway Arts Festival, Franz Xaver Kroetz's 1973 play *Request Programme*, was an intimate, site-generic theatre performance that took place in a one-bedroom apartment, a contrast to the company's larger, more expansive site-specific productions that were staged with the express purpose of foregrounding significant Cork city locales and landmarks. Directed by Kiernan, the play starred Eileen Walsh in a solo performance, and performing only a few feet from a small, voyeuristic audience that silently observed her going through a series of domestic rituals which ended with her taking her own life. Contrasting the compressed intimacy within which Eileen Walsh performed versus the cavernous space her former *Disco Pigs* co-star inhabited, it would seem, at least in this particular case, that Enda Walsh and Pat Kiernan have perhaps once again borrowed, unconsciously at least, from each other's theatrical visions and vocabulary.

By discussing the ways in which different categories of space are (and aren't) demarcated in the texts of *Disco Pigs* and *Misterman*, I have attempted to show links between Walsh's prescription of scenic and dramatic space in these texts and his early development as a playwright in Cork. Given Walsh's close collaboration with Pat Kiernan and other members of Corcadorca Theatre Company in the mid to late 1990s, as well as his experience as a performer, it should be no surprise that Walsh would access these experiences in developing his approach in order to determine more and more specific ways that space can, in multiple ways, behave as a prime element of his dramaturgy. As such, his writing has moved beyond simply crafting a highly theatrical language. From a child's bed in *bedbound*, to an empty swimming pool in *Penelope*, to the dilapidated industrial space in the 2011 version of *Misterman*, Walsh has shown since his apprenticeship with Corcadorca a more directorial prerogative in his playwriting through the prescription of scenic space, and has backed that prerogative, on several occasions, by directing his own work. By doing so, I would suggest that Walsh behaves as much as an auteur-director as he does a playwright, and strives to articulate, through his play texts and his approach to staging, a theatrical vision that is uniquely and entirely his own.

Works Cited

Balme, Christopher B. *The Cambridge Introduction to Theatre Studies*. Cambridge: Cambridge University Press, 2008. Print.

Hanrahan, Johnny. "Theatre in Cork/Cork in Theatre, an Exercise in Perspective." *Druids, Dudes and Beauty Queens*. Ed. Dermot Bolger. Dublin: New Island, 2001. 92-103. Print.

Kiernan, Pat. "Pat Kiernan in Conversation with Ben Hennessy and Ger FitzGibbon. *Theatre Talk*. Eds. Lillian Chambers, Ger FitzGibbon, and Eamonn Jordan. Dublin: Carysfort Press, 2001. 167-180. Print.

Leach, Cristín. "Cillian Murphy and Eileen Walsh Talk About "Disco Pigs."" *Audioboo*. Audioboo, 13 Feb. 2013. Web. 02 Sept. 2013.

Llewellyn-Jones , Margaret. *Contemporary Irish Drama & Cultural Identity*. Bristol: Intellect Books, 2002. Print.

Singleton, Brian. "Am I Talking to Myself?" *The Irish Times* 19 April 2001: 12. Print.

Walsh, Enda. *bedbound & misterman*. London: Nick Hern Books, 2001. Print.

---*Disco Pigs* & *Sucking Dublin*. London: Nick Hern Books, 2001. Print.

---.'Enda Walsh in Conversation with Emelie FitzGibbon." *Theatre Talk*. Eds. Lillian Chambers, Ger FitzGibbon, and Eamonn Jordan. Dublin: Carysfort Press, 2001. 471-480. Print.

---.'Forward." *Enda Walsh: Plays One*. London: Nick Herns Books, 2013. vii-ix. Print.

---. *Misterman*. London: Nick Hern Books, 2012. Print.

---.Personal interview, 28 April 2008.

Weaver, Jesse. ""The Words Look After Themselves": The Practice of Enda Walsh." *Irish Drama: Local and Global Perspectives*. Dublin: Carysfort Press, 2012. 129-139. Print.

2 | Entertainment and Dystopia in Enda Walsh's *The Ginger Ale Boy*

Ian R. Walsh

Variety entertainments and the world of show business can be identified throughout Enda Walsh's work. *Penelope* is structured around a talent contest which features singing, slapstick and a very memorable quick-change act; the trio of Cork men in *The Walworth Farce* are presented in a style that *"resembles the three stooges"* (Walsh 7), *Lynddie's Gotta Gun* begins with a party clown walking on stage with a big fish and *The Small Things* opens and closes with the classic red velvet curtains and timpani drum of the music hall. And these are only some of the more obvious examples. In his landmark essay "Entertainment and Utopia" Richard Dyer, using the example of musicals, argues that entertainment functions as escapism by offering "the image of "something better" ... that our day-to-day lives don't provide" (20). He identifies this utopianism of entertainment as being contained "in the feelings it embodies" (20) presenting the spectator with "what utopia would feel like rather than how it would be organized" (20). In this chapter I will specifically locate how the popular theatre traditions of the ventriloquist and music hall double act are fundamental to an understanding of the dramaturgy of Enda Walsh's plays. The escapism offered by performance as entertainment is presented repeatedly as a deadly pursuit by Walsh in his dramas and yet in the skill and exuberance that is demanded of actors in the enactment of his plays he cultivates a feeling of utopia in the audience. I contend that Walsh draws on the tradition of popular entertainments as a dialectical dramaturgical device that enables him to interrogate the efficacy of performance in relation to its contradictory dystopian and utopian effects. I will examine Walsh's *The Ginger Ale Boy* in relation to this contention and argue that this early piece in its use of the performance strategies of variety entertainments serves as an adaptable dramaturgical model that can be identified in his subsequent works.

The Ginger Ale Boy was produced by the Cork-based theatre company Corcadorca at the New Granary Theatre in 1995 and later transferred to Dublin's Project Arts Centre and the Belltable in Limerick. The play was directed by Pat Kiernan and starred Walsh himself in the lead role of Bobby, under the stage name of Eanna Breathnach, the Irish language form of his name. It tells a tale of a 28 year old who wishes to make it in show business as a ventriloquist. But the champagne corks never pop to celebrate his success, he must instead make do with the cheap fizz of ginger ale. For the play does not chart his rise to success but his descent into failure and mental collapse. On this journey we encounter a host of bizarre characters that inhabit his imperfect world including his overly ambitious mother, silent father, duplicitous manager, Danny, and Love Interest, who is reluctant to perform the functional role suggested by her title. The form is episodic with much of the action narrated and remarked upon by the characters directly out to the audience. A chorus of supernumerary actors and dancers called the "Community" also perform numerous acting roles, songs and dance sequences that add, interrupt, and comment on the action. Walsh has revealed how the writing process was rough-and-ready in approach, driven primarily by the pragmatic concerns of the company:

> I had an idea of a play about a ventriloquist who has a nervous breakdown. A musical comedy! Pat encouraged me to write it ... but I had to keep everyone in the group happy ... so the play's shape and characters were decided on what we had in the room. It had songs in it because the guy who wrote the music had to be kept busy and out of the pub. It had dance routines because there was a couple of restless dancers wanting to choreograph something/anything. Everyone wanted a monologue. Fair enough. It was pretty makeshift stuff. I had no idea what I was doing. The Ginger Ale Boy's a mess but it has some ability in there, I suppose. The production was fantastic though and that was all Pat. (VII)

Walsh's play is thus conceived not only in terms of a driving action (the breakdown of a ventriloquist) but also as a showcase of the various performance skills of the company. Oliver Double writes that "a variety show was not bound together by a narrative or even a theme. Each act stood for itself" (12). Much has been written on Walsh's command of storytelling and narrative but little has been written on his proclivity for the inclusion of variety entertainments in his plays and what these routines offer the playwright. For Jesse Weaver, "Walsh emphasizes that the process of storytelling is carried out through the performance of the play's action rather than on a faithful and literal interpretation of the language" (134). A similar emphasis is echoed by Lisa Fitzpatrick who writes: "Walsh's work is concerned with the nature of performance itself, and the plays must be seen and studied in performance—the texts alone will not do" (451). What the variety entertainments offer Walsh is a means to tell a story that is rooted in the immediacy and pleasure of live performance. He is by no means unique in this and follows a long established mode labelled by the director Peter Brook as "Rough Theatre". Brook observed "Every attempt to revitalize the theatre has gone back to the popular source" (68). Interestingly, Walsh frequently acts as a director of his own work and his playwriting could be said to be led by a directorial instinct which sees the play in terms of a series of theatrical "bits of business" rather than in terms of developing narrative. The playwright-director here becomes an unseen master of ceremonies that determines what is on the playbill. Gerry Colgan in his *Irish Times* review of *The Ginger Ale Boy* identified this trait in the playwriting observing that, "The parts do not add up to a coherent whole, but are of interest in their own episodic right. The treatment and the acting breeze along hypnotically for some 90 minutes of non-stop inventiveness' (Colgan 13). The problem of overall coherence that Colgan identifies is something that Walsh would later solve in subsequent works by marrying this fragmented variety style to a more classical dramatic structure of an impending crisis instigated by a prophecy of doom (the shared dream of the suitors in *Penelope*) or the arrival of a stranger entering the space (*The Walworth Farce, New Electric Ballroom* and *Ballyturk)* or simply and effectively the immediate threat of violence/death (*Lynddie's Gotta Gun, How These Desperate Men Talk, bedbound, Chatroom, The Small Things*). In the dramaturgy of Walsh's later works the variety sequences are also more carefully woven into the fabric of the play, intensifying the crisis as they serve increasingly desperate characters to distract themselves from the inexorable resolution demanded by the dramatic form. This structure it seems is happened upon in *The Ginger Ale Boy* marrying the pragmatic concerns of the company's need to showcase its skills coupled with the driving action of the play: Bobby's breakdown that follows the classical rise and fall of a doomed hero. But the crisis in the action in this early play is not made as immanent or poignant as in the more mature work. Or as Fintan O'Toole in his review for *The Irish Times* put it: "The play has … one of Aristotle's elements of tragedy—pity but not the other—fear" (10).

But variety acts in their status as a routine—a patterned behaviour—also function to reinforce a recurring dialectic in Walsh's work between order (performance) and chaos (reality). The performance of routine repeatedly offers salvation but delivers self-destruction to his characters. The control and sanctuary promised by an ordered existence separate from chaos and unpredictability of other people mutates into lonely solipsism, self-loathing and inevitable explosive violence.

But these routines as variety acts also serve to delight and engage the audience often offering some light relief from the dark foreboding atmospheres created in the plays. Double in his history of British variety theatre identifies the "display of skill" as key to the pleasure of this type of entertainment for audiences. It was this spectacle of ability that attracted the Futurist, Marinetti, to the variety stage, writing:

> The authors, actors and technicians of the Variety Theatre have only one reason for existing and triumphing: incessantly to invent new elements of astonishment. Hence … an excited competition of brains and muscles to conquer the various records of agility, speed, force, complication, and elegance. (Double 159)

In *The Ginger Ale Boy* we have no shortage of displays of skill. The play begins with a big song and dance number: Bobby's flamboyant "bisexual transvestite" manager, Danny, *"singing, as the DANCERS dance"* (5). And just before the close of the play we are treated to a talent contest *"shown in a ridiculous collage as the COMMUNITY perform songs, dances, jokes etc."* (37). Surprisingly, the one skill that is most anticipated by the plot is never delivered. The play does not have a ventriloquist act despite being a drama concerning a ventriloquist. The dummy, Barney, in the piece is played by another actor—a female actress, Bríd Ní Chionla in the original production. Therefore the skill of animating the inanimate object (the dummy) is never on offer. Further to this we are not even shown a mock ventriloquist act with the two performers. Instead Bobby narrates the act to the audience describing his process and ability:

> Then I begin. It's me and Barney. We're mixing new material with old. I'm cutting a word too long and adding that one word too less. The words are flashing in front of my eyes … I grab them and I speak them out. From him or me. I speak words now, though you can't tell, can you? My lip-control is flawless. My tongue connects with my hand and it becomes Barney's tongue. His head pivots on my hand. To me, Barney's become alive. With lever and rope, yes, but most of all … its me … I'm the one who's woken him. A twist of

my hand is all it takes and a pinch of the lever, and with that look,
Barney's always there for me. (Walsh 8)

Ventriloquism is here made all the more poignant by its absence. Its
metaphorical significance is stressed and is key to the understanding of
this early piece as well as to Walsh's subsequent work. Steven Connor
writes:

> Ventriloquism is one of the most pervasive metaphors by which
> issues of identity ownership and power have been articulated
> within a culture of performance. It could be said that all
> performance is broadly ventriloquial, in a double movement
> whereby the performer gives his or her voice to another, and, in
> the process, takes the voice of that other into him—or herself.
> (Connor 88)

In Connor's reading and in Bobby's narration of the act it is clear
that ventriloquism offers Walsh a vehicle in which to interrogate the
efficacy of performance—the delight of skill and control but the fear of
losing oneself in the playing. The dummy and vent act can act as a
metaphor for this very indeterminate nature of performance. This is
something that O'Toole highlights in his review of the play:

> The ventriloquist's dummy, though usually employed for
> children's entertainment, has always had an unmistakable air of
> menace. Like some kind of humanoid automaton it occupies a
> disturbingly uncertain space—a machine with a human voice, a
> moving statue, a cruelly wooden parody of human gestures. It is a
> mockery of human gestures. It is a mockery of human
> individuality and the dialogue between the dummy and the
> ventriloquist is a parody of conversation. A man talking to himself
> with his hand up the back of a gangly doll may be funny, but he is
> also inevitably an image of madness. (10)

Helen Davies in her study of ventriloquism echoes O'Toole's notion
of the dummy as human automaton but sees the relationship in terms
of representations of power and performance rather than conversation.
She writes,

> the ventriloquist's puppet is often a simulacrum (or "copy') of a
> human being but, more importantly, the dummy is compelled to
> recite a script authored by another

and for Davies

> in the specific context of the dummy/vent performance,
> ventriloquism is an illusion of abnegated autonomy on the part of
> the ventriloquist as s/he orchestrates her/his own lack of control
> (18).

Throughout Walsh's work we see this dummy /vent "illusion of abnegated autonomy" or "orchestrated lack of control" staged as a means to interrogate the power of performance to order behaviour (the ritual, routine and script) but also submit to disorder and chaos (the unpredictable reality of other people and the unruliness of live theatre). This is most obvious in *The Walworth Farce*—where two sons must spend their days acting out a farce scripted and controlled by their abusive father who uses the daily performance to rewrite his past in order to escape the trauma of memory and of the present. This same pattern is evident in the earlier *bedbound* in which Daughter similarly must construct her Dad's invented past through performance. While in *Penelope* suitors at the bottom of a swimming pool compete to out perform each other in order to win Penelope who, looking down on them, appears as a puppet master, but is herself that most famous example of "abnegating autonomy" in her loyalty to a long-absent husband. The characters of Man and Woman in *The Small Things* narrate the dystopian world of their childhood in which Woman's father and the "chip-shop man" began making dummies of the townsfolk by cutting out their tongues so they may speak for them and maintain order. Man and Woman tell their story in fragments with the pace of their delivery controlled by time—the ticking of clocks, the call to action of sounded alarms and the expectation of timpani drums.

In *The Ginger Ale Boy* the dummy/vent relationship and its inherent "illusion of abnegated autonomy" or the controlled play of lack of control is represented via substitution and the split subjectivity that can be captured in the double act. The dummy Barney stands in for or substitutes for Bobby in crucial scenes: his date with Love Interest and his big break interview with Television Woman. Bobby speaks the lines from his bedroom located on a higher level upstage while Barney mouths the words and interacts with the other characters on the un-localized apron space downstage. Thus Bobby is at once absent (in body) and present (through speech) in these pivotal scenes. But full presence is demanded at such turning points where his actions will determine his success in love and the realization of his ambitions. His lack of presence is his undoing. Both the date and the interview are a disaster. Bobby does not commit himself to the present reality but chooses to remain distant through performance.

In their relationship as Dummy/Vent Bobby and Barney present a classic double act of straight man and clown but in these substitution scenes by standing in for each other they also present themselves as a doubling act. Anthony Roche has established the use of the double act in Irish drama from Yeats through Beckett to Kilroy as a recurring trope writing,

> the tendency in Irish theatre has been away from the idea of a single leading man and towards the sharing of the stage space between two male protagonists, neither of whom predominates. (48)

The most famous example of a double act at the heart of a contemporary Irish play is that of Gar Public and Gar Private in Brian Friel's *Philadelphia here I come*. In this play the double act is also a doubling act of split subjectivity: two actors play two aspects of the one personality. We have the public and the private persona of Gar O'Donnell portrayed simultaneously. In many ways *The Ginger Ale Boy* could be read as a rewriting of this canonical Irish play. The two plays stage the attempted rites of passage of a young man (whose split persona is represented by two actors) becoming an adult and moving on both literally and figuratively. They both also contain father figures that cannot communicate with their sons and ambiguous endings. And most importantly to my argument here they both contain a device borrowed from the variety theatre to serve their dramatic design in terms of both plot and theme—with Friel using the double act and Walsh using the ventriloquist routine, itself a twist on the double act. But Gar Public and Gar Private are never confused for one another and are portrayed as a classic double act in which two contrasting figures usually, one serious and the other comic, struggle to complete various ridiculous routines while either sparring with or supporting each other or doing a combination of both. Tony Whitehead suggests that "the classic double act of straight man and clown is also predicated on the conflict between the realism of the world as we know it (conformity or pragmatism) and the fantasy of the world as we would like it to be (anarchy or wish-fulfilment)" (Peacock 51). In *Philadelphia* Gar Private is easily identified as the inner anarchic clown full of wish-fulfilment while Gar Public shows the outer pragmatic mask of the conformist. In the common ventriloquist act the dummy is assigned the role of the clown and the ventriloquist is the straight man. However, in the substitution scenes where Barney stands in for Bobby, Walsh confuses this relationship and it is unclear which is the clown and which the straight man. Indeed, by the end of the play Bobby is presented as becoming a dummy—his face is smeared with make-up and he gives in to silence.

The original production twisted the representation of the "male" double act even further casting the female actress Bríd Ní Chionla as

Barney. Traditionally the dummy puppet is a boy and the ventriloquist acts as surrogate parent to the puppet. This is something made explicit in the mother's line when Bobby first receives the dummy as a gift from his Aunty: "You reached down and picked up Barney like he himself was a little toddler" (Walsh 29). Connor suggests a reason why the dummy is predominantly represented as a male child:

> One might suggest that the reason boys became the favoured form of ventriloquial dummy was because they allowed for the exercise of this violence in a way that little girls or animals could not. For little girls and animals are supposed to be helpless and innocent and we are conventionally outraged when they are hurt. Little boys, those famed repositories of slugs and snails and puppy-dog's tails, are never innocent, or never wholly so. (88)

Bobby is identified as a *"boy/man"* (Walsh 5) in the opening stage directions and this duality is given physical representation when we consider Barney as representative of the "boy" part of Bobby's identity. Although this, of course, becomes confused as the play develops when the double act transforms into the doubling act already mentioned. Connor in his psychoanalytic reading of the ventriloquist act identifies this very trait that is made explicit in *The Ginger Ale Boy* when he writes:

> Paternity is often an issue in such routines; often the ventriloquist attempts to supply the place of the figure's real father, who is said to be elsewhere. The ventriloquist fathers himself, in a not-quite-bodiless vocal birth, in which the child never in fact leaves the ventriloquist's body (indeed, the ventriloquist is partly inside the body of its figure). (88)

In the first production it was obvious that the boy/dummy was a woman. This play on gender roles further destabilizes the representation of a fixed identity in the piece. In playing against gender type the performativity of the actor's adopted persona is highlighted. The fixed self of Bobby is fragmented and refracted in these other double selves of the dummy Barney that is played by a woman. Another meta-theatrical layer and twist of the premiere production was Enda Walsh himself playing Bobby under his own acting persona of Eanna Breathnach. None of the reviewers of this early work name Eanna Breathnach as Enda Walsh in their critiques but instead treat them as two separate people praising Breathnach for his acting and Walsh for his promise as a playwright. In this then Walsh himself in the first production could be considered to be a double ventriloquist. The issue of paternity and ventriloquism is also explored outside of the Bobby and Barney relationship in the depiction of Bobby's parents. The mother is a particularly dominant force who pushes her son to be famous. He functions as her puppet to be manipulated. She repeatedly states how Bobby's fame will serve as vehicle for her escape from Ireland, "Europe's coal bunker" (Walsh 26), to the happiness of her native "Anglia" (Walsh 38). Bobby will be her salvation. This is made clear when she tells of the day that her sister Daisy left her father's dummy, Barney, for Bobby: "And when you opened that suitcase, love ... ooooooohhh ... to see that face...Just like baby Jesus, except real" (Walsh 29).

If his mother can be read as a ventriloquist, Bobby's father is even more obviously a silent dummy. He is an absent figure that is never given an embodied representation on stage and as such is a diegetic character that is only animated (given life) in the words of others. Further to this Bobby tells us that his dad "hasn't spoken for about two years" (Walsh 11) and later that he catches his father mouthing to the television: "Four o'clock on the hottest day of the year and there he sat mouthing Karl Malden's lines on *The Streets of San Francisco*" (18). The father thus serves to underscore the continual dialectic between presence and absence in the play. He is not present for his son and communication is impossible. However, unlike Gar O'Donnell in Friel's *Philadelphia* Bobby does not will his father to speak. He instead enjoys his father's silence stating "there are worse things than staying quiet in life. I think so, anyway" (Walsh 11). The father's absence and silence is a welcome contrast to his Mother's garrulous overbearing presence. Parents, such as those in *The Ginger Ale Boy*, depicted as both domineering and defeated are recurring figures in Walsh's drama (most obviously in *The Walworth Farce*, *bedbound* and *The Small Things*). Parenting serves as another example of a ventriloquial performance wherein people who have children must follow a script forced upon them by culture and society. Such a script demands that they should instantly become assured, kind, strong and selfless automatons that serve their children's needs. The parents of Walsh's plays resist this role and are presented with all their human failings.

The final scene of *The Ginger Ale Boy* ends ambiguously. Bobby declares to his dummy, Barney: "Have all my words come down to this? (*Long pause*). Where's the song and dance to see us through, hey, Barney? (*Long pause*.) This is it. There's nothing left to say" (Walsh 38). He then attempts to work the dummy but "his heart and mind aren't able" (Walsh 38) and the dummy falls from his hand. The stage directions tell us that he sits holding a "*bunch of daisies*" and "*allows failure to take him*". His mother approaches him "*but can't comfort him*" (Walsh 38). "*A strong yellow light*" comes up on them, "*Blackout*" and "*End*" (Walsh 38). It is this yellow light which brings ambiguity. The colour yellow has earlier in the play been associated with silence and death. Bobby has told us of his father's butterfly collection "framed up in the hallway". And how the butterflies are "all a yellow colour". As already mentioned, Bobby's father is an absent figure who no longer speaks. Thus this final image of the play could be read as tragically deterministic where the ambitious Bobby is left to inexorably repeat the fate and failure of his father. But the colour yellow has also been associated with joy and release through an earlier speech by his mother in which she spoke of how when she was first with his father and moved to Ireland she felt "spread before me at grabbin" distance was a life of wonderful ambition' (28). This optimism is married to the colour yellow when a few lines later she tells us about "these yellow butterflies that your Dad would arrive in with after work and he'd let them fly about the house. It was so beautiful" (28). Further to this she associates baby Bobby's arrival with hope, bringing the colour yellow into the dull grey of the world. She does this in the following passage that would make a Freudian swoon:

> But when I lay you down on my bed, Bobby, you lit up the house in a light of your very own. So we learnt to look out, didn't we? Out at the others and we planned to turn that grey back to what's right. Your dad too stuck those butterflies behind that frame ... "And one day I'll let them go! One day when it's colour I see!" That was our plan, Bobby. Still is with me. (Pause). (29)

The yellow light at the end of the play through its association with the butterflies thus captures the complicated feelings of mental breakdown mixing failure and release. For Bobby himself the colour yellow is triumphant. He tells us early on:

> So this is my life you're in apparently. It's all too simple when I think of it. There's me and Barney, Mother and Danny and my girl. And all of us just trying to keep our heads above to catch that bright canary yellow. (18)

In the closing moments we know Bobby will not be the success he hoped for but he will no longer be a dummy forced to perform a script written for him by others. The final yellow lighting cue offers transcendence but we are unsure if this is the transcendence of hope or the ultimate transcendence of death.

Such ambiguous endings are common in Walsh's work. In a review of *The Walworth Farce* for *The Canadian Theatre Review* Kim Solga writes of how she is disturbed by how the play suggests "That performance might augment and reproduce, rather than rehearse in order to assuage, the traumas of the past? (90) She then ends her review disturbed by the dystopian vision projected in the performance asking: "Can theatre, it seems to ask, really allow us to stage, to purge, to deal, and then to move on? Because nobody in *The Walworth Farce* moves on—although every character plays to survive (Solga 89). Eamonn Jordan in his article also on *The Walworth Farce* would seem to answer Solga's concerns when he writes:

> Bizarrely, dysfunction does not necessarily win out. That is where the affirmation emerges in a curious way, as diasporic dystopia on offer is contested by constructive creativity, inventiveness, and the free spirited nature of the performances. The assuredness, exuberance and the commitment of the performers wins out despite the chaos. The production becomes a celebration of performance. (Trench 135)

Jordan's point also rings true for the end of *The Ginger Ale Boy* and I would argue for the majority of Walsh's work. I would further Jordan's stance by claiming it is the use of variety entertainments as structural and thematic device in the dramaturgy that allow for this simultaneous presentation of a dystopia but the feeling or affect of utopia. In this, for all their darkness Walsh's plays in their commitment to entertainment function as what Jill Dolan has labelled "utopian performatives" (8), which she explains "spring from a complex alchemy of form and content and location, which take shape in moments of utopia as doings, as process, as never finished gestures toward a potentially better future" (8). She also claims that "Utopian performatives exceed the content of a play or performance; spectators might draw a utopian performative from the most dystopian theatrical universe" (Dolan 8). Thus Walsh's plays confront the multivalent nature of performance. They depict how performance can be a toxic distraction, an unhealthy sanctuary for the vulnerable and traumatized as well as an effective means of control. But in the performance of this dystopian theatrical universe these plays also invite us to witness amazing displays of skill and frenetic inventiveness that leave us still marvelling at the beauty of humanity even when it is at its most ugly.

Works Cited

Brook, Peter. *The Empty Space,* London: Penguin, 1968. Print.

Colgan, Gerry."The Ginger Ale Boy, Project Arts Centre", *The Irish Times,* September 8, 1995, p.13. Print.

Connor, Steven. "Violence, Ventriloquism and the Vocalic Body", *Psychoanalysis and Performance* edited by Patrick Campbell and Adrian Kear, New York: Routledge, 2001

Davies, Helen. Gender and Ventriloquism in Victorian and Neo-Victorian Fiction: Passionate Puppets, Basingstoke: Palgrave Macmillan, 2012

Dolan, Jill. *Utopia in Performance: Finding Hope in the Theater*, Ann Arbor: University of Michigan Press, 2005. Print.

Double, Oliver. *Britain Had Talent, A History of Variety*, Basingstoke: Palgrave, 2012. Print.

Dyer, Richard. *Only Entertainment, Second Edition*, New York: Routledge, 2002. Print.

Fitzpatrick, Lisa. "Enda Walsh." *The Methuen Drama Guide to Contemporary Irish Playwrights*. Ed. Martin Middeke and Peter Paul Schnierer. London: Bloomsbury, 2010. Print.

Jordan, Eamonn. "It Would Never Happen On *The Waltons*: Enda Walsh's *The Walworth Farce*.", *Staging Thought: Essays on Irish Theatre Practice and Scholarship*, Ed. Rhona Trench, Oxford: New York: Peter Lang, 2012. Print

O'Toole, Fintan. "Second Opinion: Watch My Lips" *The Irish Times*, September 12, 1995, p.10 Print.

Peacock, Louise. *Slapstick and Comic Performance: Comedy and Pain*, Basingstoke, Palgrave, 2014.

Roche, Anthony. *Contemporary Irish Drama, Second Edition*, Basingstoke, Palgrave, 2010. Print

Solga, Kim. *Canadian Theatre Review*, 145, Winter (2011): pp. 89-91

Walsh, Enda. *Enda Walsh Plays: One*, London, Nick Hern Books, 2013. Print

---. *The Walworth Farce*, London, Nick Hern Books, 2007.Print

Weaver, Jesse. "'The Words Look After Themselves': The Practice of Enda Walsh." *Irish Drama: Local and Global Perspectives*. Ed. Nicholas Grene and Patrick Lonergan. Dublin: Carysfort Press, 2012. Print.

3 | Pig is/is not Runt: Gender and Shared Identity in the film adaptation of *Disco Pigs*

Kevin McCluskey

Historically, film adaptations of Irish plays have drawn on a very narrow selection of representations. From the US film company Kalem's silent versions of Dion Boucicault's melodramas to Brian Desmond Hurst's Synge adaptations, the positioning of picturesque rural locations as places harbouring the narratives of the "real" Ireland has been prevalent. Another major trend—an interest in adapting both mainstream commercial successes and canonical texts, has meant that the scope of what Irish theatre has to offer beyond the Abbey Theatre has been under-explored in cinema. From Alfred Hitchcock's *Juno and the Paycock* to Emmet Dalton's films with the Abbey Players and John Ford's *The Rising of the Moon* and *The Plough and the Stars* it is clear that, where film adaptation is concerned, the Abbey has historically served as something of a synecdoche of Irish performance practice. Jim Sheridan's 1990 film of John B. Keane's *The Field* arguably marks a turning point in the re-examination of Irish plays in its significant re-working of Keane's play to explore redemption, justice, and a destructive heritage of violence inherited from the colonial past. Since *The Field* we have also seen low budget films of plays that are not products of the Dublin theatre scene, including versions of Abbie Spallen's play *Pumpgirl* and the all-women theatre group Trouble and Strife's devised piece *Now and at the Hour of Our Death* (the film version is called *Silent Grace*), as well as Enda Walsh's *Disco Pigs*. *Disco Pigs*, first staged by the Cork-based company Corcadorca, presents an eruption of violence and sexuality and a retreat from mimetic representation in its exploration of a relationship between two teenagers. This chapter argues that, through the reworking of his play as a screenwriter Enda Walsh, alongside the director Kirsten Sheridan, revisits the play in order to explore the struggle between a developing female identity and the forces that seek to define and contain it. These influences include the competitiveness and violence stereotypically encouraged in males in society, and the state's influence through education and reform systems. This chapter will argue that, in re-exploring his play on screen, Walsh also explores pressures facing Irish youth along gendered lines, focusing on the similarities and differences brought to light when female and male identities conflict. The addition of new characters, the changes in performance from stage to screen, and how the editing and camera work of the film explore male-female power dynamics will be explored. I will look at how the film incorporates concerns in Irish society surrounding anti-social behaviour and suicide in the younger population, comparing the language and story of the original play with the changes made in the adaptation process. This chapter will reveal how aspects as seemingly minute as costume decisions can have a marked impact on the movement from stage to screen.

First performed in 1996, *Disco Pigs* sees two teenagers—the male Pig and female Runt, narrate events in their lives in Cork as they look forward to celebrating their seventeenth birthdays. Born on the same day, the pair have an intense relationship, appearing to share a grotesque and violent worldview which they communicate to the audience in an invented language of slang and baby talk occasionally punctuated with pig noises. Walsh's script gives no instructions for set design—occasional directions such as one calling for "*sounds of a quiet bar*" create impressions of locations, but otherwise the sense of space and place is controlled by the bodies and performances of the two actors (168). The play shifts from Pig and Runt's collective narration of past events to their present interactions and reactions, with all knowledge of the past and of other characters made available to the audience only through Pig and Runt's descriptions and impersonations. Like Owen McCafferty's *Mojo Mickybo* and Marie Jones's *Stones in his Pockets,* Walsh's play belongs to a large group of plays from the 1990s that emphasized narration within performance, with two actors given the responsibility of conveying a larger world of events and characters through a variety of metatheatrical techniques. The frantic pace of the piece coupled with the language and the shifting levels of narration obscures any sense of a conventional plot structure. Loosely speaking the play hinges on the transformation of Pig and Runt's relationship from one that is rather childlike in their games and language to one that is fraught with sexual tension and animosity, with Pig viewing Runt as something that belongs to him after kissing her. Runt also changes, desiring something approaching normality when she envisages having a social life that exists apart from her friendship with Pig. In the final moments of the play the pair describe a final act of violence in which Pig, seething with jealousy at the sight of a boy dancing with Runt, kills the boy in a nightclub. Following Pig's violent act Runt runs to escape from Pig. As Pig repeatedly shouts "stay!" Runt delivers her final speech, ending the play on a note of hopefulness that is nevertheless shadowed by uncertainty:

> **Runt.** But is OK now, all right. (*Beat.*) Runt, she calm ... calm down ... an I watch ... da liddle quack quacks ... I look ... at the ducks ... as they swim in the morning sun ... in the great big ... watery shite ... that is the River Lee. Where to? (188)

This moment suggests both Runt's liberation from Pig's influence and her effort to reject a world rife with male violence carried out in the pursuit of "ownership" of a female. From the words "I look" onward Runt abandons the language she shared with Pig. Walsh's final stage directions, with the light fading first on Pig and then on Runt, does suggest an end to the disastrous but dynamic relationship shared by the two characters. However, Runt's "where to?" suggests a loss of direction as much as it suggests the emergence of new possibilities; with this ambiguity there also exists the possibility that Pig and Runt could resume their relationship. Up until these final moments there is little sense that the work is "about" one character more than the other—both are onstage throughout the performance and are each given long soliloquies revealing their thoughts to the audience earlier in the play. In comparison to the treatment of the characters onstage, Sheridan's 2001 film adaptation positions Runt as the central character. Through the introduction of new material and the direct dramatization of characters that were previously only present through Pig and Runt's impersonations, Walsh and Sheridan re-explore the character of Runt in terms of her struggle to define herself as a separate entity from Pig. This struggle is largely a gendered one revolving around oppositions between female socialization, expectations surrounding romantic and sexual relationships, and masculine violence. Walsh's screenplay and Sheridan's film also appears to establish an opposition between objective realism and fantastical theatricality that runs parallel to the split that occurs in the relationship between the central characters.

The film's shift from the play's telling mode to a showing mode involves the inclusion of additional characters and locations. This is a typical practice in stage-to-screen adaptation, but unlike film versions that expand upon and continue the realistic dramaturgy of a source text, the film of *Disco Pigs* is more comparable to works that adapt prose fiction with unreliable narrators. This is crucial for what the audience experiences as "real"—unlike the play, the world of the film is not thoroughly and consistently mediated by Pig and Runt. In portraying these additional characters with other actors onscreen, Sheridan's film places the audience at a remove—we observe the behaviour of the characters Pig and Runt, but we now see it in a context of the reactions of a wider group of characters and society at large. After a year and a half working on the screenplay Walsh, recognizing that "the whole logic of that performance world the characters inhabit is very difficult to transfer to film", settled on a final draft that he was satisfied with, with his ultimate approach summarized by his remark that "the rules have to change so much. In the play they don't talk to anyone, but in the film I needed to bring them into different worlds" (Patrick 18). It is this "different world" that represents a marked shift in how these characters are treated onscreen. Walsh's play, with its numerous shifts between time periods as Pig and Runt collaborate in their narration, in many ways corresponds to Martin Puchner's identification of an anti-mimetic stance that prioritizes language in modernist drama. Puchner writes that

> [d]iegesis redefines what we see and thus conditions our perception and reception of the theater. In doing so, it mediates the theater through an art form much more acceptable to modernism, namely, literature. (25)

Walsh's valorization of language and his eschewing of a realistic set supports the achronological structure of the piece, with the play epitomizing Nicholas Grene's statement that in contemporary Irish drama "mimetic theatrical space is more or less eliminated" (65). Aside from the change in visceral impact—having a violent action described verbally is markedly different to seeing it acted out—the camera and its tendency toward objectivity and the presentation of interactions without the constant mediation of Pig and Runt means that the film largely rejects the play's prioritizing of verbal communication, seeking other ways to explore Pig and Runt and their relationships with each other and with the wider world.

The film covers the birth of Runt and her first meeting with Pig as a baby, moving on to show them as teenagers and inserting occasional flashbacks to their childhood. As in the play, the pair gets into trouble repeatedly through such actions including robbing and vandalizing an off-license and playing sexually humiliating pranks that involve Runt dancing with a boy before Pig sneaks up and pulls their trousers down. Unlike the play, on film these acts are shown to lead to sanctions. Acting on advice from teachers, Runt's parents send her to an all-girl reform school outside Cork. This separation proves to be disastrous for Pig's already volatile mental state. Pig leaves home and tracks Runt down at her new school, taking her away from it and returning to Cork to journey through the streets and clubs of the city. Here, the film follows what is described in the play—Pig sees Runt dancing with a boy (on film this character Marky has been expanded through other interactions with Runt) and beats him to death in a night club. Following this, Runt flees the scene to escape from Pig. The film ends rather differently—whereas the play ends with Runt having escaped from Pig, on film Runt does not outrun Pig. Instead, they journey to a beach together. Runt then smothers Pig, but he seems to agree to her doing this—in his writing on the film Pat Brereton characterizes the scene as an assisted suicide (414). In a final voiceover monologue Runt says:

> It's like I really do want for something else, yeah? That silence again. And so I know that he, too, is silent and safe. And Runt alone. She calm. And you know? The sun—it really is a big beautiful shining thing. But where to, eh pal? Where to?

Though the "where to?" mirrors the final lines of the play, the context of Pig's death and the final image of Runt walking along the beach as the sun rises is arguably a more optimistic ending; here, the absolute finality of Pig and Runt's relationship suggests more strongly that Runt will explore her own identity away from Pig in a way that will bring her contentment. Brereton argues that "[l]ike many dystopic texts, most of the narrative is framed around various forms of dysfunctional environments, which are not conducive to character development, much less any form of self-actualization" (414). The dysfunctional environments in the film include the reform school, the night club culture, and the home lives of Pig and Runt. I would argue that, not only does the ending gesture toward the beginning of Runt's successful self-actualization, but that the film adaptation is largely structured around Runt's previous failed attempts to seize authority over her own identity, all of which are presented in terms of struggles involving gender and the expectations of society.

One way in which the narrative of the film is focused more on Runt is through the presence of Runt as a voiceover narrator in the opening scenes. Whereas the play opens with Pig and Runt frantically describing their births by mimicking women in labour and saying vulgar lines such as "An my mam she pain no more! Sorta happy wid wat she fart out", the film opens with Runt narrating only her birth (Walsh 163). Slow organ music and soft lighting accompany images of a baby in the womb. Runt begins speaking her narration serenely—her words "I make up my mind to stay in this lovely warm pink goo. The thumpety-thump of the heart—my only true pal" already suggests that to be born and to enter the world involves the relinquishing of safety and comfort. A tunnel effect with a circle of light is shown when Runt is about to be born, with the camera moving toward it to suggest the baby arriving in the world. The screen fills with white light which then fades to show a shot of the baby being held and washed in the hospital. The move from soft lighting, gentle camera movements and ethereal music, to the dank lighting of the hospital ward, signifies a leap into harsh naturalism. The film will repeatedly explore the movements between fantasy and reality, for example when it cuts to scenes showing Pig and Runt's shared vision of themselves dressed as a king and queen. Though the film opens and closes with Runt's voiceover narration and the plot is more centred on Runt's ordeals, it must be stressed that the entire film is not concerned with showing us only Runt's subjective experience—she is not comparable to what Brian Richardson would term a "generative narrator"—a character in stage drama who narrates their subjective recollection of events that are then performed (152). Indeed, in his application of narrative theory to the film Dióg O'Connell argues that "from the opening sequence the audience is plunged to the "subjective levels" of characterization in narrative terms" and notes that "[m]uch of the narrative is internally focalized, either from Pig or Runt's point of view" (118). While it is true that the narrative occasionally switches between the points of view of each character, the film is undoubtedly more concerned with the growth of Runt as a character than it is with the tumultuous and perhaps even stubbornly regressive state of Pig's interior life. Showing Runt alone in her crib for a few brief moments, Sheridan uses point-of-view shots to show the world through a baby's eyes—the ceiling above the crib and the almost grotesque close-ups of cartoon characters on the walls are one of few instances in the film where Runt's gaze is shown. When Pig is placed in the crib next to her a music cue and a close-up of the two babies holding hands across the divide establishes the central relationship—Runt's existence and exploration of the world on her own has now been interrupted, and will remain so until the closing moments of the film. Sheridan and Walsh emphasize the importance of this first encounter in the closing moments of the film—following Pig's death, there is a cut to the close-up of the babies' hands, a book-end of sorts that lends symmetry to Runt's character arc as it shows her once more in a world without Pig.

The uncertain borders between an extremely close interpersonal bond and the absorption of two people into a shared identity is explored throughout the film. Onstage the language of Pig and Runt is more obviously distorted and artificial, and as such the entire world described to the audience is also distorted. On film Pig and Runt's shared methods of communication are more comprehensible and less frantic, primarily because the camera takes over from the descriptive function of the language. Language and accents were a concern for Walsh and Sheridan during the making of the film, with Sheridan remarking on the subtitling of the film *Ratcatcher* and the reshooting of *Trainspotting* with clearer dialogue for US audiences as possibly setting a precedent (Shields 13). The use of animalistic grunting and even the names Pig and Runt (their real names are revealed to be Darren and Sinead) are dehumanized and also ungendered, though it is significant that the name Runt, signifying weakness and smallness, is applied to the female character. The genesis of the play involved Walsh reading Marjorie Wallace's book *The Silent Twins,* a non-fiction work exploring the identical twins June and Jennifer Gibbons and their rejection of communication with anyone except each other and their formation of their own language and social cues (Patrick 17). Like Pig and Runt, the Gibbons' relationship also escalated into crime and violence. Whereas Pig and Runt's narration onstage is a collaborative act of authorship demonstrating shared language, thoughts, and concepts, the film emphasizes this collective identity in other ways. Even the trailer for the film highlights the blurring and confusion of boundaries and identities, with the words *Pig, is, Runt,* and *isn't* flashing across the screen in different orders. In an interview Sheridan said that she watched a recording of Cillian Murphy in the stage version after she finished directing the film. Comparing Murphy's performance in the play to his work in the film, she said that "It was much more lustful than I expected; the sexuality was much more lust than babies. For me they were like two babies." (Shields 13). Following on from this comment, it is clear that the film emphasizes that the bond between Pig and Runt is forged before they are conditioned by the outside world. The film version, more strongly than Walsh's play, suggests that societal expectations surrounding gender, sexuality, language, and behaviour come to intrude upon the central relationship—confronted with the possibilities to adapt or self-destruct, Pig gravitates toward destruction and Runt towards change.

Though the adaptation expands the visual schemata from that of the original play, Sheridan still seeks to visually retain the sense of a universe shaped by Pig and Runt's intense bond. Interesting visuals include the image of Pig and Runt holding hands through a hole in the wall between their houses, echoing the scenes of them as babies. In the first half of the film Sheridan frames Pig and Runt together in shots, drawing attention to them in various ways; for example, in a scene at the beach overhead long shots show the pair sitting together in an otherwise empty space. This technique is repeated in the film, with the couple decentred in the frame. The editing in earlier scenes establish Pig and Runt's synchronized routine—one shot shows their houses side by side, bisected only by a small brick wall. Sheridan shoots the exterior of the houses symmetrically, showing Pig and Runt enter their homes in step with one another, opening the doors and gates in the exact same way and closing them at the same time. When the relationship between the characters change, so does the approach to framing and editing.

> **PIG.** Why I kiss da honey lips a Runt? An now all dat I put my gob to is Runt
> I take an tase. I close da eyes an see da inhide a Runt legs. ... an Runt she give one mo moan an Pig he pour inta da Runt. We man an woman now. (179)

After Pig kisses Runt he delivers the above monologue detailing his sexual fantasies. The speech on film is lifted verbatim from the play text. The moment represents a clear change in the central relationship. Reflecting this change through cinematic techniques, Sheridan begins to film the front of the houses from other angles, with the movements of the characters no longer synchronized through editing. When Pig's anger and frustration worsens, jump cuts and handheld camera movements externalize his loss of control and his confused sense of reality.

The loss of a singular identity involves both a descent into animalistic traits and an abandonment of individuality that, for Runt, also involves the rejection of expectations of heterosexual femininity.

This can be read even in the costumes in the film. In the original stage production both actors wore white costumes signalling a uniform identity—promotional stills showing Cillian Murphy and the original Runt, Eileen Walsh, shows both actors with short haircuts and dressed in suits, suggesting Runt conforms to stereotypical notions of masculine appearance—an appearance that does not require Pig to similarly alter outward signifiers of his own gender (NUIG Archives Website). The film often shows the pair wearing very similar long coats with the hood up to obscure part of the face. Changes in Runt's clothing and appearance accompany changes in her character. We see this in the film's treatment of Pig's changing attitudes toward Runt. Onstage, Pig spontaneously kisses Runt in the aftermath of a prank they have played at a night club—Pig's change toward viewing Runt in a sexual light is soon after presented in the aforementioned monologue. Walsh emphasizes the importance of this moment in the structure of the play—the stage directions read *"Music. Pig stands out"* before Pig delivers the monologue, detailing his sexual fantasies about Runt (178). This moment is crucial in that it departs from the method of the two characters sharing the task of narration, affording the audience a glimpse into Pig's mind as separate from his interactions with Runt. On film the move from a telling to a showing mode facilitates a more gradual portrayal of the shift in the relationship. The film's first major suggestion of this change is with a scene in Shandon Church in which Runt tries on a skirt while Pig stands outside. When Pig re-enters and sees Runt in the dress the music rises and his facial expression changes, followed by a cut to a slow tracking shot moving toward Runt. Runt is heard saying "OK?" but her lips do not move. When Runt tells her that she's beautiful the music stops and we are brought back to reality with Runt's response: "Fuck off." In establishing the central conflict of the film—the struggle of the female character to define herself in an oppressive environment—this scene, particularly through the use of camera movements and music, demonstrates rather explicitly Laura Mulvey's theory of the male gaze in narrative cinema, emphasizing the act of looking (which the audience also partakes in) in the fictional world of a film. Mulvey writes that:

> In a world ordered by sexual imbalance, pleasure in looking has been split between active/male and passive/female. The determining male gaze projects its phantasy on to the female figure which is styled accordingly. In their traditional exhibitionist role women are simultaneously looked at and displayed, with their appearance coded for strong visual and erotic impact so that they

can be said to connote to-be-looked-at-ness. (837)

Pig's reaction to Runt in this scene is associated with her change in costume, a change that foregrounds here the "to-be-looked-at-ness" that Mulvey identifies. In this scene the editing, the discontinuity of sound and image, and the movement of the camera, all serve to show us Pig's view of Runt. Later, Runt will again explore traditionally feminine styles when she braids her hair and dresses up at the girl's reformatory. Significantly, this second exploration of femininity in the company of other women is not accompanied by the lingering shots and music of the earlier scene. This latter scene is suggestive of a monologue in the play in which Runt imagines having a female friend that she can dance with and confide in: "Maybe we dress before in my room! Maybe we chit chat an I say, I don fancy, Frankie, no, ohhh does it really show?" (185). Whereas onstage the characters author their story together, on film Pig is frequently the bearer of the gaze. He is repeatedly shown in the act of looking—watching Runt as she interacts with other people at school and in night clubs. In one scene he stands with a camera filming a couple kissing at school—after the couple notice him doing this, he asks them to continue, lifting the camera back up to continue recording. This moment typifies Pig's experience in the world—he is a voyeur, placed at a remove and lacking in understanding or empathy, trying to observe and shape the relationships of other people, first through subjecting them to his gaze and later through his use of violence. Through the absence of other actors the dramaturgy of the play effortlessly suggests that Pig and Runt exist in a world cut off from everybody else. On film Pig is more obviously the would-be creator of this closed-off world—his speech in which he fantasizes about returning from outer space with a laser and killing everyone except for himself and Runt is a reflection of how his actions repeatedly prevent Runt from interactions with other people, confining her to socializing only with him regardless of her own desires.

Runt's scenes in the reformatory in particular have a sombre realistic quality to them, with subdued camerawork and naturalistic lighting, in contrast with the fast-paced editing style and vibrant soundtrack of modern songs that are present in other sequences. The displacement of one style by another can be disruptive, and indeed some reviews of the film did criticize this approach as being both uneven and symptomatic of the film's stage origins (Ward 38). However, I would argue that the disparity in styles reflects the opposing trajectories of the characters. As Pig travels to meet Runt, he tells a story to an old man about Runt as a child being placed by her father in the boot of a car overnight as punishment for misbehaving. The whimsical music and the bright and exaggerated colour scheme of this memory scene is a clue that it is fantastical—in this tale, Runt is placed in the wrong car and travels all around the world with the owner of the car, before returning home to Pig. This story, which is not in the play, is interesting both because it suggests Pig's tendency to retreat into fantasy but also because it repeats Pig's narrative of Runt returning to him. There is a darker undercurrent to the story; prior to the section about Runt travelling the world, the memory shows Runt being beaten by her father as Pig stares at the television. The unreliability and instability of Pig as a character and his repeated forays into his own imagination mean that all that he says has a shadow of doubt over it, but nevertheless this moment places Pig as merely yet another oppressive male figure in Runt's life. When Pig appears alone onscreen the filmmaking approach often changes. Arguably Cillian Murphy's reconceptualizing of his stage performance onscreen is tasked with the theatricalizing of the film. We see this when, following Pig's change in feelings toward Runt, the film cuts to Pig alone in his bedroom, delivering the monologue explored earlier in this chapter. The moment is a pause in the action of the film, with the length of the speech and absence of a listener in the scene drawing attention to the theatrical roots of the film; the male/female struggle of Pig and Runt's relationship becomes an opposition of other styles, of the subdued and the frantic, the theatrical and the cinematic.

None of this is to suggest that the world that Pig and Runt are shutting out is a perfect or even healthy place either. Authority figures are repeatedly shown to be corrupt, irrational, or barely present. The head of the reformatory is shown as condescending and abusive, slapping Runt's friend Margaret during a meeting called to discuss the behaviour of both girls. A teacher at the school mocks a student who has difficulty reading aloud in class, humiliating him in front of his peers, and one of the authorities at the school brands Pig "a lost cause" in a discussion about whether or not Pig and Runt will respond to being separated. Clearly, although the film suggests a necessity for their relationship to end in order for Runt to establish her own identity, the society in which she is entering into is also presented as cruel and stifling—here, Brereton's description of the text as dystopic is apt. The push-pull between a unique and intense relationship with its own linguistic and behavioural codes and the expectations of wider society induces anxiety in the pair; the camera even reflects the breakdown in their relationship, with Sheridan abandoning her carefully composed shots that emphasize symmetry in favour of a mix of wildly different styles, most notably in the use of jump cuts and loud sounds of a heartbeat accompanying Pig's anguish when he discovers that Runt has been sent away. The strength of Walsh's adaptation is apparent when one considers how he expands Pig and Runt's social sphere. The humiliated male student, the violence and death sparked by a sense of ownership of another person, the discarding of Pig as a "lost cause", and even the addition of Pig's death and the characterization of it as a suicide situate the film in a context of crises in masculinities. These crises, as demonstrated in the film, also represent a threat to the wellbeing of women. In his work on masculinities in Irish stage drama Brian Singleton writes that the Irish male "was the subject of scrutiny by the emerging playwrights of the 1990s who configured abject males surfing on the social margins but in a personal and spiritual wasteland"; with the film of *Disco Pigs*, Walsh shifts the change in Pig and Runt's relationship from being a unique and rather personal implosion to being one that reflects on the fraught experiences of young men in an ever-changing society (15). Listing *Disco Pigs* among other Irish films in which "the school environment is a key contributing factor to the young male protagonist's unhappiness", Debbie Ging's *Men and Masculinities in Irish Cinema* identifies a range of issues surrounding masculinity-in-crisis, from the education system to unemployment, continually changing social mores and hegemonic notions that see the intertwining of masculinity with both violence and a reserved attitude toward emotional expression (67). By having Pig choose to die in the film version, Walsh adapts his own work in a way that reflects changing concerns between the original production and the time of the adaptation process. Suicide among male youth became a great matter of concern in the mid to late 1990s in the Republic of Ireland. A July 2006 Oireachtas report entitled "The High Level of Suicide in Irish Society" notes a greatly accelerated increase in suicide committed by young men in the period of 1989-1999 (17). The National Suicide Research Foundation emphasizes the disparity in the suicide rates of males and females, stating in 2002 the ratio of male to female suicides was over 4:1, with an increased ratio in younger age groups (The Male Perspective 7). Thus, though the film suggests hope in Runt's future, it raises awareness of a devastating trend among young Irish men, implicitly indicting the education system and gendered attitudes toward the behaviour and rehabilitation of troubled youth. Runt clearly suffers as the object of Pig's gaze, but Walsh rejects a black-and-white depiction of a male-female/victim-victimizer dynamic in favour of a more nuanced exploration of male emotional turmoil.

Walsh has stated that "what motivates me in theatre has always been to get close to characters who're on the edge of madness, or have entered it. It invigorates me to think that we're all the same ... The job of a playwright is to bring an audience close to characters they don't want to feel close to" (Pilny 221). On film, other characters are shown reacting in a puzzled way to Pig and Runt's way of speaking—in this sense we have an audience substitute or a guide to how to respond—something that is unavailable to an audience member of the play. Clearly the audience's proximity to characters who are on the brink of madness is less of a concern for Walsh in his work for the screen. Runt's acknowledgment of a need to escape in the closing moments of the play is the only instance onstage that contains any judgment of the central relationship from a critical or distanced perspective. On film, the inner world of the central relationship is repeatedly placed in opposition to the outside world. As such, some of the new characters appear as banal. A meeting between the parents of Pig and Runt and the school principal opens with the lines "It's simply not a healthy relationship. I mean you have to separate them, for their own good." The obviousness of the line coupled with the fact that the shot composition and editing is more conventional in these scenes suggests that, even though Pig and Runt's relationship is destructive, it has an element of creativity that is absent from their surroundings. Comparing the play, a frantic two-hander with actors working in close proximity to conjure some sense of an entire world through just their bodies and their words, with the film, which can explore as much as it wants through the apparatus of the camera, reveals just how radical the stage to screen adaptation process can be. Though the experience of theatre as a live event cannot be substituted, through the adaptation of *Disco Pigs* Walsh has created a new encounter with the same characters, expanding our view of events with a less uncomfortable proximity to "madness", but in a way that, I would argue, sheds new light on the original text whilst existing separately as a work that makes use of the language of cinema to explore both issues of gender and problems in Irish society at large.

Works Cited

Brereton, Pat. "Nature Tourism and Irish Film." *Irish Studies Review* 14.4 (2006): 407-420. Print.

Disco Pigs. Dir. Kirsten Sheridan. Renaissance Films, 2001. Film.

Ging, Debbie. *Men and Masculinities in Irish Cinema*. Basingstoke: Palgrave Macmillan (2013). Print.

Grene, Nicholas. "The Spaces of Irish Drama." *Kaleidoscopic Views of Ireland*. Eds. Munira H. Mutran and Laura P.Z. Izarra. São Paolo: Humanitas (2003): 53-73. Print.

The Male Perspective: Young Men's Outlook on Life. Ireland: Suicide Prevention Office (2003). Web. April 18th 2014. <http://nsrf.ie/wpcontent/uploads/reports/YoungMensStudy.pdf>

Mulvey, Laura. "Visual Pleasure and Narrative Cinema." *Film Theory and Criticism: Introductory Readings*. Eds. Leo Braudy and Marshall Cohen. Oxford: Oxford University Press (1999): 833-44. Print.

National University of Ireland Archives Blog. Web. 21 April 2014. <http://nuigarchives.blogspot.co.uk/2011/06/cillian-murphy-returns-to-galway-arts.html>

O'Connell, Díóg. "Narrative Strategies in Contemporary Irish Cinema: 1993-2003." PhD Thesis. Dublin City University, Dublin. 2005. Print.

Patrick, Jon. "'Transformer'—Interview with Enda Walsh." *Film Ireland* 82 (2001): 17-18. Print.

Pilny, Ondrej. "The grotesque in the plays of Enda Walsh." *Irish Studies Review* 21.2 (2013): 217-225. Print.

Puchner, Martin. *Stage Fright: Modernism, Anti-theatricality, and Drama*. Baltimore: Johns Hopkins University Press (2002). Print.

Republic of Ireland. Houses of the Oireachtas. Joint Committee on Health and Children. *The High Level of Suicide in Irish Society* 2006). Web. 30 April 2014. <http://www.nosp.ie/oireachtas_report.pdf>

Richardson, Brian. "Drama and Narrative." *The Cambridge Companion to Narrative*. Ed. David Herman. Cambridge: Cambridge University Press (2007): 142-155. Print.

Shields, Paula. "Animal Harm: Kirsten Sheridan on *Disco Pigs*." *Film Ireland* 83 (2001): 12-14. Print.

Singleton, Brian. *Masculinities and the Contemporary Irish Theatre*. Basingstoke: Palgrave Macmillan (2011). Print.

Walsh, Enda. "Disco Pigs." *Far From the Land: Contemporary Irish Plays*. Ed. John Farleigh. London: Methuen (1998): 159-189. Print.

Ward, Nada. "Film Review—Disco Pigs." *Film Ireland*. 83 (2001): 38-39. Print.

4 | The Representation of Vulnerability in Enda Walsh's *Sucking Dublin* and *Lynndie's Gotta Gun*

Lisa Fitzpatrick

Sucking Dublin and *Lynndie's Gotta Gun* are two examples of Walsh's minor work, from different stages of his career. *Sucking Dublin* was first printed with the critically acclaimed and popular *Disco Pigs*, and was first produced by the Abbey Theatre's Youth Outreach department in 1997, the year after Corcadorca's tour of *Disco Pigs*. Directed by Sarah Thornton following workshops with Youth Outreach Centres in deprived areas of Dublin, it was performed at the Samuel Beckett Theatre and at two other venues and has rarely been remounted. Most recently, the New Theatre performed it in February 2013 to lukewarm reviews. It is not published in the collection of Walsh's *Plays: One*, though other work written around the same time is included: *The Ginger Ale Boy, Disco Pigs, Misterman,* and *bedbound. Lynndie's Gotta Gun*, which is in the same collection, is a 5-page playlet that was first performed in 2005 at a conference in Lisbon by Artistas Unidos as part of a collection of sketches inspired by Harold Pinter. Its debt to Pinter's *One for the Road* is apparent, though refracted through Walsh's characteristic grotesque and clownish humour. It was first performed at the same time as a number of his more critically significant mid-career plays: *New Electric Ballroom* premiered in September 2004 at the Kammerspiele in Munich (and in 2008 by Druid Theatre Company); *The Small Things,* and *Chatroom* in 2005, and *The Walworth Farce* in 2006.

A recurring issue in Walsh's work is human vulnerability and responses to that vulnerability, and in this essay I am mainly concerned with its representation and performance in these two plays. In defining the term, I'm drawing on work by Judith Butler, Adriana Cavarero, Erinn Gilson and Ann Murphy. These scholars all argue that vulnerability to harm and to care are an aspect of the human condition that provokes responses of violence as well as of tenderness, and use this idea to explore the ethics of interpersonal relationships. While earlier plays like *Sucking Dublin* and *Disco Pigs* represent violent characters and their victimization of others, in later plays Walsh's characters repeatedly create performances and stories that make sense of their experiences of hurt or threat. The characters in *Walworth Farce* or *The New Electric Ballroom* rehearse and perform the moments that lead to their withdrawal from contact with the world, and this instinct towards isolation is present in nascent form in *Disco Pigs*. Darren and Sinead make up animal nicknames for each other and a shared *parole*, essential elements in their creation of "... a whirl where Pig an Runt jar king an queen! ... we make a whirl dat no one can live sept us 2" (Walsh 173). In *The New Electric Ballroom*, a small humiliation drives Breda and Clara to live within the walls of their family home, where they endlessly re-enact their moment of shame. In *The Walworth Farce* Dinny and his sons enact the story of Dinny's leaving Ireland, a tragic story recast as a farce in which Dinny is recreated as a self-taught brain surgeon, and Sean and Blake enact all the other characters, using wigs, small props, and the wardrobe as the off-stage space. As Dinny says, "What are we, if we are not our stories?" (Walsh 82). This later concern with levels of fictionality in performance is apparent in *Lynndie's Gotta Gun*, where the eponymous Lynndie tells her version of the war she is engaged in, where she casts herself a friend and hero rather than a torturer and executioner. In the earlier *Sucking Dublin*, the characters' violence towards each other is treated in a more naturalistic way, focusing on their various responses and their positioning within the group as perpetrator or victim. Both plays, however, address the question of who is vulnerable and how that vulnerability is expressed and internalized.

Taken together these texts open interesting questions about vulnerability, representations of gender, and sexual violence. The issue of bodily vulnerability has been a concern for feminist theory for some time, in both theoretical and sociological texts that examine the construction in discourse of women as weak and vulnerable, and the material consequences of such constructions. Physical vulnerability is often associated with the body's penetrability, making the female body normatively more vulnerable and thus more strongly associated with vulnerability of all kinds—including, in Christian teaching, a weakness towards sinfulness as well as harm.[1] The penetrability of *all* bodies is somewhat obscured by this emphasis on the female, while the corresponding configuration of the male body as *in*vulnerable may also be significant in the formation and normalization of oppressive relationships. Erinn Gilson argues that:

> ignorance is no mere lack of knowledge but rather is actively produced and maintained... ignorance of vulnerability is a pervasive form of ignorance that underlies other oppressive types of ignorance, all of which depend essentially on a form of closure. If this is the case, then the perilous effects of ignorance can be attenuated only through the cultivation of a certain kind of vulnerability, namely, epistemic vulnerability. (Gilson 308-309)

All the theorists distinguish between vulnerability and helplessness, a crucial distinction since one is only sometimes helpless, but always vulnerable. Gilson's essay proposes that ignorance of this shared vulnerability facilitates brutal responses when others are perceived as vulnerable. In *Sucking Dublin* Steve dominates the others through his capacity for sudden and unmotivated physical violence and emotional abuse, which emerges whenever they show weakness. Like *Disco Pigs*, *Sucking Dublin* sets the action in a small closed group of people in a dystopic urban setting, giving most of the characters nicknames that reflect their physical or mental attributes (Little Lamb, her boyfriend Lep and his sister Fat), and charting the chaos and speed of violence as it bursts out from the banal street language of the dialogue to physical form. *Sucking Dublin* is generally less inventive in its use of language than *Disco Pigs*, and missing the extraordinary energy of the more famous play.

The opening scene is set in Steve's council flat during Little Lamb's 18th birthday party: the lights come on full with loud music and the sight of the characters dancing. The flat is described as "a smartly decorated council flat" (Walsh 33) secured with a heavily bolted metal door. Outside the local community protests against Steve's presence: he is a heroin dealer who has killed their "dirty junky little cunts of kids"

---

[1] The "sealed" quality of the female virgin body is important in Christian iconography because, like the male body, it is conceived of as closed and invulnerable. The stories of virgin martyrs focus on the women's invulnerability to Satan and to doubt, despite the dreadful tortures which are typically inflicted upon them. See, for example, Karen A. Winstead, *Virgin Martyrs: Legends of Sainthood in Late Medieval England*, Ithaca & London, 1997.

(Walsh 51); their roars of "Out Out Out" punctuate the action. Steve shouts abuse back at them, taunting them that they can't get past his security door. A tension soon emerges between Steve and his girlfriend Amanda, who is Lamb's older sister: in the opening scene Steve flirts with Lamb but when Amanda interjects "Good looks are in the family!" he replies, "Looked in the mirror lately!" It becomes apparent that Amanda's desire for Steve is far greater than his for her; she is enthralled by him and his crude rejection of her only feeds her obsession. Meanwhile, Lep (short for Leper) is so drunk he has vomited on himself and passed out; this elicits tenderness from the gentle Little Lamb but irritation and violence from Steve. Fat eats, constantly: this action provokes contempt from Steve but Fat ignores him, absorbed in the action of consumption and (occasionally) defecation.

The first scene of physical violence emerges quite rapidly from Steve's response to the increasing drunkenness of his friends: he puts on devil horns and jumps up from behind the sofa, roaring loudly and alarming everyone in the room. He "roars into [Lep's] face again", repeatedly; Lep responds "Get fuckin off ya spastic! Jesus! He's mad Amanda! [...] Shit me knickers there!" As the scene continues, with Steve also getting drunk and moving in with apparent affection towards Little Lamb, his mood switches without warning. While dancing to "Happy Birthday To Ya", his playfulness turns to kissing her as she "folds into him, pissed and giggling", then:

> he suddenly loses it and kisses her more, feeling her up and placing her on the coffee table. Her sitting with her back to the audience. Steve gets down and begins to rape Little Lamb. She calls out Lep's name. She flops down on the coffee table her head facing the audience. Steven's actions are clumsy and lost but he goes at it really hard. Amanda looks on completely petrified. (Walsh 39-40)

When he stops, Little Lamb begins to cry and "wanders" over to the door, which she unlocks; Fat and Lep also leave. Amanda begins to clean up while Steve sits on the sofa.

Amanda refers to Steve's rape of Little Lamb, though she doesn't call it rape, in the closing scenes where she describes her longing for him "I want him to touch me now. I look at the same big fat hands that wrestled my little sister down last night" although her own thoughts sicken her "He's made the word "love" filth in my book". He tells her he will "break your fuckin face wide open! Like ya know I can, like ya know I will!" Towards the end of these scenes they fight physically, and Steve

*"grabs the teddy bear and rips it to pieces and forces it into her mouth
while hitting her"* (Walsh 54).

Steve's violence towards Amanda and Little Lamb, and the implicit
violence of his heroin dealing, can in each case be read as his response
to the represented vulnerability of the characters. Amanda's
vulnerability is in her unremitting desire for him, while Lep and the
local addicts are dependent upon him for access to the heroin they
crave. Little Lamb is constituted in every way as vulnerable: her name
suggests innocence and defencelessness, as does the name she gives her
daughter (Little Dove). Her love for Lep, covered in vomit and
unconscious with drugs and drink, marks her as undiscriminating and
generously non-judgemental. Finally Steve's comment that she looks
only about fourteen marks her as physically childish, small, and
relatively helpless in the face of the acts of violence visited upon her
during the course of the play. Little Lamb's odyssey around Dublin with
her baby brings her to a fast-food restaurant where she sits weeping
and reflecting on the place she comes from, where she sees "men who
look like sad dogs walkin about with nowhere to go", "women workin all
day long for no money", her mother is afraid to leave the flat and her
father promises "the world on five hundred pounds" (Walsh 42).
Throughout her odyssey around Dublin city centre she is alone,
accompanied only by her helpless infant, heightening her
characterization as fragile and imperilled. The city is represented
aurally as a violent place of threat and danger, unfriendly and uncaring.
Lamb is abused by passing men and women, accosted by a beggar,
propositioned by a group of friends "Get over here and sit on his face,
will ya gorgeous?!" (Walsh 47), and finally beaten up by a young couple.
Covered in blood, she decides to leave Dublin and announces to passers
by that she must leave Dublin and is looking for the way to the airport.
The final scene sees her in the airport, deciding to leave Dove behind
"for someone ta be a good mammy and daddy!" The pram is left alone
on stage as Lamb walks off and the lights come down. Her vulnerability
is gendered in her tenderness for Lep and for their baby, and the kinds
of violence the city visits upon her. But Walsh's main focus does not
appear to be on gender; Lamb is vulnerable but so is Lep, and so is Fat,
and in a different way, so are Amanda and Steve. Yet in Steve he creates
a character who is unable to respond positively to others, and who
shows no weakness until, left alone on stage when Amanda leaves, he
sits on the sofa and cries (Walsh 54).

The fact that it was written around the same time as *Disco Pigs*
makes it tempting to read Steve and Amanda's dysfunctional

relationship as another version of Pig and Runt's. Like Pig and Runt, they engage in acts of violence that Amanda witnesses and tolerates, and they part at the end in a moment that suggests that Amanda has realized she must extract herself from the little world of their apartment, while Steve—like Pig—is left bereft. But while Pig and Runt find solace and support in each other, *Sucking Dublin* offers a comfortless world in which those who are weak are ruthlessly exploited. Even Lep, who claims to love Little Lamb, fails to protect her from Steve or any of the other violence she experiences. Although the play sets up certain moments of sensory shock for the audience, such as the opening with sudden and simultaneous lights and loud music, or the repeated on-stage scenes of brutality, which are similar to those in *Disco Pigs*, it lacks the latter's moment of epiphany. Little Lamb realizes she must leave Dublin and she sets off for the airport and then, apparently, for the southern European coast but as she goes, she abandons Little Dove in a pram at the airport. Although Lamb states that this is the best possible decision for both herself and her child, the preceding scenes suggest the opposite.

Walsh's work is often concerned with the nature of violence but it rarely represents rape on stage. There are references to rape and sexual violence in *The Small Things*, but represented diegetically in the testimony of Woman. In that play, genocidal violence erupts from society's attempt to impose order. It progresses from the imposition of nonsensical regulations through the silencing of the population by cutting out their tongues, to the final massacres survived only by Man and Woman. There is a clear implication that the women are raped either before or after they are mutilated. Woman says that all the women were "made silent and one at a time taken to the woods" (Walsh 191). She recounts an experience of sexual assault when she is dragged away from her mother and into the woods "He opens my mouth ... I feel him inside my mouth and feel him drag at my hair. Face pressed to ground and punching and fucking in equal measures, you know that sad scene" (Walsh 192). She describes herself as having been "in a baggy swimsuit" (Walsh 192), the phrase evoking the underdeveloped body of the vulnerable child. Verbs like "drag", "punch" and "fuck" communicate the physical fear and panic of the assault, the "sad scene". The description is vivid and communicates a range of bodily experiences through language, but it involves no mimetic representation.

In contrast, in *Sucking Dublin* the mimetic performance of rape occurs early in the play and emerges from the verbal violence of a rough scatological and truncated dialogue that communicates the intoxicated exhaustion of the characters. The sense of threat that is present from the start from outside the domestic space suddenly erupts inside that supposedly secure and familial apartment, rupturing the natural affection of friendship and sibling relationships. The stage directions give no indication of the duration of the scene, which is always significant in the shaping of audience responses to representations of violence. But it indicates the violence of the actor's movement in the phrase "goes at it really hard", and in the frozen terror of the other characters. Little Lamb's drunken defencelessness is signalled by her inability to resist: she "flops" down on the coffee table, her head thrown back so that the audience can see her face. This position potentially creates a morphological sense of her disorientation and physical discomfort, quite apart from the pain of the rape. It is a marker of Steve's power that nobody intervenes or protests, but it also performs the shock of sudden violence in a presumed safe space and the sense of confusion created by such a transgression of normal social behaviour.

Taken together, *Sucking Dublin* and *Lynndie's Gotta Gun* raise two different issues about the assumption of female vulnerability. In *Sucking Dublin*, the image is normative in that it represents the vulnerability of a young female character to sexual violence. But *Lynndie* offers a more complicated representation of vulnerability in taking for its focus the crimes committed by Lynndie England at Abu Ghraib. The naming of the eponymous character and her characterization as an American soldier make that identification unavoidable, while the other two characters' generic names of Man and Boy position them both as representatives of the non-individualized, non-Western subjects of violence in American-controlled Iraq. They are revealed in the Man's opening lines as father and son. Lynndie England has been represented in a couple of plays, including Judith Thompson's *Palace of the End* and *My Pyramids*, her story was covered extensively and she has been interviewed by the international press including a major piece in *The Guardian* in 2009. Her active engagement in the torture of prisoners, while shocking in any circumstances, was almost certainly received as more so because of her gender.

Cavarero points out that it is difficult to make the argument that the women committing these acts of torture were vulnerable parties (106), but exploring their behaviour within a conception of vulnerability as an essential human quality allows for the complexities of the situation to emerge without reverting to stereotypes that seem to situate woman as victim (or man as aggressor). This sketch doesn't explore the issue to any extent, relying as it does on our extra-diegetic knowledge of the character and of the history of these events. This sketch was performed at a conference and was written for a specific context, so it has two existences: as a piece of grotesque brutality outside its historical context and as a commentary on the brutality that ordinary people, finding themselves unexpectedly powerful, will visit on others.

The lights come up on a man, standing on stage, terrified, looking towards the wings. Lynndie enters dressed as a children's party clown and carrying a large fish with which she "smashes the man in the face" knocking him to the ground. When he protests that he doesn't understand what he is doing there, she "slaps him on the head with the fish", then turns and leaves. She returns to hit him on the head with a frying pan, again knocking him down; she leaves and returns again with a "large cream cake", which she fires into the man's face (Walsh 187). The ensuing dialogue is the circular, Kafka-esque exchange of the interrogation room: the Man must give her the information she seeks, but what that information actually is, is classified. So he must guess correctly: what does Lynndie need to know to save his life and that of his child? His wife has already been taken by the soldiers because, the Man says, "You thought she had information, I suppose" (Walsh 189). Lynndie orders him "Tell me what you know"; when he says he doesn't know anything she calls him a liar and tells him "Every man has information" (Walsh 188). Since this is true, the man must agree with her, but in doing so he must incriminate himself. The dialogue evolves absurdly yet convincingly:

> MAN. ... I'm sure I don't have specific information. The information you want.
> LYNNDIE. How would you know that?
> MAN. Well, why don't you tell me what information you want to hear and I'll tell you whether I know it or not.
> LYNNDIE. Well, that would be Classified. Are you trying to get me in trouble with my superior? (Walsh 188)

The play ends with a gag: Lynndie aims and fires a gun "and a little flag comes out with "Bang" on it". The Man laughs "from exasperation" and thanks her, whereupon she draws another gun and shoots him dead (Walsh 191). She watches him bleed, then takes off her clown nose and puts it on his face. A ten-year-old boy walks on stage; Lynndie reloads the gun and points it at him as the stage goes to black. The fate of the child is thereby left to the imagination of the audience. The audience's temporary relief at the falseness of the gun heightens the shock of the sudden shooting and the threat towards the child.

In this very brief piece, Walsh returns again to the stories that we tell ourselves in order to survive, a central motif in his work. Lynndie's story situates her as a person motivated by the desire to help others and to make friends: travelling a long way to save people who—like the Man—turn out not to be as grateful as she had expected. In his portrayal of Lynndie, Walsh's dialogue echoes the self-justifying narratives of those accused of the Abu Ghraib abuses: their good intentions, the lack of gratitude of the Iraqi people, their sense of outrage at coming under attack from local forces. Juxtaposed with the Man, beaten and humiliated, separated from his wife and son, Lynndie's accusation "You've just got no idea of the sacrifices we're making, FUCKER!" (Walsh 190) speaks to the tragic absurdity of the conflict and to the forces that drive human beings to deny their shared vulnerability. Michael Billington, reviewing Druid's 2008 production of the piece, wrote that *Lynndie* "explicitly echoes Pinter's *One For The Road* even down to the torturer's need for approval; but, although too palpably Pinteresque, it is vividly directed by Sarah Lynch and packs a polemical punch" (online).

The torturer's need to be liked by her victim indicates the shared vulnerability of the two characters. Her frustration with his fear and her insistence that they should be friends, even lovers, is revelatory of her delusions but also, perhaps, of all torturers, bound to their victims by the intimacy of the infliction of pain on the subject body. The need to be liked and accepted reveals the vulnerability of the torturer, even as the spectators empathize with, and fear for, the endangered body of the victim. Walsh's Lynndie is not unlike the unnamed soldier in Judith Thompson's *Palace of the End*, whose monologue details examples of torture at Abu Ghraib and rages against the "Rakees" who fail to appreciate the generosity of their American liberators. Situating Walsh's character in this historical and social context—that of the actual individual and her biography as recorded in the press—develops a more complex sense of her as terrorized like her victim. Lynndie is aware that the Man might complain about her, and aware of the possibility of getting into trouble with her unnamed superior. But in addition to the hierarchy within the army, the spectator might be aware of the reports of rape of female soldiers by their comrades in the US Army: in 2011 Lucy Broadbent reported that "a female soldier in Iraq is more likely to be attacked by a fellow soldier than killed by enemy fire" (online). Her report is just one of many published in the past five years, identifying both women and gay men as targets for predatory sexual violence by their fellow soldiers. Thompson's play *Palace at the End* hints at this:

her unnamed character is filmed having sex with her boyfriend at his
insistence, the other soldiers doing the filming (20); and she
experiences "hazing" when she first joins the prison team (19). Like
Walsh's character, Thompson's soldier also deludes herself with the
idea that she is a martyr, "I am like Joan of Arc" (Thompson 10).

Walsh's Lynndie is costumed as a children's clown and opens the
show with moments of slapstick comedy that are threatening because of
their speed, violence, and the apparent fear of their target. The play
opens with a man on stage, staring towards the wings, out of breath,
and looking terrified. His breathlessness communicates the
physiological nature of his fear and this communicates affectively to the
audience. This tense opening is undercut to some extent by the
slapstick props: a large fish, a frying pan, and finally a cream cake. But
the ludicrous props in this context merely heighten the humiliation of
the victim. As the play continues the closed game of the torture
chamber forces the victim to tell Lynndie that he likes her:

> **MAN.** Tell me you didn't shoot him [his son]?
> *A pause*
> **LYNNDIE.** Tell me you like me first.
> *A pause*
> **MAN.** I like you.
> **LYNNDIE.** "I really like you, Lynndie.'
> *A pause*
> **MAN.** I really like you, Lynndie. (Walsh 191)

In attempting to force the victim into complicity with his abuser,
Lynndie's actions expose the reliance of the torturer on the tortured.
When the man is shot—as he always inevitably will be—Lynndie takes
off her red nose and places it on his face.

The play was performed by Druid Theatre Company in 2008, at the
Galway Arts Festival, in a lunchtime double bill with *Gentrification*,
while Walsh's *New Electric Ballroom* was performed as an evening
show. The unpublished *Gentrification* which was directed by Thomas
Conway is a dialogue between a fictionalized Walsh and his neighbour
Henry, and is also reminiscent of Pinter's work; it captures a sense of
the helpless vulnerability of children, and thus the protective
vulnerability of their parents. As noted above *New Electric Ballroom*
addresses issues of human vulnerability and the limitations it can lead
to: both self-imposed, and cruelly imposed upon others. The idea of
developing a story that represents and protects the Self from the moral
consequences of its own actions are central to both plays: Lynndie
imposes her narrative of heroism and friendship upon her victim and,

in a more absurd dramatic universe, Breda and Clara allow the motif of love betrayed to become the basis for their identities and behaviours, while imposing their dreadfully blighted world view upon the life and happiness of their younger sister Ada.

Walsh's recurring themes of violence and of human vulnerability are variously reflected in these two plays: in Steve's brutality towards the vulnerabilities of his friends and girlfriend; in the depicted indifference of the general public towards the small figure of Little Lamb and her baby, and in the brutality exhibited by Lynndie towards her prisoner. These performances of violence centre on the vulnerabilities of the victims and, at times, representations of violence are structured to arouse the audience's sympathies, such as the brutality of the on-stage rape in *Sucking Dublin* and the moment in which Lynndie produces a fake gun, relieving the tension only to immediately shock with the murder of the Man and the possible murder of the child. Meanwhile, like many of Walsh's characters, Lynndie engages in a fictional self-representation in which she is the victim. While Walsh's more acclaimed works explore these issues in their complexity, these minor works illustrate his various approaches to the issue at different stages in his career, and the insistence in his mid-career work on characters who define themselves in and through the stories they tell themselves and others.

Works Cited

Billington, Michael. "Galway Arts Festival: Small but Perfectly Formed" *The Guardian* (28 July 2008). Available online at http://www.theguardian.com/stage/2008/jul/30/galway.arts.festival. Last accessed 28/1/2015.

Broadbent, Lucy. "Rape in the US Military" *The Guardian* (9 December 2011). Available online at http://www.theguardian.com/society/2011/dec/09/rape-us-military. Last accessed 28/1/2015.

Butler, Judith. *Precarious Life* (London: Verso, 2006)

Cavarero, Adriana. *Horrorism* Trans. William McCuaig. (New York: Columbia University Press, 2009)

Dolan, Jill. *Utopia in Performance* (Ann Arbor: University of Michigan Press, 2005)

Gilson, Erinn. "Vulnerability, Ignorance, and Oppression" *Hypatia* 26:2 (Spring 2011): 308-332

Irish Playography Website www.irishplayography.com. Last accessed 10 January 2015.

Murphy, Ann V. *Violence and the Philosophical Imaginary* (Albany: SUNY Press, 2013)

Thompson, Judith. *Palace of the End* (London: Oberon, 2010)

---. *My Pyramids* (adapted from *Palace of the End*. Unpublished)

Walsh, Enda. *Disco Pigs and Sucking Dublin* (London: Nick Hern Books, 1997)

---. *Lynndie's Gotta Gun* in *Plays One* (London: Nick Hern Books, 2011)

---. *The New Electric Ballroom* in *Plays Two* (London: Nick Hern Books, 2014)

---. "The Small Things" in *Plays One* (London: Nick Hern Books, 2011)

---. *The Walworth Farce* in *Plays Two* (London: Nick Hern Books, 2014)

Winstead, Karen A. *Virgin Martyrs: Legends of Sainthood in Late Medieval England* (Ithaca & London: Cornell University Press, 1997)

5 | FIERCE WORDS / BRUTAL DEEDS: Abjection and Redemption in Enda Walsh's *bedbound*

Kay Martinovich

> Harping on misery, and only wearing herself out ... And she never finishes it—
> Why doesn't she finish it and have done with it? For God's sake!
> "Dolly" from Bailegangaire by Tom Murphy

In Tom Murphy's play *Bailegangaire* (1985) the character Dolly is furious about her grandmother's inability to end her story about "the town without laughter." "Mommo" is a master storyteller; yet this particular narrative involves the accidental deaths of her grandson and husband, for which she was partly responsible. The story repeats in an ongoing cycle that continually stops short of the moment of truth; that is, Mommo admitting to her culpability in those deaths. Her account begins anew each day while Dolly and her sister Mary grow ever more weary of waiting to hear what exactly happened thirty years previously. The traumatic events cause Mommo to be physically and emotionally confined—to her bed and to a story that never ends.

Similarly Enda Walsh's *bedbound* (2000) features a woman bound to a bed, who is also engaged in re-telling a past filled with suffering and violence. By the conclusion of Walsh's play, the characters "Daughter" and "Dad" have finished their stories, but talking them through does not lead to the end of the trauma they suffer. Daughter is forced "ta start over"; and while listening "*to the silence for a bit*" she begins again, the play concluding with her line "Go" (Walsh 34). Other parallels exist between *bedbound* and *Bailegangaire*: Daughter is disabled by polio, Mommo by senility. Daughter and Mommo both reside in the bed, traditionally a place of comfort and safety that becomes a space of overwhelming anxiety and fear. Dad, like Mommo, has difficulty finishing a story where he must admit blame for the acts of violence he committed against his family. Lastly, Daughter and Mommo struggle to deal with distressing events of the past and, with only the tiniest of hopes, seek a kind of redemption in the repetition of their narratives.

While *Bailegangaire* is a sublime piece of storytelling, *bedbound* is a sucker punch to the gut, and an electrifying and ferocious piece of theatre. The play was first performed in October 2000 at the New Theatre, produced by the Dublin Theatre Festival, and directed by the playwright himself. The role of Dad was played by Peter Gowen, and that of Daughter by Norma Sheahan, whose fiery picture graces the front of the Nick Hern Books version. Following its premiere, the play was produced at the Edinburgh Festival in August 2001 with Sheahan reprising her award-winning role as Daughter and Liam Carney recast as Dad.[2] Subsequently, *bedbound* was translated into several languages and toured Europe. The show opened in London in January 2002 at the Royal Court Jerwood Theatre Upstairs with the Edinburgh cast, and then transferred to Dublin in February 2002. Reviewers of these productions expertly expressed the play's intensity: "carries a memorable whack" (Moroney); "It is like watching a dam burst" (Gardner); "the piece is as fierce and frightening as, at just one hour's running time, it's brief and brusque" (Nightingale); "uncomfortable, unforgettable tour de force" (Spencer). Trapped in the bed and with each other Dad and Daughter are left with nothing except to try and fill the stifling silence between them.

Not unlike Walsh's other plays *The New Electric Ballroom* and *The Walworth Farce*, the primary activity of *bedbound* revolves around repeated reconstruction of events of the past, which include the violent actions of the brutal, sadistic Dad and the tragic circumstances that result in Daughter's debilitating disease. The play is also an assault on the senses: in the opening moments of the play, the lights start to come up on a large box onstage when suddenly the front wall of the box comes crashing down to the floor, revealing a "small child's bed inside" (Walsh 9). Two figures are seen in the bed, a 50-year old man in a worn, creased suit and a 20-year old woman, whose "back is twisted ... obviously crippled" (Walsh 9). Dad and Daughter are on opposite sides

---

[2] In 2000, Norma Sheahan won the Evening Herald Dublin Theatre Festival Best Actress Award and a Best Actress nomination in The Irish Times/ESB Irish Theatre Awards.

of a small bed in a shuttered room, cut off from Cork City and the rest of the world. Through their storytelling they both participate in a re-playing of the traumatic events of their life. In turn, they speak noisily, incessantly, urgently, desperately: Dad, an ambitious furniture salesman turned entrepreneur, recounts how he built a furniture store empire while murdering associates along the way; Daughter describes in ghastly detail the day when, as a 10-year old girl, she fell down a concrete hole filled with excrement, and becomes infected with the polio that caused her paralysis. Daughter's anguish worsens when her dad, shamed by his daughter's illness and his wife's weakness, builds walls in their home to shut them out from the outside world, leading to a type of imprisonment of her and her mother. Soon thereafter Daughter watches her mother die next to her. In Walsh's monologue-driven play, Daughter "acts out" various characters in her dad's stories. When not taking part in these stories, the silence becomes too deafening for her. She finds comfort in reciting aloud from a *"worn filthy softback novella"* that her now-dead mother used to read to her, contrasting her dismal life in a vomit and pee stained bed with that of the story's fairy-tale princess, Katie (Walsh 13). The play is a race to the finish of horrific stories, with neither Dad nor Daughter able to find rest or solace from the other.

Walsh's *bedbound* evocatively draws attention to the concept of abjection by way of its images of shit, piss, blood, puke, muck, murder, and a corpse as well as its language of violence. Abjection is Julia Kristeva's term for the horror and disgust that humans experience when faced with filth, bodily excretions, or the dead. The abject both repels and fascinates. Kristeva developed her theory on abjection in *Powers of Horror: An Essay on Abjection* (1982) wherein she describes the abject as that which is not of the body, nor completely outside the body. In other words, the abject is on the border between states of the body's processes, and does not adhere to order or rules. Kristeva writes that excretions of the body—blood, pus, and feces—mark the boundary between life and death:

> A wound with blood and pus, or the sickly, acrid smell of sweat, of decay, does not signify death. ... No, as in true theater, without makeup or masks, refuse and corpses show me what I permanently thrust aside in order to live. These body fluids, this defilement, this shit are what life withstands, hardly and with difficulty, on the part of death. There, I am at the border of my condition as a living being. My body extricates itself, as being alive, from that border. Such wastes drop so that I might live ... dung signifies the other side of the border, the place where I am not and

which permits me to be ..." (Kristeva 3)

The body's excretions, once part of the life of the body, are tossed away. These excretions do not signify death, as Kristeva writes, they are visible remainders of what must be disposed of in order to continue living. The body frees itself from the waste so that it can live. And yet, what causes horror and disgust is the idea that these excretions disturb the already ambiguous border between life and death. The abject then is the in-between space of subject (the self) and object (that which is cast off from the subject). The living body may remove itself from that border, but the peripheral contact is continual.

In *Powers of Horror*, Kristeva also addresses abjection and the breakdown of boundaries in terms of language and the law. For example, what she calls the "language of violence" throws out the rules of linguistics such as proper grammar and sentence structure thereby functioning more like the "violence of poetry" where "linearity is shattered" (Kristeva 141). Furthermore, for Kristeva any crime is abject because it highlights the "fragility of law"; premeditated murder, though, is even more abject, she writes, because it accentuates that fragility more acutely (Kristeva 4). Those things that operate outside the "rules" of language or the law are subject to abjection.

In this essay, I examine abjection in Walsh's *bedbound* by way of the language of violence, the murderous male impulse, and the disfigured female body. I argue that the bed becomes a space of abjection in that Dad and Daughter, confined to the bed, represent the homicidal compulsion on the one hand and the traumatized abject body on the other. Dad operates outside the rules of law, whereas Daughter is the disabled body, the body in filth, the body in shit, the vomiting body. The bed becomes the ultimate space of abjection by its housing of the corpse of the mother, the very space in which Daughter and Dad both struggle to exist.

Walsh integrates the abject into his use of language by way of destabilizing the distinction between reason and the body. In fact, Walsh rarely uses the language of reason here—instead favouring psychological (internal) language (what is going on inside characters' heads, that then gets verbalized), and bodily (external) language (what is happening in the moment). Kristeva explains that the abject in language allows for the performative aspect of language, when language can act violently. Further, she explains that an abject literature can involve a "language of violence, of obscenity," which is certainly present in Walsh's text. In abject literature, she states that narration is replaced by the "crying out theme of suffering-horror." This theme of suffering-horror, she writes, is the "ultimate evidence" of abjection within literary representation, or for purposes here, dramatic representation (Kristeva 141).

Walsh uses the repetition of words and slashes in the text to indicate a severing of language, stoppage in thought, and strokes of violence. The slashes used in the text may also be thought of as a "language of trauma"—even though they happen between words. This "language of trauma"—most commonly used by victims to describe and to testify to the violence used against them[3]—allows Daughter to speak, even if in a disjointed way. Slashes occur in two monologues of Daughter—those moments when her dad has fallen silent and she "*begins to panic*" (Walsh 12, 20). In her first monologue, she utters:

> He stops/it stops/his panic putting an end to him and a start to me/I see that silence/oh Christ/fill it fast!/feel it race towards me all full of the lonliness/think fast of of of of of /my body!/my body ache is what I feel now/that fills my head/that packs the silence with the smell of dust and piss/. (Walsh 12)

Daughter is not only afraid of silence, but also is fearful of speaking, represented by slashes in the text. No space exists between phrases. The two-page monologue goes on like this—as she tries to describe her abjected existence. Her words coming out like vomit, uncontrollably:

> I feel the words line up and use my mouth like a cliff edge/they jump/fall fast with an ugly-scream/my body ache/the smell of piss and shit/stunted and twisted girl/mouth an angry hole/me the dust mite is what I am/I can feel me sit in me and must know that this is my body/but no control/mouth like a cliff edge. (Walsh 12)

Daughter acknowledges that her mouth has no control over the words coming out of her, similar to the body's excesses. She also knows she must keep speaking her torrent of words, for if she stops talking, she will stop "being." This is exemplified later in the same monologue when she says: "I fill the silence   ...   /for what am I if I'm not words?/I'm empty space is what I am/what am I if I'm not words I'm empty space/" (Walsh 13). In this two line passage, she first asks the question, "/for what am I if I'm not words?/" which is highlighted by Walsh's use of a question mark and a slash. Daughter answers herself in the next line, "I'm empty space is what I am." In her second iteration of

---

[3] See Didier Fassin and Richard Rechtman, *The Empire of Trauma: An Inquiry into the Condition of Victimhood*, transl. by Rachel Gomme, (Princeton: Princeton University Press, 2009), p. 187.

the question, both the question mark and the slash are absent, and she answers her now rhetorical question all within the two slashes, "/what am I if I'm not words I'm empty space/". This line is repetition with subtle, but significant, revision. If the first time is a working through of the question and answer, the second time is an acknowledgment and awareness of her state, that she is nothing—she is not even visible ("empty space")—if she does not speak. If she were to stop talking, she believes she would negate herself out of existence. In so doing, she would be casting herself off from herself, putting herself in a state of abjection.

In the character of Dad, known as "Maxie," Walsh unites verbal violence with psychological violence in his attack on the other characters in the play, especially his daughter. For instance, Maxie assaults Daughter verbally by stating to her outright that she is dead as far as he is concerned. He then proceeds to use psychological violence in building the walls around her—loudly constructing them in her presence scaring her, and further isolating her from his life.

'How's the daughter, Maxie!" "Sure my daughter's dead, Dan Dan! She died when I was up in Dublin!..." I get home in the evening with a car full of plasterboard and start at the walls! Thump pa thump pa thump pa thump pa thump pa thump!! Your space getting tighter and tighter! I feed ya bits of lunches I've robbed off Dan Dan! For a while I think of killing ya straight off! But this seems the better option. Of course it does!! Keep ya alive I can think of what to do next! (Walsh 31).

The incessant exclamation points underscore the violence in Dad's actions as well as his extreme emotional state. The language of violence is clearly revealed through Maxie's blatant expression of his thoughts of killing her and the "thump pa thump pa thump," which becomes an aggressive, recurring refrain in the play's final pages. The words even start to run together, Maxie saying his head is going "thumpa-thumpathumpa thumpa thumpa" (Walsh 31). The language of violence is jarring and corresponds with Dad's physical acts of violence used against his co-workers.

The character of Dad, named Maxwell Darcy, is a murderous psychopath driven to succeed at all costs. At 15 years of age, he began working in the stockroom of a furniture store where he discovers his passion for salesmanship. By the age of 23, he becomes the owner of the furniture store albeit gained by killing his boss, the stuttering seventy-year-old Mr. Dee. Waiting at a bus stop Maxie says, "I smile the smile of a friend" to Mr. Dee but before long he is cunningly planning a way to get rid of him (Walsh 16). Maxie spills odourless paraffin oil on the odour-impaired Mr. Dee, knowing he would light his daily cigar and blow himself up. Maxie says, "I hear the tear of the strike. And I walk from the small canteen for the storeroom as Mr. Bee explodes into 'fla fla flames' and lights my future upwards" (Walsh 17). Maxie's premeditated crime is exemplary of Kristeva's description of abjection and the law, mentioned earlier. Abjection is also "a hatred that smiles … a friend who stabs you" (Walsh 4). With his "friend" out of the way, Maxie takes over Robson's Furniture Emporium. Yet the ever-ambitious Maxie sets his sights on Dublin. There he plans to open three stores on the same day. Scheduled to open the third "Maxie's Furniture Super Store" at 11am, Maxie discovers his worker Brian has not opened the store in time. His daughter plays the roles of the other men in Maxie's life, here playing Brian. Maxie is livid at being shamed in public and the press, and proceeds to knock Brian's head in:

> **DAD**. Oh fuck. Oh Jesus. (*He suddenly screams.*) "BRIAN!! BRIAN YA LITTLE FUCKER!! Is it not eleven o'clock and the doors still shut?!
> **DAUGHTER**. We're all over the place, boss!
> **DAD**. "Shut it! SHUT IT!! Shut your hole!!" I grabs hold of his hair and run! What's got into me?! I run through the shop smashing his head from wardrobe to table from cabinet to wall unit! I feel hair coming off in my fingers so I grab tighter! SCHLAPP!! I take him to the office and open the door with his fucking head! SCHMAAAK! "Ya little fucker! Make a fool a me will ya! We'll all have a laugh at Maxie, is that it!!" Schmack! Schmack schmack! SCHMACK! SCHMACK!" (Walsh 29-30)

Maxie returns to Cork City, quickly after newspapers splash pictures of him "bent over Brian and smashing his head ta mush!" (Walsh 30). Once home, he sees only the "fucked up body" of his polio-stricken Daughter and everything that is "wrong" with his life (Walsh 30). He vows to rise again, but cannot for the "SHAME" his wife and daughter have given him (Walsh 30). Infuriated with his wife who "did this" to him, he goes to the hardware store and buys building materials to partition off his wife and daughter from the rest of the house. Now that his home life is compartmentalized and contained, he can move on; and within ten years he is on top again with his furniture business, and Dan Dan—his associate and van man—by his side. He tells his loyal worker, "Ten years of good years, Dan Dan! Ten years and the nightmare of Dublin has fucked off to someone else entirely! … Ten years and the people of Cork City FUCKING GENUFLECT IN FRONT OF ME!" (Walsh 31). On the job delivering furniture with Dan Dan, Maxie expresses that he wants "no fucking mistakes now," but Dan Dan accidently drops the expensive wall unit outside the house of its new owner (Walsh 31). Back inside the van, Maxie becomes so enraged that he slits the throat of his best mate. With no other options and nowhere else to go, he is forced to join his daughter in the walled off room in the back of the house. All of his successes abruptly end as a result of his sadistic and brutal behaviour, part of which was directed towards Daughter.

Throughout her life, Maxie's daughter has been "abjected" by him. He attacks her gender when she is born; he verbally abuses her because of her disease; and he physically "abjects" her by walling off her bedroom from the rest of the house, and by extension, the rest of the world. Here the concept of abjection also means the condition of being cast down, which happens with often-marginalized groups like women and the disabled. When Maxie decides he needs "an ally" in the furniture business—meaning a son, he goes "at the wife all doggy style ... my first ever fuck ... Nine months later and it's all push push pushing!" (Walsh 24). When his daughter is born, he cries out, "Not a son at all but a girl! ... Fuck!" (Walsh 24). While he is disappointed, he is also "undaunted" and proceeds to raise her like his son, getting her to read baby books on furniture, "pop-up books about chairs and tables" (Walsh 24). She is still a child when he starts to think of them running the business together, and thus renames the store. "Robson's Furniture Emporium" becomes "Maxwell Darcy and Daughter" (Walsh 25). However at the age of 10 tragedy befalls her when, at the beach with her Mam, she goes for a walk by herself.

> I left Mam lying on the beach. That would be the last time I would see her as a healthy girl....The soft sand sent spitting from my heels. My skinny arms and legs a mad blur ... And then I felt no ground underneath me ... And I fell down into this big hole. And right up to my waist I was covered in shit. I soon stopped trying to catch any clear air and just breathed in the shit air. I had a little puke. Puked up the cola bottles I ate on the bus. I wiped my mouth of the puke with a hand covered in shit. I spat the shit out and started to climb up a little ladder out of the concrete hole. And I didn't even cry. And that's the story of the day I got the polio. From then on everything went mad, didn't it? And ya know a day doesn't go past where I think I should have stayed in that place. How fucking happy I'd be. ...Why is it that's a clear picture and nothing else is? Do you have any answers for me, Dad? (Walsh 26-27; emphasis added)

At the beach, she is enjoying her Mam, the sun and the sand, but her life, as she has known it to this point, ends as soon as she falls into, and gets stuck in a filth-infested hole. This immersion in waste is what Kristeva calls "the contamination of life by death" (POH, 149). For Kristeva, "fecal matter signifies ... what never ceases to separate from a body" and thus "gives rise to abjection" (POH, 108). Daughter's *"clean and proper body"* has been polluted by her fall into the hole and subsequently, by her identity as a polio victim. Abjection is made visible by Daughter's disfigured diseased body, and as a result Maxie treats her as "revolting." He calls her "ya stumpy bitch!", "you fuck", "you little bollix", and "ya little puke" (Walsh 14-15). In a particularly cruel exchange he mocks her paralyzed condition:

> **DAD.** I'm not here for you, ya know! (*He goes to get out of the bed*).
> **DAUGHTER.** Don't go!
> **DAD.** I can walk!
> **DAUGHTER.** Don't!
> **DAD.** I could!
> **DAUGHTER.** Don't!
> **DAD.** I could do what I want! My legs are in great shape! (Walsh 14-15).

He ridicules his daughter by bragging about his own good health. Yet what is underneath the mockery is blame and shame. Maxie blames his daughter for getting the polio, which gives rise to his blaming her for ruining his life. He tells her, "I see how the polio has sent things wrong in *my* life! And I look at the wife who did this! ... WHAT SHAME YOU GAVE ME!" (Walsh 30). Maxie's daughter is abjected a third time, and most grievously, when he wants nothing more to do with her or her Mam. He builds the walls around them; he feeds them leftovers from Dan Dan's lunches. Maxie's treatment of his wife and daughter has everything to do with the shame that he believes they brought on him. Daughter's position in the play is one of powerlessness—at least to her dad. First she has no one that cares for her and second her status as "daughter" means nothing. Third, she wrestles with the belief in a fairytale ending—what her mam always promised would happen someday—whereas her circumstances grossly dictate otherwise. This fairytale belief is a reminder of the failures of her life as a woman attributable to her sick, cruel Dad. Lastly, Daughter is unable to move forward or to imagine an alternative future other than the fantasy life of a princess given that she is physically and emotionally bedbound.

The bed is a space of abjection for it is the place where Daughter and Dad live, sleep, and piss. The bed is "heavily stained and grubby" and Daughter's face is "filthy, her hair is tangled and manky" (B, 9).

Leakages of Daughter's body spill into the bed such that her body and the bed become one. Daughter says: "body a thick duvet lump/smelling my body smell/all stale/ give a little puke then/watch the puke take to the duvet where once was flowers but now all muck/all is muck and dust/" (Walsh 12). The bed becomes a definitive space of abjection however when the corpse of Maxie's wife—and Daughter's Mam—is found there. The corpse, for Kristeva, is the "utmost of abjection" (Kristeva 4). The trauma of seeing the corpse collapses all boundaries between life and death. Writing on the subject of abjection, Dino Felluga explains that "what we are confronted with when we experience the trauma of seeing a human corpse (particularly the corpse of a friend or family member) is our own eventual death made palpably real" (Felluga). Maxie begins to slowly kill his wife and daughter. When he finds the dead body of his wife, he has partially succeeded in his attempt. He says, "I see Mam lying all hollow and dead like a doll. When I lift her up you look at me. You don't know who I am. And I take your Mam's body out" (Walsh 32-33). Daughter not only sees the corpse of her Mam but she was "living" next to it for who knows how long. The end of the story for Maxie—and the part of the story that his daughter has not heard before—is the moment of finding his wife and then hearing the cries of his daughter:

> Your crying and the busy outside. And I stop. (Pause.) I stop and listen and what I hear is silence then. (Long pause.) And it's the first time in my life I've got room for silence. I stand with the tiny body of your Mam and let the silence clean me out for a bit. (Pause.) And then—and then it starts as a tiny thing in my mouth. I swallow it and it fills my stomach. And then my brain gets hold of it and it fills my everything. I have fear. It's fear. And I'm afraid of my life outside. And I place your Mam on the ground and turn back until I arrive back at the bed. And I get into the bed and face you as I do now. And this is me talking. This is really me talking now. And I don't have words for you. I don't have the right words for you, love. I just want to sleep and get back to the silence but I can't. (Walsh 33)

Maxie is reduced to silence, evident by the three pauses within five lines (which happens nowhere else in the playtext). He has no words for his daughter, and immediately after this passage the stage directions read, "*He is overcome*" (Walsh 33). He has committed one crime after another until he is forced to "abject" himself in the same space as his daughter. The bed as a place of abjection also becomes a place of "recovery"—of recovering the past and trying to make amends in the present. By repeating and reconstructing the past, Daughter and Dad try to make sense of their own and each other's traumatic past in the in-between space of abjection and the bed. When the daughter kisses her dad on the forehead, and he returns the kiss, there is at least in part, an attempt at a coming together between them. This physical act of shared kindness, small though it may be, offers a glimpse of hope for the daughter, and maybe a tiny step towards attaining some sort of redemption for the father.

Enda Walsh pushes the boundaries of representation on the stage. His plays often exist in a Beckettian landscape by way of their humour and bleakness, and by the characters' struggle to find meaning in their existence. They are also provocative in the sense that the playwright's use of images, situations, and language are at once outrageous and transcendent. Undoubtedly Walsh writes what he wants to see in the theatre:

> I don't like seeing everyday life on stage: it's boring. I like my plays to exist in an abstract, expressionistic world: the audience has to learn its rules, and then connect with these characters who are, on the surface, dreadful monsters. (Costa)

Maxie in *bedbound* is one such "monster," who verbally and psychologically harms his daughter. Because of his foul words and deeds, Daughter becomes abjection itself. She has no name, and thus no identity in the world of the play, except as a stand-in for the fairy tale princess. Daughter is known only as someone in relationship to a parent, and with her Mam dead, in relationship to a father who wants nothing to do with her. Maxie is his daughter's persecutor; and yet, in the closing moments of the play, the hint of a "human being" starts to appear. By Daughter and Dad's re-construction, revision, and making sense of their traumatic past, a bit of room is made for a kind of reconciliation in their relationship to each other and to society.

Works Cited

Costa, Maddy. "One Man and His Monsters." *The Guardian.* 17 September 2008.Web. 26 November 2014.
<http://www.theguardian.com/stage/2008/sep/18/theatre.drama>.

Fassin, Didier, and Rechtman, Richard. The Empire of Trauma: An Inquiry into the *Condition of Victimhood.* Trans. Rachel Gomme. Princeton: Princeton University Press, 2009. Print.

Felluga, Dino. "Modules on Kristeva: On the Abject." *Introductory Guide to Critical Theory.* Purdue U, Jan 2011. Web. 28 November

2014.<http://www.purdue.edu/guidetotheory/psychoanalysis/kristevaa bject.html>.

Gardner, Lyn. "Bedbound." *The Guardian*. 5 August 2001. Web. 26 November 2014. <http://www.theguardian.com/stage/2001/aug/06/theatre.edinburghfe stival20013>.

Kristeva, Julia. *Powers of Horror: An Essay on Abjection*. Trans. Leon S. Roudiez. New York: Columbia University Press, 1982. Print.

Moroney, Mic. "Bedbound." *The Guardian*. 9 October 2000. Web. 26 November 2014. <http://www.theguardian.com/culture/2000/oct/10/artsfeatures2>.

Murphy, Tom. *Bailegangaire. Plays: 2*. London: Methuen Drama, 1993. Print.

Nightingale, Benedict. "Bedbound Review." *Bedbound at the Royal Court Theatre*. January 2002. Web. 26 November 2014.

<http://www.royalcourttheatre.com/whats-on/bedbound/?tab=4>.

Spencer, Charles. "Hypnotic Tale of Murder and Ruin." *The Telegraph*. 17 January 2002. Web. 26 November 2014.

<http://www.telegraph.co.uk/culture/theatre/drama/3571946/Hypnotic-tale-of-murder-and-ruin.html>.

Walsh, Enda. *bedbound & Misterman*. London: Nick Hern Books, 2002. Print.

6| Through a Glass Darkly: Identity, Language and Performance in Enda Walsh's *Chatroom*

Kevin Wallace

Behaviour on the internet can be a dark mirror image to human social interactions in what has been termed more and more often "real life". Douglas Heaven asks, what is the internet for, and answers sarcastically: "Meeting new people. Bullying them mercilessly. Sharing a video of yourself playing guitar. Sharing a video of yourself masturbating. Buying books. Buying drugs. Registering a vote. Requesting a murder" (44). The crucial difference between interaction in cyberspace and in the real world, "meatspace" in internet jargon (Parry 318), is that the on-line interactions lack all social cues related to the body (gesture, intonation and facial expression). What Enda Walsh's *Chatroom* dramatizes is the gap between community and communication in these two spheres. In a production of this play the audience are privy to the physical dynamics of its six performers, something that the characters are blind to.

This article will examine how *Chatroom* treats the complex issues of teenage identity and cyber-bullying. It will focus on how the dramaturgy of the play creates ambiguity and uses it to introduce empathy in a space devoid of it. *Chatroom* could be considered a political play because it shows the impact of internet bullying, and is structured to force the audience to see the person on the other side of a username. In the UK the National Society for the Prevention of Cruelty to Children (NSPCC) says that 4,500 children contacted them due to cyber bullying in 2013 (NSPCC, "Bullying and cyberbullyingFacts and statistics"). In Ireland a study by Brian O'Neill and Thuy Dinh found that 4% of 9-16 year olds in their study's sample say that they experienced bullying online, and that: "Up to a quarter of 15-16 year olds (24%) also say they have bullied others [online, with nearly] half of those who have bullied others online ... also being victims of cyberbullying" (O'Neill and Dinh 1). Chillingly O'Neill and Dinh also found that 19% of the children surveyed who had experienced cyber-bullying "felt guilty about what went wrong, adding to their sense of victimization and vulnerability" (O'Neill and Dinh 10). These figures are significant in the context of discussing *Chatroom*, because they show that victims of cyberbullying internalize its effects and stigmatize themselves.

Chatroom is also one of a number of Irish and British plays dealing directly with suicide and identity crisis from the ten year period between 1996 and 2006. It premiered in March 2006 at the National Theatre in London, during its NT Connections season (Walsh 195). The Connections series according to John F. Deeney has been designed to create a space for teenagers to debate social issues, especially with regard to citizenship, on the National Theatre's stage. Although not unproblematic the Connections series has opened a space where issues for young people can be staged in a significant cultural space (Deeney 332-335). *Chatroom* in its depiction of cyberbullying is perfect for the Connections remit but it is also potentially problematic itself because of its use of common tropes (and *clichés*) about teenagers. What is most interesting about this play is that it picks upon some of the issues depicted in Walsh's 1996 play *Disco Pigs*. While there is a gulf between the two plays, technologically and aesthetically, there is also a resonance. *Disco Pigs* is duologue, a lyrical polyphony of dialect, a fractured and refracted version of the Hiberno-English spoken in Cork city, but also reminiscent of an idioglossia, or gibberish language, shared by baby twins. This sense of a shared identity teenage community, separated from and in opposition to the rest of the world, and the ease at which violence erupts from that identity is what links these plays.

Chatroom, more than anything else, is a play about teenage alienation. It examines this through the lenses of adolescent depression, identity crisis and internet bullying. It focuses on six adolescents "all around fifteen, sixteen ... all middle class kids of varying wealth growing up in and around Chiswick [in London]" (210). The first four, William, Emily, Eva and Jack meet in the virtual space of an internet chatroom and come together out of teenage angst and disillusionment with adults. However, the play focusses on Jim, a depressed teenager who has come to the chatrooms to seek help. He meets Laura in one of the other chatrooms, but her help, which mainly consists of supportive listening, is insufficient for Jim. He comes across the first four teenagers in another room. These four, the two boys and then two girls separately had been discussing murder. William wants to kill J.K. Rowling, as an act of rebellion against all of the adults who "[are] trying to keep children young ... and don't want children to think for themselves" (200), and Eva wants to kill her mother (203-204).

When the opportunity to take advantage of Jim arises Eva and William quickly cease seize upon it. They play the role of counsellors and use the facelessness of the chatroom to attempt to confuse and control Jim. Their bullying of him relies solely on the textual, and what is most troubling about this situation is that *Chatroom* reflects how the internet being a purely textual space can construct identities that constantly reduce persons to pure symbols. However the abuse inflicted upon Jim by William and Eva is no less damaging than physical violence. Arguably it is even more detrimental because they are attempting to distort Jim's view of reality and of himself. Through this manipulation he becomes tied into what William terms his "cause" (212-213). Yet for all of Jim's vulnerability in many ways the characters with the greatest identity problems are his bullies, William and Eva. William begins the play in a conversation with Jack where he condemns adult writers for trying to control children through fiction. He trolls the Harry Potter chatroom looking for support for an assassination attempt on J.K. Rowling (200). Meanwhile Emily and Eva debate how Britney Spears "sold their childhood soul[s]" (201-204). Both William and Eva struggle to find a cause or purpose for themselves. William lists the punks and other teenage "rebels" as political activists in revolution against the establishment, however the only "cause" that he has in the play is orchestrating the suicide of Jim (221-223). Jim's taking of his own life in public becomes not only a twisted power-game for two disaffected teenagers but also a parody of a political protest. Maggie Inchley notes that William's voice is articulate, intelligent and persuasive (Incheley 338-340). She notes further that "without a positive outlet, becomes twisted, convoluted and deceptive, demonstrating the most distrusted features of the voice, and skilled in the arts of manipulation that its speaker has himself condemned in the adult world" (Incheley 339).

Although the world inhabited by the six teenagers in *Chatroom* is formed and controlled by words it is Jim's body that is the central matter of Eva and William's attention. Indeed what the play exposes is the power of language to pacify and control the body. Michel Foucault argues that the body, "its forces, their utility and their docility, their distribution and their submission" are always at issue in discourse (Foucault 24-26). Indeed it is Foucault's central argument that a discourse's mechanisms for control of people's minds are always focused on controlling their bodies (Foucault 305-308). One might point out that today internet bullying is not always as anonymous as it is presented in *Chatroom*. Yet the same principles remain: damage to the textual or symbolic self is as wounding as any physical attack and perhaps even more dangerous.

The anonymity of the Web allows for roleplay, hoaxes and identity scams. In this play despite it being a performance based around text-based communication, at its heart is a dramaturgy based upon role-play and the mutability of identity. The first moment of crisis for Jim is during the Passion play where he plays St. John, the surrogate son of the Virgin Mary. However Jim is confronted with his "failure" as a real son to his mother due to the role reversal between him and the character he plays. In the Passion play St. John is accepted by the Virgin Mary although he is not her biological son, whereas Jim is rejected by his mother (who is playing the Virgin Mary) even though he is her biological son.

It is worth noting also that William, Eva and Laura all role play as counsellors online, Eva and William in order to encourage Jim to commit suicide, and Laura to do the opposite. As well as having a straightforward or naturalistic representation of internet support groups and internet bullies these two voices also correspond with the Good and Bad Angel archetypes of morality and passion plays. Passion plays were a staple of medieval European drama. They staged the crucifixion of Jesus of Nazareth, usually as part of an Easter pageant (Banham 841). Although these plays had a ritual or religious significance as a part of a pageant they also had a social significance (Banham 702-706). In *Chatroom* the social significance revolves around Jim's mother and her control of her son. The pageant play becomes a means to effect that power relationship and to reinforce the social role that Jim has been *playing* in his family—the runt of the litter. Although the Passion play is only a small detail in Jim's backstory it looms large in *Chatroom* firstly as a central event in Jim's personal crisis and secondly as a theatrical conceit. The concept of performativity is central to the dramaturgy of this play, and the mirroring of Jim with his role-play as St. John highlights this. In a discussion of role-play in the work of Frank McGuinness, Eamonn Jordan notes that "play gives rise to a liminal consciousness that disturbs as much as it distorts, that provokes as much as it perverts and that re-states dissent as much as it resists" (Jordan 197). Jim's catharsis during the passion play is a traumatic eruption that both underscores his role in the family and that undermines it. His mother had castigated him for being unable to weep as St. John and then verbally abused him as being "just like his father", a failure to her. What followed that was an excessive performance of weeping not because his mother commanded it but because Jim had realized the irony of his role-playing of St. John.

The other major moment of role play in the piece is Jim's video at the end of the play. For Inchley it is a deeply ambivalent moment in the text. She argues that "it was a fantasy from which Jim's own voice had been notably absent. Unable to find a wholly satisfactory means of self-expression its author was deposited back into childhood" (Inchley 340). In this film Jim re-enacts the traumatic moment at which his father abandoned him and his family. When he was six Jim was at the zoo with his father and while Jim watched the penguins his father disappeared. The play itself echoes with this loss and the trauma it created for Jim. This is dramatized with the echoing of the request to tell "me about the day your father went missing" (208; 221). This trauma is the heart of the play. It is also the centre of the role-play in the text. Jim is forced to repeat this trauma in order to exorcize it, role-playing the cowboy that lost his childhood at the end of *Chatroom*. Eva and Laura role-play counsellors, Eva's inadequate performance marked after hearing the story of how Jim's father went missing with the stage direction: "EVA *looks bored*" (223).

Jim's docility is a central concern for all the other characters in the play. William and Eva focus on Jim when he enters their chatroom. They emphasize the negative aspects of his life and eliminate Jack and Emily's dissenting voices. William and Eva both of whom blame celebrities for their lack of any "cause" in their life see convincing Jim to commit suicide as their new personal purpose, equal in status to the rebellion of punk rock or a civil rights movement. Through their playing as counsellors they distort and pervert the concept of teenage rebellion, citing the performance of Jim's future suicide as a "statement".

WILLIAM. But you know, Jim, maybe the more public you make it, the more of a statement you'd be making (235).

For William and Eva in particular a teenager is not a full human being. Reflecting society's double standards, they have internalized the idea that a teenager is a "sub-person" (234). This is interesting given the kind of programming BBC3 have been producing since the mid-

2000s that merges the teenage and horror genres, shows like *Being Human* (2008) and *In the Flesh* (2013) as well as Channel 4's *Misfits* (2009), which variously present teenagers as vampires, werewolves, mutants and zombies, all of them struggling with the conflict between their identities and "normal" humans. The discourse of "monstrous teenager", whose humanity is questionable, has been incorporated into British culture. Indeed the moral panic about Jamie Bulger's murder focused upon the potentially desensitizing effect violence in popular culture might have on teenagers (Cohen viii-xi). Ironically, it seems that, in the two decades since this horrific crime, moral panic could be argued to have contributed to a discourse that dehumanizes teenagers.

This discourse has a dual effect in *Chatroom*. On the one hand the depiction of Eva and William has a terrifying resemblance to Jamie Bulger's murderers who led a vulnerable person, a child in this case, to his death purely because they could. On the other hand this discourse is the very tool that these cyber bullies use to dehumanize Jim and perversely reframe his public suicide into an act of self-assertion for Eva and William, something that gives *their* lives and identities purpose. Inchley suggests that "Under William's tutelage, the other teenagers make [Jim] prey to the exploitative representative strategies they have learned from a cynical adult culture" (Inchley 340). This argument however creates a simplistic binary between the adult and teenage world. It could be argued otherwise that the whole system of representation itself is implicated in this lack of empathy, rather than it being simply modelled behaviour. William's rather perverse view of culture and his place within it are problematic within this line of argument also. Rather like Jim's decision at the end of the play to, as Inchley puts it, " [seize] the means to represent himself" (Inchley 340), Eva and William are attempting to usurp Jim's agency, to make him docile (in the Foucauldian sense) and thus substitute their control over Jim for the lack of agency in their own lives.

Walsh is walking a tightrope in term of portraying a *clichéd* or stereotypical view of teenage psychopathy. However Walsh is trying to deal with a very real and very present crisis regarding social interaction on the internet. For the holocaust scholar Hannah Arendt evil is not extraordinary but rather banal (Arendt 289). The anonymity or rather, and more pertinently, the facelessness of communication on the internet allows and in fact encourages human relationships without empathy. Like Arendt's view of the Nazi Adolf Eichmann, this allows for a kind of *clichéd* thinking where people and ideas are reduced into meaningless rhetorical devices. The political economy of the World

Wide Web is based upon dehumanization, as it facilitates this banal lack of imagination, the failure to see the person behind the numbers or the username. On the internet the user does not relate to another person but rather to an image or to text, to a symbol, to bytes of information detached from the person that they signify. The psychoanalytic theorist, Jacques Lacan, terms this function of language *aphanasis*, the process by which an object is eclipsed by the symbol, or sign, representing it (Lacan 216-229). This is clearest on the internet where a person is reduced to a name—a hollow textual signifier—text that can be reshaped or removed without a second thought. *Chatroom* interrupts that detachment by performing the split between "real life" communication and internet based relationships on stage. It subverts the dehumanizing logic of faceless communication, and in this way *Chatroom* could be seen as a piece of didactic theatre, a moralizing play designed to teach the audience to empathize with the person on the other-side of the screen. However this begins to breakdown with the *dénouement* of the piece—Jim's video and performance in McDonalds.

The piece is an attempt at protest art, a protest for a lost childhood (241). He re-performs the day his father left him alone in the zoo when he was six years old, and disappeared from the family forever. He dresses up in a children's cowboy costume, replete with a sheriff's badge and toy revolvers, and plays the song "Rawhide" while standing in his costume on a table in a McDonald's restaurant. Jim enacts the exact opposite of William's cause, instead of being frustrated at being "kept young" Jim wants to repair his traumatic childhood. However this performance is quite problematic, the central issue here is that it plays out the same tropes that both William and Eva were using to advocate for Jim to commit suicide. It uses pop music, the mass cultural setting of McDonalds and takes the form of a video "starring" all the characters in the play. Furthermore if we can consider Eva and William to be chilling depictions of the banality of evil inherent in cyber-bullying today, then we can also see Jim's act of rebellion as itself banal. It relies on citation of the song *Rawhide*, itself the theme song of a TV Western from the 1960s. It could be argued that the impact of the song in this context relies on the lyric "Don't try to understand "em | Just rope, throw, and brand "em", which underlines the gap between adult and adolescent cultures and expresses the dissatisfaction that all the teenagers seem to have with adults. Inchley argues that through Jim's film the values of: "heroism, fantasy and mythology were mixed with commerce and commodification. [It is an] act of identity construction that spoke of both the potential and the impossibilities of self-definition for contemporary teenagers" (Inchley 340). However it cannot be denied that the space in which this self-definition occurs is a McDonalds, the costume used is a generic children's cowboy outfit, and the song is a theme tune that has been used in multiple films, TV shows, adverts and parodies of the above. The film runs the risk of stripping Jim of any identity of his own, and thus reinforcing William's argument that the teenagers "[are] all clichés" (211). His final monologue notes the ghosts of all the teenage suicides watching him "buy some chicken nuggets and Coke and find a table" (240). Arguably however, what saves it from this is that Jim's performance is a "failure". It is an imperfect reproduction of the mythical mass consumer society that Inchley references. Moreover, in the space created by that failure of representation the public space becomes a site for the reparative, a place or moment of specific psychological healing. It reclaims the almost anonymous social environment of any other McDonalds as a bulwark against the dehumanized anonymous and individuated "social medium" of the internet.

In *Chatroom* the internet functions as a meeting place, a space of exclusion, a space of revelation, and simultaneously both a space of conscience and a space devoid of empathy. The internet in *Chatroom* is a site of perfect liminality and Walsh extends this through play and role-play. From the beginning of the piece cyphers (characters without depth, identity or meaning) are to the fore. The characters' names are hollow substitutes for actual people. Lisa's line "You can call me Laura" (208) emphasizes that the role of the internet in this play is to both connect the characters and to keep them separated. It underlines how the effect of *aphanasis* discussed above works to dehumanize through the creation of disconnection in the chatrooms rather than bringing them together. Moreover, the references to celebrities, to Britney Spears, Punk Rock, Roald Dahl and J.K. Rowling, are depthless and hyperbolic. These symbols, rather than individuals, substitute for the real adults that the teenagers (specifically William, Eva and Jim) feel are persecuting them (in both Eva and Jim's cases, their mothers). In *Chatroom* the relationship between the self and the Other (the issue of radical alterity) becomes the central issue of the plot and is indeed the main concern of the dramaturgy.

For the anthropologist Roger Keesing radical alterity is "a culturally constructed Other radically different from Us" (Keesing 310). The adults cited by William and Eva in their diatribes at the beginning of the play act as a site for that radical alterity on to which all the negative associations and ideas that the teenagers are unable to integrate into their own identities can be projected. This is not merely a social action by the teenagers (an act of differentiation) it is also a function of language (especially given that this is a play about the internet where all communication is textual and not embodied). Thus this projection is not only because of, but also about, the symbolic order. On the one hand the characters are caught in this alienating discourse where subjectivity becomes perpetually reductible, where William is able to equate the punk cultural movement with Jim's suicide, where J.K. Rowling, Roald Dahl and Britney Spears are responsible for that frustration, and where a person suffering depression becomes a toy that children play with. However, on the other hand the audience sees this gap between the person and the communication being dramatized, and thus the absent in internet communication (the human behind the text) becomes present.

Walsh brilliantly uses metatheatre to expose the hidden acts of role-play and bullying on the internet. For Eamonn Jordan, this use of metatheatre is bound-up with play, as he says, "play is about make-believe, about release and about the establishment of a space of transition, of working out and of recognition, [it is] most of all a protective and insulating strategy" (Jordan 244) This is quite clearly the case in *Chatroom*. Jim, Eva and William are all using the virtual space of the internet to remake themselves, thus it becomes a clearly transitional or liminal space. Victor Turner famously noted the relationship between liminality and rites of passage. In this play manipulating Jim into suicide and indeed Jim's artistic response to his depression at the end of the play are both "rites of passage". William and Eva with their sociopathic mind-sets see Jim's death as a proxy battle in their war with the establishment, with adults.

WILLIAM. It'll be a laugh. Right now, we're all he has. We're here for him 24/7 ... it will be a blast! Eva gets it, why can't you? He's our cause. Let him talk. Mess him up a bit. See how far he'll go (223).

Jordan notes further that Walsh's plays exist in a discourse of ever increasing violence on stage. He rightly points out that:

> In much of contemporary dramaturgy globally, there are increasing levels of violence and mutilation, with an escalating smudging of pleasure and pain through a fetishistic eroticization of violence. Irish playwrights are engaged with a similar type of hazing. What is recent, however, is that the distinction between pleasure and pain has been blurred ... In general the

decontextualization of pain/pleasure plus the commodification of both are increasingly the mainstay of the contemporary dramaturgy, which has as much to do with irony, as it has led to a lack of empathy available to an audience when it comes to contemporary work. Pain is alienated to such an extent that its impact is often utterly emptied of meaning beyond the frame of performance. (Jordan 245-46)

Chatroom offers a response to this increasing lack of empathy. By creating a dialectic between the performed web-based disconnection of the six teenagers and the six actors embodied presence on-stage the play forces a reconsideration of the pervasive dehumanizing effects of the internet's "social media".

Chatroom also exists in the context of British theatre after the In-Yer-Face movement. That group of plays and playwrights from the late 1990s were obsessed with the mediated self, plays as diverse as Mark Ravenhill's *Shopping and Fucking*, Martin Crimp's *Attempts on Her Life* (1997) and Sarah Kane's *4.48 Psychosis* (2000), dramatized the debilitating power of discourse to structure and destroy the individual (Sierz 30-35). This movement was also known as the New Brutalists or the Neo-Jacobeans and renowned for their spectacular and shocking use of violence on stage. This is the context in which Jordan notes the blurring of pleasure and pain and indeed the escalating trauma of theatre. At the same time many of Ireland's major playwrights were involved with a series of monologue dramas, such as Conor McPherson's *Rum and Vodka* (1992) and *Port Authority* (2001), Mark O'Rowe's *Howie the Rookie* (1999) and *Terminus* (2006), Eugene O'Brien's *Eden* (2001), as well as Walsh's own *Disco Pigs* (1996). While on the surface these plays are all radically different what unites them is their obsession with the continual construction and reconstruction of the self, the notion of individuality or subjectivity as an incomplete and incompletable process.

These plays, whether the 1990s Irish monologue or the British In-Yer-Face dramas, depict how fraught the experience of subjectivity is within the media dominated world of the late twentieth and early twenty-first centuries. They focus on how these media, which are often disembodied or abstracted from the physical world, are destructive to the characters in the plays. *Chatroom* follows on from this tradition, it attempts to do something important for theatre in the twenty-first century by dramatizing interaction on the internet. Thus the dark mirror that is web-based social media becomes a spotlight where reductive representational practices are exposed. Walsh's play is an attempt to engage with the most pervasive technology in teenage culture in the early Twenty-first century. It is an attempt to depict this sphere of instant connectedness and constant disconnection upon which the internet is structured. It is also an ambiguous play because it tries to facilitate a moral lesson, to be a social issues piece, and at the same time be more than that. The end of the play with Jim's highly commodified piece of protest art, which masquerades as a suicide note, has no definite reading. The image of Jim in his cowboy costume in McDonalds is a potential moment of victory where he, in Inchley's terms, "seizes" control of how he is being represented. However, he is simultaneously expressing the traumatic wound that he wants his "childhood back" (241), and on the contrary like William, Jack, Emily, Eva, and Laura, he runs the risk of becoming a cliché. *Chatroom* underlines the fragility of identity, and the banality of the forces that erode it. On the other hand the very structure of the play's performance revolts against the dehumanizing effects of the cyberbullying. By making the absent present, the play enacts an end of *aphanasis*, the eclipsing of the person by a symbol. *Chatroom*, a play about alienation, becomes the means by which connection and connectedness can be reasserted in an increasing unempathetic and unsympathetic world.

Works Cited

Arendt, Hannah. Eichmann in Jerusalem: A Report on the Banality of Evil. London: Penguin 2006. Print.

Banham, Martin. *The Cambridge Guide to Theatre*. Cambridge: CUP, 1995. Print.

Cohen, Stanley. *Folk Devils and Moral Panics*. London: Routledge, 2011. Print.

Deeney, John F. "National causes/moral clauses?: the National Theatre, young people and Citizenship." *Research in Drama Education: The Journal of Applied Theatre and Performance* 12.3 (2007): 331-344. Print.

Foucault, Michel. *Discipline and Punish*. London: Penguin, 1991. Print.

---. *The Birth of the Clinic*. London: Routledge, 2003. Print.

Goffman, Erving. *Stigma: Notes on the Management of Spoiled Identity*. London: Penguin, 1990. Print.

Hartsock, Nancy. "Foucault on Power: A Theory for Women?" *Feminism/Postmodernism*. Ed. Linda Nicholson. London: Routledge, 2013. 157 175. Print.

Heaven, Douglas. "Down and very dirty." *New Scientist*. Aug. 2014. 44-45. Print.

Jordan, Eamonn. "From Playground to Battleground: Metatheatricality in the Plays of Frank McGuiness." *Theatre Stuff: Critical Essays on Contemporary Irish Theatre*. Ed. Eamonn Jordan. Dublin: Carysfort Press, 2000. 194-208. Print.

Jordan, Eamonn. *Dissident Dramaturgies: Contemporary Irish Theatre*. Dublin: Irish Academic Press, 2010. Print.

Keesing, Roger. "Theories of Culture Revisited." *Assessing Cultural Anthropology*. Ed. Robert Borofsky. New York; McGraw-Hill, 1994. 300-310. Print.

Lacan, Jacques. "The Subject and the Other: Aphanisis". *The Four Fundamental Concepts of Psycho-Analysis*. London: W. W. Norton & Company, 1998. Print.

Malabou, Catherine. *The New Wounded: From Neurosis to Brain Damage*. New York: Fordham University Press, 2012. Print.

NSPCC. "Bullying and cyberbullyingFacts and statistics". *nspcc.org.uk*. National Society for the Prevention of Cruelty to Children, 25 Sept. 2014. Web. 12 Oct. 2014.

O'Neill, Brian, and Thuy Dinh. "Cyberbullying among 9-16 year olds in Ireland. Digital Childhoods Working Paper Series (No.5)." Dublin Institute of Technology, 4 Feb. 2013. Web. 1 Nov. 2013.

Parry, Ross. Ed. *Museums in a Digital Age*. London: Routledge, 2010. Print.

Sierz, Aleks. *In-Yer-Face Theatre: British Drama Today*. London: Faber and Faber, 2001. Print.

Turner, Victor. "Betwixt and Between: The Liminal Period in Rites of Passage" *Betwixt & Between: Patterns of Masculine and Feminine Initiation*. Eds. Louise Carus Mahdi, Steven Foster and Meredith Little. Chicago: Open Court Publishing, 1994. 3-19. Print.

Walsh, Enda. *Enda Walsh: Plays 1*. London: Nick Hern Books, 2010. Print.

7 | *The Small Things*: A Postdramatic Analysis

Finian O'Gorman

In February 2005, Dan Rebellato attended Paines Plough's production of *The Small Things* at the Menier Chocolate Factory in London. The production, directed by Vicky Featherstone, was part of a season of plays entitled *This Other England*. Had the production gone according to plan, Rebellato would have seen two characters, Man and Woman, recounting alternating narratives about their distant childhoods. The narratives, punctuated by alarm clocks held by both characters, would have told of a campaign waged by Woman's father to impose order on their village by removing the tongues of its inhabitants. It would have gradually emerged that Man and Woman escaped from the village to separate mountain tops, and that all that sustained their existence was the memory of their childhood love, and their ongoing compulsion to speak and to exist. However, on the particular night Rebellato was in attendance, not everything went according to plan:

> From the beginning there were noises from somewhere in the audience. I couldn't locate the source—the audience was shallow and very wide and it was hard to look round—but the interruptions became louder and soon more verbal. After about fifteen minutes of this, Bernard Gallagher, playing the man, said to his fellow actor Valerie Lilley "I think we should stop, Val". The audience burst into applause. Immediately two ushers appeared. We applauded them. They persuaded what turned out to be a very drunk guy in a tracksuit, about thirty years of age, to leave the auditorium. We applauded his departure. Then Bernard Gallagher said "let us resume" and we applauded that too. It was cathartic applause of tension and release. It was applause that marked the expulsion from a community and the restoration of order. (Rebellato)

Rebellato's experience, while unconventional, nevertheless foregrounds a number of conventions of theatre-going experience. There is the world of the audience, the "real" world, and the enclosed fictional world on stage. In conventional dramatic theatre these worlds orbit each other, but rarely engage in direct dialogue. In this case however, the drunk man unintentionally stimulated a holistic awareness of the theatre situation that moved beyond a myopic focus on the events on stage. Before "order" was restored, the audience and actors formed a "community", with a shared awareness of each other's presence.

Although unintentional in this case, the audience's awareness of the total "theatre situation" is a key aim of postdramatic theatre practice. On that night in February 2005 the postdramatic bombastically crashed proceedings from the outside. This essay argues that this incident both mirrored and overshadowed postdramatic elements of *The Small Things* that were already firmly in place. Hans-Thies Lehmann's *Postdramatic Theatre* was first published in German in 1999 before being translated into English by Karen Jürs-Munby in 2006. It identifies key developments in European experimental theatre since the late 1960s, with a particular focus on the work of experimental practitioners such as Robert Wilson, Tadeusz Kantor, Heiner Müller, The Wooster Group, Needcompany and Societas Rafaello Sanzio. According to Lehmann, dramatic theatre was based on the idea that the stage could present a "fictive cosmos": a space where the illusion of an enclosed world could be formed from the imagination and empathy of the spectator (22). This fictional whole was based on a logocentric or language-based hierarchical structure that had the words of the playwright at its centre. In contrast, the postdramatic approach favours a non-hierarchical array of elements that include what Christopher Balme refers to as:

> a preference for the visual image over the written word, collage and montage instead of linear structure, a reliance on metonymic rather than metaphoric representation, and a redefinition of the performer's function in terms of being and materiality rather than appearance and mimetic imitation. (Balme 1)

At first, it appears easy to place *The Small Things* firmly within a logocentric tradition: it was commissioned for a season of plays "inspired by the English language" (Fisher), and the structure of the play is centred on the spoken narratives performed by Man and Woman. Furthermore, reviews of the play emphasized that it was a play "of and about words" (Scott). These reviews adopt a perspective that mirrors the logocentric hierarchy Lehmann identifies as central to the dramatic tradition. In keeping with this hierarchy, in the majority of critical responses to Walsh's plays, story "telling", rather than "showing", has been identified as a central characteristic.[4] This emphasis on language in the reception of his work could be attributed to his status as an Irish playwright, and the repeated claims made that Irish drama is defined by its lyricism and storytelling. However, as already mentioned above, it is my contention that on examination Walsh's plays prove to adhere more closely to a postdramatic theatre. This essay investigates how *The Small Things* can be considered as a piece of postdramatic theatre, thus placing it within the wider context of contemporary European theatre. Such a reading emphasizes the importance of performance in meaning-making and reveals a broader, more fluid range of possible experiences and interpretations of Walsh's plays.

Firstly, it is important to emphasize that the term postdramatic does not represent a direct opposition or clear break with the dramatic tradition that has preceded it. Instead, it may be seen as an interrogation of the fundamental structures of representation inherent in the dramatic tradition. As Karen Jürs-Munby points out:

> 'post" here is to be understood neither as an epochal category, nor simply as a chronological "after" drama, a "forgetting" of the dramatic "past", but rather as a rupture and a beyond that continue to entertain relationships with drama and are in many ways an analysis and "anamnesis" of drama. (Lehmann 2)

Jürs-Munby reminds us that this is not an exercise in denial or "forgetting". With this in mind the aim of this essay is not to forget or discount the Irish cultural and dramatic tradition that Walsh is writing from. Rather, the purpose is to show the way Walsh's work represents a meeting point between Irish and European influences.

---

[4] Almost all of Walsh's plays have elicited this response from reviewers: Adam Scott's describes a "palpable relish of words" in his review of *The Small Things* (Scott); in his review of *bedbound* Jesse Weaver claims that the act of speaking seems imperative to the survival of Walsh's characters (Weaver); Michael Billington notes Walsh's "astonishing way with words" in his review of *Penelope* (Billington); a *New York Times* review of *The Walworth Farce* describes Walsh as a "master storyteller" (Brantley) and in her review of *The New Electric Ballroom*, Lyn Gardner describes Walsh as "one of the most dazzling wordsmiths of contemporary theatre" (Gardner).

The beginning of *The Small Things* calls for a postponement of any process of meaning-making on the part of the audience. An epic roll of timpani drums heralds the opening of red velvet curtains as the stage is revealed. Strange details undermine what is otherwise a conventional portrait of an elderly couple in a shared living space: the bemused expression of Man who wears child's shoes with red laces, the twelve ceramic trinkets being polished by Woman, the alarm clocks held by both characters, and the enormous window/screen on the back wall emanating a yellow-grey light (Walsh 3). In the Paines Plough production, designer Neil Warmington chose to emphasize the surreal feel to this picture by suspending everything—the table, the ornaments, the chair—above the stage (Fisher). The contrast between the mundane and the bizarre in this stage image calls for what Lehmann, drawing on Freud, terms "evenly hovering attention" (87). Rather than understanding theatrical signs immediately, the audience's perception has to "remain open for connections, correspondences, and clues at completely unexpected moments ... Thus, meaning remains in principle postponed" (Lehmann 87). Coherent meaning-making is further suspended by the first lines of speech in Walsh's play: "Window. Knickknacks. Song" (Walsh 4). These nouns are a verbal map charting Woman's limited range of actions over the course of the drama, but for the audience their significance at first remains hidden. Is Woman speaking to Man? Are her words a proclamation or an invitation to speak? She delivers her words to the window, and their chairs "sort of" (3) face towards each other: clear answers, like the furniture that surrounds the characters, are suspended and out of reach. Man's alarm clock sounds, he slaps it off and launches into a monologue about a key event from his childhood. In the monologue he is three years old, but the use of present tenses (simple and continuous) to tell the story lends an immediacy to the tale that linguistically undermines a clear, unambiguous temporal structure.

> **MAN.** ... I'm three years old and all talk is me and future ... I'm leaving behind a life that's somewhat lumpen—HEY! (Walsh 4)
> Man's use of present tenses, coupled with the uncertainty about the realism of the space he occupies, makes it unclear whether he is recalling, living, or reliving the tale he is telling. This is complicated further by the following passage, where Man describes being brought to school by his mother as a three year old:
> **MAN.** ... That hug in the classroom an unusual show of affection more to do with doing the right thing than telling me of her love, self-pity, very attractive in an old man.

> *He laughs. She laughs.*
> Oh very good! Very nice!
> *They both stop laughing.*
> I drop my school bag and reach in and hold my mother's breasts.
> **WOMAN**. Oh! (Walsh 5)

Without warning, Man quickly switches from telling the tale, to describing himself as an "old man", before returning to the narrative in the next sentence, suddenly springing the description of groping his mother's breasts. These swift verbal gymnastics, coupled with the immediacy of the use of present tenses, undermine the clarity of this passage: are we being presented with the image of a three-year-old or an old man? Is there a sexual motivation behind this action, or is it merely one of affection? The reference soon after to his mother's "tits" (Walsh 5) rather than her breasts would suggest that the former cannot be ruled out. Either way the grammatical and descriptive ambiguity combines with an implied sexual undertone to create a disorientating and slightly disturbing tone. Woman immediately follows Man's story with her own monologue and a fresh set of questions arise. Are their stories related? Are they reacting to each other? Do they respond to their clocks rather than each other? From the opening moments of the play, *The Small Things* presents a series of questions that place the setting, characters and speech between the real and the "not real", disrupting our ability to assimilate the action.

This technique is closely related to what Lehmann terms the "simultaneity of signs" (87). Dramatic theatre proceeds by communicating and emphasizing one particular signal above others at any one moment of a performance. This is in contrast to postdramatic theatre, in which there is an intentional lack of linear and singular communication of signs. In outlining this concept, Lehmann refers to events such as dance performances by William Forsythe and Saburo, where it is impossible to take in all of the events that are occurring simultaneously (88). There are no simultaneously occurring events in *The Small Things* which the audience must attempt to process. However, visual, gestural and grammatical signs simultaneously combine in a way that prevents a coherent narrative from forming. It could be argued that those signs can still be contained within the enclosed fictional space of the play, and that in this way *The Small Things* fundamentally adheres to the traditional conventions of drama. Nevertheless, throughout the performance key characteristics of the postdramatic challenge those conventions, in turn fracturing attempts to form an enclosed world on stage that is separate from the audience.

What results from this intermittent fracturing is an interesting blending of the dramatic and postdramatic: a key trait of both *The Small Things* and Walsh's later plays.

The structure of *The Small Things,* like many of Walsh's plays, is based on an interlocking series of monologues, or what Lehmann terms "monologies" (128). In his analysis, he outlines the distinction between an intra-scenic, and an orthogonal axis of communication in theatre. The intra-scenic axis of communication refers to communication between characters, while the orthogonal axis refers to communication between the stage and the spectators. Lehmann dubs the latter axis the "theatron axis" after the Greek word used to designate the place of the spectators (127). While theatrical discourse can be addressed to both axes, a characteristic common to all forms of monologue is that the intra-scenic axis recedes in comparison to the theatron axis. According to Lehmann, this process of recession is emphasized in postdramatic theatre to the point where the intra-scenic axis can almost disappear in order to raise communication on the theatron axis to a "new quality of theatre" (127). Hence the need for a neologism to highlight the difference between a postdramatic and dramatic understanding and use of monologue. The essential difference is between speech that takes place "in the theatre" and that takes into account the theatre situation, and conversely, a theatre that has "withdrawn behind the fourth wall and which lets smoothly functioning dialogical communication take place there" (128). A reading of the speech acts in *The Small Things* as monologues allows for a wide number of interpretations, all of which can be accounted for and contained within the enclosed fictional space of the play. For example, it is suggested in the closing lines that Man and Woman inhabit separate houses on two mountains facing each other:

> **WOMAN.** ....! The house in the distance on top of
> that mountain. Our two houses blinking over at each
> other ... over the ... ? ... (Thinks) Oh the world
> that was there, that's enough. ... (Walsh 18)

From a dramatic point of view, this may be seen as an effective plot twist; before this point in the play there are only subtle indications that, in spite of their appearance together on stage, Man and Woman do not occupy the same physical space. The emotiveness of their paralleling love stories is made all the more poignant with the realization that the characters have been talking to themselves, rather than in dialogue. This is not an unusual use of monologue in dramatic theatre, and reflects the common thesis that "monologue (or "soliloquoy", as Pfister calls it) "expresses themes such as the disruption of communication and the isolation and alienation of the individual" (Lehmann 128). An alternative reading might even suggest that Man and Woman are no longer alive, and such a reading would be supported by Walsh's admission that the play is about his mother's relationship with his dead father (Walsh *Plays ix)*.

When considered from a postdramatic perspective, the readings above are still valid. However, if the monologues are read as monologies, then the presence of the audience and of the actors, the theatrical situation, gains more prominence: Man and Woman are not only talking to themselves, but to us, the audience. A variety of readings may place Man and Woman as alive, dead, on either side of a valley, or elements of the same consciousness. However, from a postdramatic perspective we cannot ignore that the voices of the actors pass through the same theatre space occupied by both themselves and the audience. The script suggests that the characters are not co-present; they do not address each other directly, and both sets of dialogue cleverly function as autonomous monologues if read separately. Nevertheless, the actors cohabit the same theatre situation. Thus the dialogic structure and sound of the play is composed of two voices, two presences. The acknowledgement of this commingling of sound and presence allows for a multiplicity of readings that extend beyond the dramatic text alone.

One possible reading is based on the way the alternating voices of the actors not only occupy the same aural space, but construct a musical dynamic that provides a sonic structure to the action of the play. This structure can only be realized and recognized through the co-presence of the audience and the actors in the moment of performance: it must be heard to be believed. Lehmann identifies the consistent tendency towards a musicalization of theatre as an important chapter of the sign usage in postdramatic theatre (91). Man's opening monologue encapsulates several of the musical elements of language deployed by Walsh in *The Small Things*:

> **MAN.** It's been raining for the past two weeks which
> would account for dampness. Not that I could
> remember. How could I remember. Impossible to
> remember! ... We're marching me and her. Parquet
> floor zigzagging down corridors. (Walsh 4)

The repetition of "remember" not only gestures to a preoccupation with memory in the thematic content of the *The Small Things*, but allows for variation in the pace of delivery of the lines. Words and phrases are repeated in quick succession in a similar manner throughout the play. In between these incidences of repetition, which allow the actor and director to decide on the rhythmic pace of the narrative, the tenses are constructed in a way that lends a musical tonality to the delivery of lines. This essay has already argued that the use of present tenses to recall past events lends an immediacy to those recollections. The continuous form of these tenses—"been raining" "We're marching" "zigzagging"—has the further effect of adding a lyrical ring to the words through the repeated "-ing" sound, a lyricism that is augmented by the rhyming "floor" and "corridor". A more general point in relation to the tonality of Walsh's plays is the dialect he chooses for his characters. His breakthrough play, *Disco Pigs* (1997) was set in Cork, a city with a distinctive, musical accent that the playwright jokingly discusses in a 2009 interview:

> They had the maddest accent, I was going, "I have no idea what they are saying!" ... it was sort of, it was sort of like trying to learn a dialect, ... and I wrote Disco Pigs directly after it, which was my dialogue with Cork about, "Why are you talking like that?!" ... And, it's a piece about identity and, sort of, striving to be something bigger than you are, and Cork as the second city in Ireland, dramatically it's very interesting for a playwright, the city itself, the shape of it is very interesting. (Walsh, "In Conversation: Joe Dowling and Enda Walsh")

The Small Things, Walsh's first play to be set outside Ireland, is not set in a defined location but in performance the characters had distinctive North Country accents (Fisher). Northern English and Cork accents share two key characteristics. Firstly, they both have a distinctive, musical tonality. Secondly, this distinctive sound parallels the status of the inhabitants of those regions as occupying places that are outside of the political centres of power in their respective countries. However, this peripheral status is either celebrated or treated with casual indifference by their inhabitants : examples of this include the Northern Soul music movement in England in the 1970s and 80s , or the sale of t-shirts in Ireland with humorous banners celebrating the "People's Republic of Cork". Like Walsh's characters, the people of Lancashire and Cork have a self-contained culture within which their otherness forms part of the construction of their identity. Cultural or political status may or may not have influenced Walsh's and/or Featherstone's choice of the Lancashire accent for *The Small Things*. What is more important in terms of the performance of the play is the role played by the sound of words in the meaning-making process. This is a point that the playwright makes reference to in an interview in 2013 for the Art of Psychiatry Society:

> as soon as they [words] leave your mouth, there's so many variables to the way they actually sound; this is why, sort of, theatre is really complex, you know like, when a character begins to, sort of, talk it's like "blaargh" (makes an explosive gesture from his mouth with his hands), how do we then sort of, how do we then begin to read that? And sort of like, you know like, understand it? There are so many different understandings to whatever a phrase is! (chuckles) So, they're loaded, they're like bloody boils! (Walsh, "Femi Oyebode in conversation with Enda Walsh")

Walsh is talking about the multitude of possible meanings that phrases can hold but, more importantly, he is considering the way variations in sound and delivery can alter and contribute to these multitudes. This points towards the necessity of an understanding of the play that incorporates the performance experience as much as a knowledge of the playscript. The amount of possible interpretations that can be applied to the words of *The Small Things* on paper changes when those words are spoken. Therefore, the process of meaning could potentially change, not only with each new production over the years, but with each performance of the play by the same group of actors.

Walsh mentions the multitude of understandings that can be applied to words and phrases, which may lead us to question whether any fixed understanding can be gleaned from words, sentences at all? At first it appears that the sound of words further complicates these questions by adding to the layers of possible meanings. Despite at first appearing to complicate matters, one possible answer to these questions resides in a deeper consideration of the role of speech and sound in performance. In an interview for the *Guardian*, Walsh recalls a conversation with fellow playwright Sarah Kane:

> I remember once ... asking her how she was getting on with her new play. She said "I haven't started writing it yet but I can hum it." That's exactly it. You have to find the internal rhythm of a play in order to make it work. (Billington)

If we think about the rhythm and "hum" of *The Small Things* we begin to form a musical structure, where two voices form a sonic whole in an interlocking duet. As Eleni Varopolou states: " This is not a matter of the evident role of music and of music theatre, but rather of a more profound idea of theatre as music" (Lehmann 91). The play is structured around alternating monologies of almost equal length, punctuated by small sections of alternating sentences. The almost equal time given to each voice structurally reflects the harmony of their love for each other; it suggests a shared space and presence. This harmony reaches its structural apotheosis in the playing of the song *Nagasaki* by the Mills Brothers (Walsh 31). At this point, the play not only structurally reflects music, it becomes music: Man and Woman's alternating blocks of words give way to a shared appreciation of the flow of lyrics and sound. In the minutes following this harmonious high point, the monologies resume with renewed urgency before shortening in length and ultimately climaxing in a series of sharp, alternating one-line sentences. This rapid-fire crescendo at first threatens, before ultimately tearing, the structural fabric of the play: the balanced, harmonious tone is broken, and Woman disappears from sight and hearing. She is followed by Man, but not before he promises a resumption of their duet for the following morning (Walsh 40). The idea of a sonic structure underlying *The Small Things* is supported by Walsh's recollection of directing *The New Electric Ballroom* in Italy. Walsh doesn't speak Italian, and none of the cast spoke English:

> I had a translator for three days, but then I got rid of her because I didn't need her," he says, "I knew the play, they knew the play, and it was about finding the rhythm of it. We all knew the scenes, and I knew emotionally what they were trying to get at. It was a very funny experience. ... (Taylor)

It could be argued that Walsh was familiar enough with the script not to require a translator. Nevertheless, the suggestion is that the meaning of the words did not matter as much as their sound and rhythm. Given the above reference to *New Electric*, it appears possible to seek out sonic structures, not only in *The Small Things,* but in the entire range of Walsh's plays; structures that reflect and accentuate the core of the relationships between the characters on stage. For example, in Druid's production of *The Walworth Farce* (2006), the high-pitched, manic tune of Sean and Blake had a forced and warped nature, dictated by Dinny in his role as conductor. A similar structure was evident in *New Electric*, although there was more space for monologies, or solos, as Ada, Breda and Clara vied for the role of master of ceremonies. In this analysis, the play that most resembles *The Small Things* is *Ballyturk* (2014). The burden of sound production necessary for the creation of sonic structure was more or less shared by 1 and 2 in a way that reflected the deep bond of their friendship. The strain of this co-production of sound visibly grew, until 3 arrived to rhythmically, aurally and structurally tear their world apart. If we were to attend a production of the *The Small Things* in a language foreign to us, blindfolded, it is possible to suggest that while the details of the narrative would elude us, we would still be able to sense the dynamics of the relationship at the heart of the play. In 2012, Walsh's adaptation of the Irish film *Once* (2006) for Broadway won the Tony Award for Best Book of a Musical. In his acceptance speech Walsh acknowledged that, given the dark subject matter of his plays, he was the "wrong person" to take on a "delicate little love story" (Walsh). It was a humourous but, at the same time, perceptive echo of what was very likely the most common reaction to the news that he was writing the book for *Once*: fans of the film could be forgiven for having dark visions of its tranquil tone being torn asunder by a cohort of Walsh's creations. Such fears proved to be unfounded and, in the context of the musicalization inherent in his plays, Walsh's brief transition and success in musical theatre appears a great deal less surprising.

In addition to musicalization, the technical and thematic treatment of time is a central characteristic of both postdramatic theatre generally, and *The Small Things* in particular. In *bedbound, Walworth, New Electric, Penelope* (2010) and more recently in *Ballyturk,* the central characters are caught in a repetitive loop of action in a space that is outside of time. In *The Small Things* the thematic prominence of time is immediately signalled by the clocks held by both Man and Woman. As with players caught in a chess match, the ringing of the clocks trigger the back and forth of their interlocking monologies. In the shared narrative outlined by Man and Woman, time plays a central role. The day Man and Woman bond as children is the "day of the no stopwatch" (14), when all around them their community strive to "measure all that can be measured" (22); timepieces at the ready in an attempt to control time, or more broadly speaking, nature. Woman and Man see a fellow villager in a field "counting bees, counting birds, counting flies." The impulse to exert this kind of control comes from a place of fear, a feeling of insignificance against the vast incomprehensibility of time and existence. Walsh has spoken about his struggle to come to terms with these feelings in the past:

> I told [Cillian Murphy] about a ground-zero moment I had some years ago. Just after my play Disco Pigs opened in 1996 and was being picked up everywhere, I was walking over Patrick's bridge in Cork and I stopped dead still and felt absolutely terrified that I was alive and had to keep on living. The moment lasted maybe five seconds and I kept on walking. But it's a playwright's job to explore that feeling that, however many good days you may have, you are still ultimately alone and walking around in your own

private universe. (Billington)

Compartmentalizing and naming time is a way of exerting a measure of control over something that is vast, intangible and immeasurable. This attempt mirrors what Lehmann identifies as an essential component of the Aristotelian tradition of dramatic theatre: the rule of the unity of time (158). A central aspect of this rule is that,

> to the same degree as time and action attain an internal coherence, seamless continuity and totality of surveyability, this same unity draws a distinct line between drama and the external world. ... Gaps and leaps in the continuum of time, on the other hand, would immediately function as points of intrusion for external reality. (Lehmann 160)

According to these principles, beauty is analogous to order and rationality. In Lehmann's analysis the unity of time outlined by Aristotle, and later further developed by others such as Pierre Corneille, was upheld in order to prevent precisely the reception that postdramatic theatre strives to instigate: "free-roaming imagination uncontrolled by the dramatic process ... [and] the outbreak of the imagined reception in Lord knows what other spatial and temporal spheres (161)." The ubiquity of this correlation between time, unity and order is evident in the anecdote that opens this essay: the drunken man ruptures the unity of the spectacle being surveyed by the audience, and, following his expulsion, "order" is restored (Rebellato). Maintenance of order, prevention of "free-roaming imagination" and mis-communication: all of these are central characteristics of the campaign waged by Woman's father and chip shop man. In this way their efforts mirror those of the writer: to manipulate characters into an aesthetically pleasing, easy to assimilate whole that ignores the variability and unpredictability of "real life." On the level of the dramatic text of *The Small Things*, the unity of this whole is corrupted by another unquantifiable variable of human existence: love. The scientific order imposed by the dictatorial duo is undermined by a series of motifs drawn from nature; the scattered array of leaves in the forest and clouds in the sky form a natural, creative space where love can blossom. Against a backdrop of mechanically prohibited speech, meaningless and idle small talk forms the basis for a deep bond between Man and Woman. These contrasting images are poignant, and instigate an engagement with the theme of time through symbol and metaphor. However, an extra layer of rupture is required in order for *The Small Things* to engage with the subject of time on a postdramatic, as well as dramatic, level.

One of the possible ways this type of rupture is achieved is through the clocks held by Man and Woman. They can be assimilated on a dramatic level as psychological props for the characters, symbols of their shared existence or, perhaps implausibly, as a way for them to ensure that their narratives remain in time with each other in their separate mountaintop abodes. An alternative reading of the clocks can be gleaned from the role they play in performance. The ringing of the clocks stimulates an awareness of the imperative placed on the actors to perform. Every theatrical performance is subject to a given timeframe, and in this way *The Small Things* is no different. The alarm clocks act as a reminder of the timeframe imposed on the performance and thus awaken the audience to the "time of the performance text": a sense of time that incorporates the "total real and staged situation of the performance ... in order to emphasize the impulse of presence always inherent to it" (Lehmann 154). An awareness of the time of the performance text adds an extra dynamic to the monologies in the play. Every act of communication has an unspoken "comfort zone" of temporality, mutually agreed upon by each participant and dictated by social mores. For example, in most Western cultures a chance encounter with an acquaintance requires small talk to fill the appropriate length of time of conversation. Similarly, most theatrical performances are a standardized length of time that audiences submit to through their attendance. In the Aristotelian model outlined by Lehmann, this length of time has a unity that aims to make the time of the performance text disappear. However, in *The Small Things*, the audience is confronted with the overt presence of time. Time controls the characters and in turn the characters, through the performance time, have control over the audience. As we realize that the characters are caught in a repetitive loop we are confronted with the possibility that we too could be caught in the confines of this repetition (Walsh 40). Walsh brings us to the precipice of the repetitive abyss his characters have fallen into without casting us in completely. At the close of *The Walworth Farce*, *The New Electric Ballroom* and *The Small Things*, the lights in the auditorium brighten, and as we leave we are left merely to imagine the repetitive stasis of Sean, Ada, Man and Woman. We continue upon the apparently teleological paths of our lives. However, at certain, repeated moments—our daily commute, lunch breaks, dinners, holidays, trips to the theatre—our own "real" lives may come closer to those characters than we had believed to be possible; the rhythm of their existence may not seem so different to that of the lives we lead.

Lisa Fitzpatrick argues that the reason Walsh's work has received comparatively little academic attention to date is that it does not easily fit within the contemporary Irish repertoire, or the scholarly narratives of contemporary Irish theatre:

> His fascination with stories and storytelling does not result in plays like McPherson's The Weir, or work that sits within a storytelling tradition. Rather, Walsh's work is concerned with the nature of performance itself, and the plays must be seen and studied in performance—the texts alone will not do. (451)

Through a close reading of The Small Things, this essay has attempted to respond to Fitzpatrick's prompt by foregrounding the importance of performance in the analysis of Walsh's oeuvre. Interestingly, The Small Things did not attract a great deal of critical or public attention at the Galway Arts Festival in 2005, and it is likely that its more overt postdramatic tendencies may have alienated some audience members. Walsh's subsequent successes in Ireland—The Walworth Farce, The New Electric Ballroom, and Penelope—retained traces of the postdramatic but, crucially, each play was anchored by narratives and tropes familiar to Irish audiences: lonely emigrants, rural villages, Greek classics. However, Walsh's most recent productions in Ireland, Misterman and Ballyturk, represent a noteworthy return to the more overt aspects of the postdramatic found in The Small Things. The quintessentially Irish sounding title of Ballyturk suggested the familiar, but in many ways this was Walsh's furthest departure from a traditional Irish drama. This was reflected in individual audience reactions to the play, which emphasized a connection with the experience of the performance rather than an overarching "message". Audience members used adjectives such as "speechless", "exhilarating", "zany", "drained", "heart-wrenched" and "scared" (Galway International Arts Festival). From this perspective, Walsh's work represents an important moment in Irish theatre history. The success and growth in prominence of experimental theatre groups such as Anú, Brokentalkers, and Pan Pan has created a growing polarity between tradition and experimentation in Irish theatre. On one side there is the conventional drama, with a focus on well-written and structured stories, and on the other there is a conscious rejection of the writer, the script, and in some cases the stage. In their blending of conventional Irish drama and the postdramatic, Walsh's plays are a meeting point between these polarities. The critical and financial success of Ballyturk, described by Michael Billington as the "hottest ticket at the 2014 Galway International Arts Festival" (Billington), is a clear indication that Irish audiences are embracing a change in mainstream Irish theatre. The question is, where will this change take us? Are we at the dawn of a new era in Irish theatre or, as *The Small Things* seems to suggest, condemned to repeat the narratives of our past?

Works Cited

Balme, Christopher. "Editorial." *Theatre Research International* 29.01 (2004): 1-3. *Jstor*. Web. 7 Dec. 2014.

Billington, Michael. "Enda Walsh: "Pure theatre animal" explores solitude and the void below." *The Guardian* 18 Sept. 2014: n. pag. Web. 6 Dec. 2014.

Billington, Michael. "Penelope." *Guardian* 26 July 2010: n. pag. Web. 24 Feb. 2015.

Brantley, Ben. "Theater Review: The Walworth Farce." *New York Times* 19 Apr. 2008: n. pag. Web. 24 Feb. 2015.

Fitzpatrick, Lisa. "Enda Walsh." *The Methuen Drama Guide to Contemporary Irish Playwrights*. Ed. Martin Middeke and Peter Paul Schnierer. London: Bloomsbury, 2010. Print.

Fisher, Philip. "Theatre review: The Small Things at Menier Chocolate Factory." *British Theatre Guide*. N.p., n.d. Web. 6 Dec. 2014.

Galway International Arts Fesival. "*Ballyturk* Audience Reactions @ Galway International Arts Festival 2014." *YouTube*. N.p., n.d. Web. 7 Dec. 2014.

Gardner, Lyn. "Edinburgh Festival: The New Electric Ballroom." *Guardian* 4 Aug. 2008: n. pag. Web. 24 Feb. 2015.

Lehmann, Hans-Thies. *Postdramatic Theatre*. London [i.e. Abington: Routledge, 2006. Print.

Rebellato, Dan. "10 Audiences I have known." *Dan Rebellato*. N.p., 10 Oct. 2014. Web. 24 Feb. 2015. <http://www.danrebellato.co.uk/spilledink/2014/10/21/10-audiences-i-have-known>.

Scott, Adam. "The Small Things, Menier Chocolate Factory, London—Reviews—Theatre & Dance." *The Independent*. N.p., n.d. Web. 5 Dec. 2014.

Taylor, James C. "Irishman Enda Walsh doesn't let words get in the way." *Los Angeles Times* 8 Nov. 2009: n. pag. Web. 7 Dec. 2014.

Walsh, Enda. "Acceptance Speech: Enda Walsh." The Tony Awards. Beacon Theatre. 10 June 2012. Speech.

---. "Femi Oyebode in conversation with Enda Walsh." Interview by Femi Oyebode. *Youtube*. The Art of Psychiatry Society, 27 July 2013. Web. 24 Feb. 2015. https://www.youtube.com/watch?v=jPOnVlLlWzo>.

---.”In conversation: Joe Dowling and Enda Walsh.” Interview by Joe
    Dowling. *Youtube*. Walker Art Center, 25 May 2010. Web. 24 Feb. 2015.
    <https://www.youtube.com/watch?v=BCJdK-U1Q-4>.

---. *The Small Things*. London: Nick Hern Books, 2005. Print.

Weaver, Jesse. "Review: Bedbound." *Irish Theatre Magazine* 12 Aug. 2011:
    n. pag. Web. 24 Feb. 2015.

---, "'The Words Look After Themselves": The Practice of Enda Walsh."
    Irish Drama: Local and Global Perspectives. Eds Nicholas Grene and
    Patrick Lonergan. Dublin: Carysfort Press, 2012. Print.

8| Fantasizing About Truth: Re-membered Histories and Performance in *How These Desperate Men Talk*

Nelson Barre

One man holds a gun to another man's head, demanding that he recount his past transgressions under threat of execution. But the man under threat can stop his would-be murderer by simply asking "Is this the truth?" This is the world into which an audience is thrust in Enda Walsh's play *How These Desperate Men Talk*. The playwright presents the world of the play as the first layer of understanding a reconstruction of memory within a performative space. The man under the gun must satisfy his aggressor through a retelling of a shared personal history. This act highlights questions of truth and the slippery nature of recalling past experiences, especially in moments of stress and mortal danger. The body and brain strive to survive, willing the psyche to do anything to stay alive. The play, however, does not solely rely on this first level of performance. Instead, Walsh's world exposes the human tendency to protect oneself from the past by re-creating it, amending the undesirable events to portray a preferred history. If a person can fully embody the performance of the past, then he or she becomes master of the story and the one in control of the narrative and its truth. In this play, the question of verity becomes the focus of the dialogue as the men craft personal versions of their memories in hopes of discovering what really happened. But is that enough to salvage the meaning/purpose of their lives? To answer this question, I will explore Walsh's reconsiderations of memory versus reality and how the characters within this play utilize reconstructions of the past to remember[5] and revise personal history. Restructured narratives and the necessity of maintaining the veracity of the story provide the fractured structure in which these men search for truth and survival. Using this frame, *How These Desperate Men Talk* presents a world where the characters' sole desire is to find what is "true" in their recollection of the past.

Walsh's play follows the repeated framework of one man controlling another by forcing him to recall a memory. But there is a twist in Walsh's work: the men have been playing this game for a long time now and continually replay the scene as a process of individual and communal (re)discovery.

> **DAVE.** Your mother!? Haven't we done that before?
> **JOHN.** Well, I don't know!
> **DAVE.** I'm sure we have used your mother ...
> **JOHN.** Really?
> **DAVE.** A little time ago.
> **JOHN.** Are you certain?
> **DAVE.** Certain? No, I'm not certain.
> **JOHN.** Then just use it! USE IT! CARRY ON!
> (132)

The titular characters, Dave and John, are "two middle-aged men of similar appearance ... they are men from suburbia" (Walsh 131). The common names of Dave and John do little to differentiate them from any middle-class man happily living a daily routine. The main tension of the scene stems from the fact that John is holding a gun firmly against Dave's head, forcing him to perform. Fear of death drives the alleged need for truth; that is to say, the men have created this scenario in hopes that they will re-member better if their lives depend on it.

The audience is meant to catch up with the story as the play moves along; the narrative starts with references to an anniversary and to the stalking of a young woman which eventually shifts into a narrative of detestation for John's mother (or whoever happens to be the object of their scorn in a given iteration of the story). Walsh relieves the audience when the men drop out of the intensity of the scene so they can comment upon the developments in Dave's confession. The men constantly ask whether a certain version of their story is "true" or comes closer to their memory. As the play progresses, however, we discover that these men do not actually remember the events that transpired.

---

5 In her essay "Possession," Suzan-Lori Parks uses the term "re-member" to mean something that is reassembled, parts of a body put back together (4-5). My usage of the term relies on that same notion.

JOHN. The details are fine. Mother's not right. It was good but completely wrong.
DAVE. Are we getting any closer to who it is we're blaming?
JOHN. We must be. We've been doing this for quite a long time now. We must be closer.
DAVE. Unless we're repeating ourselves.
JOHN. Well, let's say we are repeating ourselves every so often ... you'd still imagine that we're bound to come across some resemblance to truth, right? (137)

The men repeat the same scripted dialogue with only minor adjustments as a means of discovering their culpability to the past and its consequences. Walsh then replaces the physical threat of death with the metaphysical deconstruction of the characters' psyches. The men fear not knowing the truth. In response, they recreate the circumstances of interrogator and detainee out of necessity to find the reality of their memory and the purpose of their lives.

Their continuous performances are all in service of assigning blame. The playwright never enumerates the incident in any detail beyond the fact that someone followed a young woman in a park only to murder and leave her body in the bushes for the ducks to find the next day. To find a suitable subject worthy of blame, the eponymous men turn their gaze to others. Both men feel as though they are coming closer to the truth of the matter; however there is no indication of their specific involvement in the crime. John and Dave need to find a reason for the alleged murder, a vindication for what they have truthfully pursued through play-acting. By enacting their version of the past, they can make the story real and perhaps escape culpability. However, the only authorities the audience ever hears about are the titular characters themselves. In a sense, this story only exists within the confines of the room in which the men perform. By refashioning the memory so often, they seem to have forgotten this fact. They do not even remember if they were the ones to have killed the woman in the story, which leads an audience to wonder whether a woman ever existed or if the entire story was imagined. This scenario which the two men have collaboratively invented and continue to repeat may simply exist in their constructed world of alleged responsibility.

To extend this argument, one must consider whether the threat is entirely imagined. Paul Ricœur states "memory begins deliberately with an analysis turned toward the object of memory ... it then passes through the stage of the search for a given memory ... we then move from memory as it is given and exercised to reflective memory, to memory of oneself" (Ricœur *xvi*). The process of remembering and forgetting is distinctly and inextricably human. Dave and John suffer from this need for self-reflection; both are helpless against the possibility that they may not even be the people who committed the crime. They could simply be exploring their own personal revulsions through repetition of an imagined murder. As such, John's power is purely constructed and only as real as the story the two men have re-enacted countless times. Dave's verbal creation of the world ostensibly holds more sway than John's physicality, but that is where the fear of bodily harm inspires the mind.

Rather than reduce the play to metaphysical ponderings, Walsh presents the men as explorers of memory and reality through performance of remembrance. The play puts a death threat on the search for purpose through repetition. Do the men remember what happened, or have they warped their actions in their thoughts so completely that they would not recognize what is "right" even if they stumble upon it? Like Walsh's other works, *How These Desperate Men Talk* questions whether anyone who tells a story ever fully discloses the truth. The act of re-membering the past is subjective and therefore impossible to impartially recount. This fact begs the question: is a performance of memory ever reliable even if it has been rehearsed hundreds of times? The dramatic tension of this play is built on these questions, the exploration of the past and how its repercussions extend into the present of the performance.

Like Samuel Beckett before him, Walsh's work constantly refers to the process of re-membering the past through words and memories[6]. Thomas Postlewait's argument that "The inner chronology in Beckett's art functions not as an escape from the present by means of the fullness of memory, but as a sad reminder of the present moment cut off from past experience" is echoed in *How These Desperate Men Talk* (Postlewait 474). The characters cannot ever truly remember the past and so are only interested in the truth as they remember it. The pair find their *raison-d'être* in the process of creating a version of reality from memories of the past rather than the attainment of truth. This essay argues that Walsh's dramaturgy does not solely rely on the claim that, for Beckett, "Time reveals but one countenance, thus refusing—

---

[6] Scholars have written extensively on Beckett's use of memory. For further reference, consult James Olney's article "Memory and the Narrative Imperative: St. Augustine and Samuel Beckett" (1993), Sabine Kozdon's *Memory in Samuel Beckett's Plays: A Psychological Approach* (2006), and Seán Kennedy and Katherine Weiss's *Samuel Beckett: History, Memory, Archive* (2010).

even in death itself—to grant release and salvation" (ibid). Instead time and repeated performance grant agency to characters who simultaneously rely upon and deny the fictionality of their memories. As with any historian, the narrative of the past as told in the present is necessarily influenced by the one telling the story at that moment. For John and Dave, re-membering the past becomes its own form of release and salvation—even in its necessity for endless repetition.

By giving the men agency in revising the past, Walsh complicates our understanding of the relationship between reality and fiction both in the play itself and in the active re-membering of history. Every part of the performance is meant to serve the "truth" of the past, but there is no unified, unbiased retelling. John and Dave argue about the purpose of replaying the scene:

> **JOHN.** This is very good.
> **DAVE.** Yeah?
> **JOHN.** I'm enjoying this.
> **DAVE.** Really?
> **JOHN.** All this mother stuff, I like it.
> **DAVE.** Yeah, but you like the priest one too.
> **JOHN.** The priest version was good but this has more truth about it.
> **DAVE.** Really? You think this might be the truth?
> **JOHN.** Well, that doesn't matter, does it?
> **DAVE.** Doesn't it?
> **JOHN.** The exact truth hardly matters, Dave. Are you joking!
> **DAVE.** Of course, sorry. Then we're searching for what exactly?
> **JOHN.** Difficult to say. We are definitely searching, though!
> *John clicks the trigger on the gun. Dave quickly continues.*
> (133-4)

The intent and intensity of the performance is paramount to both men. The characters simultaneously seek to subvert the truth of the past and also to uphold it through performed memory. The main problem is that they do not know what the truth is. Instead, the men must restructure their memories and hope to hit on something "true." By taking control of the past through their retelling of it, the characters display agency and the creative need for self-preservation. But what happens when the truth comes out? Or as J.L. Austin posits in his book *How to Do Things with Words*, "Can saying make it so?" (7). In a situation where words create reality, who defines what is right? Can simply repeating a faulty history enough times make it seem real? Would the men be able to recognize when/if these deviations were made? Does it even matter to the men if they ever stop searching? For these men, the beauty is in the communion not in the outcome.

By highlighting the process of re-membering, *How These Desperate Men Talk* blends storytelling and creating history. As with any story which has been repeated, even once, the original always differs from the subsequent iterations. John and Dave follow a carefully crafted set of lines, but each iteration changes in intonation and content as they approach or recede from their perceived version of the past. Diana Taylor, in her book *The Archive and the Repertoire*, explains this evolution of performed myth as "the transfer of performances [which] outlasted the memory of their meaning, as populations found themselves faithfully repeating behaviors that they no longer understood" (Taylor 50). In a sense, the characters have created a world out of words that may or may not be "true." As the men admit, they do not know what they need to finish the story correctly. Early in the play, John is the one who says the "*exact* truth hardly matters" (134), but later it is Dave who says the same words (143). This recognition presents a complicated notion for characters within a play who ostensibly have no recognition that their words were actually given to them by an author. Ignoring that fact, however, provides an even more insidious possibility for the eponymous men: they are the authors of their own repressed truth.

In their attempts to escape from ignorance, Dave and John follow what appears to be a strict regimen of ritualistic repetition of their history[7]. They perform their roles in an effort to create, to take control of their world when it seems to otherwise have dwindled to just their small room. Like artists searching for a muse, the men find both inspiration and devastation in the act of myth-making. The instability of thought leads to further difficulties in assigning a singular meaning to repeated actions. When the past can be interpreted in several ways, there will undoubtedly be many versions of performance. To complicate matters further, Michel de Certeau argues that, "Performances are tools manipulated by users and are the evidence of a creative agency that facilitates the construction of identity" (21). Walsh builds his play around this idea—that every repeated performance of the men's skewed

---

[7] I use the term ritual to mean a repeated, performative (often quotidian) act that has meaning on both a personal and communal level. As described by Roy A. Rappaport in his book *Ecology, Meaning, and Religion*, "Ritual tends to be stylized, repetitive, stereotyped, often but not always decorous, and they also tend to occur at special places and at times fixed by the clock, calendar, or specified circumstances" (175-76). Catherine Bell's *Ritual Theory, Ritual Practice* also notes the necessity for ritual as a form of individually appropriated meaning-making (222).

memories creates a new version of the pair's history. This point begs questions of cultural memory concerning subjective revisions of history as told by various groups. Without the repetition and ritualization of past events, history could not be created. It is only through the inherently revisionist nature of re-membering that a person or group creates an identity. The difficulty in maintaining authorial integrity over the "original" becomes apparent when a story has been performed as often as the one in *How These Desperate Men Talk*.

Returning to the necessity to create, repeat, and revise, neither John nor Dave knows how the story they repeat actually occurred. However, they pursue the truth as if they could define it, as if reality was not a subjective part of their personal experience and memory. Several times throughout the play, the men both note the creative process of their storytelling:

> **DAVE.** Like you gave life to her somehow.
> **JOHN.** Like she just existed from that moment on.
> **DAVE.** Right, you imagined her and there she was. (131)

Each man is able to offer ideas and edits, suggesting an art to the invention of their memories. But in the second iteration of the story, John slightly alters the telling where he states "I imagined her and there she was" rather than Dave (140). The men hardly recognize these instances when small changes are made, simply accepting them as part of the process. Their modus operandi hinges on how they feel in the moment—like actors who perform onstage and have to "feel it" or else their performance falls flat. John and Dave simultaneously understand and forget the power they can wield with words. While it may seem a small inconsistency, these men have built their lives around precision. Their ability to recall the exact words is a mnemonic feat, but they are still unable to actually re-member what led them to their current situation. Similar to Diana Taylor's argument about repeated behaviour, these men no longer know their purpose apart from enacting the expected behaviour which will allegedly produce an epiphany for their salvation.

To circumnavigate their forgotten function, the men insert a repeated mantra at the start of each version of the memory: "How simple and true and right" (131, 140, 144). This phrase sets the parameters of the world—it is about correctly recounting a story. The repetition of these words each time the men play the scene emphasizes their dedication to truth and accuracy, even though the expression subversively indicates their inability to remember. In short, they admit defeat each time they play the scene. Technically there is no wrong version as neither man knows for sure what is real, but it is a battle between the ability to re-member the past and the desire for survival. Their partly improvised scene has become codified through repetition and requires the identification of their act as "simple and true and right," otherwise the process deteriorates. Without the belief that they are searching for reality, their existence would lose its meaning in relation to each other and the imagined world beyond their fractured memories.

As authors of their own version of truth, the men prefer to weave a complex tapestry of story rather than actually coming to a conclusion. With this love of tale-spinning comes the tendency toward embellishment or even playing for an audience. However, the only audience for Dave is John and vice versa. As such, the men serve as the only participants in the story and therefore the only contributors to the creative process. But this fact is made more personal as the story presents mostly a confession by Dave about John. Throughout the performance, Dave describes how John felt—"You hated your father" or "You felt no pangs of guilt" (133, 135). Dave describes the interiority of John's character, something he could not possibly know from personal experience. And yet, Dave is expected to provide the emotions to which John must agree. This role grants him both the responsibility and the power to dictate the past as it is re-membered in the performance. However, John appears to utilize the fear of execution as a means for forcing this outpouring of imagined thoughts and feelings. John demands that someone else provide him with the responses he is meant to have regarding experiences from his life. This fact inserts yet another layer to the already palimpsestuous retelling and revising process of the men's performance. Under the duress of the gun Dave must perform for his own survival and also for John's forgotten emotions. Their search for a version of reality through a faulty attempt at re-membering the past provides little hope that these men will ever find their answer.

Even with the constructed, underlying meaning of the performance, the two men differ in their alleged purpose for performing the scene. Dave seems to be in favour of finding a satisfactory ending and John prefers the searching. The performance tires Dave each time due to the requisite intensity and words he must produce at gunpoint. He protests: "I can't be doing this indefinitely, you know!" to which John replies: "What are you talking about! I've got a gun! Of course you can!" (137). Neither man, however, even knows if there is a bullet in the gun.

DAVE. Did we have a conversation as to whether we believed there was a bullet in the gun?
Pause
JOHN. I'm not too sure.
DAVE. Do you think there's a bullet in there?
JOHN. It's safer to believe that there might be a bullet. (139)

There is safety in fear. If they ever decided this was not the case, there would be no need for the endless repetition and re-membering of the past. Without a bullet, Dave has no reason to fear for his life and could invent lies. But terror elicits alleged truth, which is the reality the men so desperately want. In this way, John and Dave are living out fantasies of revenge against anyone and everyone whom they could possibly construe as antagonist. Instead of ever achieving their goal, the need for control and compartmentalization over the shared history becomes its own reasoning. The constructed framework of the memory drives John, even when he recognizes his uncertainty of its origins. John is certain of one thing: they must continue to re-member the story. And because he has the gun, he is in a position to say when and if they go on with the performance.

In this way, John uses the gun to control Dave's storytelling to combat the existential crisis of re-membering the past through ritualized performance. But over the course of the play it seems that he does not wield any real power, and not merely because the gun may or may not be loaded. Most of the story is told in the second person, putting John in a precarious position of authority and ignorance, because Dave does all the re-membering on John's behalf. Dave dictates and John can only improvise off the creative impulses provided. Dave is also the one with the agency to change the meaning and content of the story because he lists the events which led to the woman's murder. The scene resembles an improvisation exercise, but it is one in which certain references and words combine to connect to the one person who John blames for the woman's murder in the story.

Thinking of the play as an extended improv proves useful in locating the level of dedication and accuracy the men are willing to endure. Normally a pair of improvising actors would know the rules of their scenario and would react based on the details provided by their partner. Walsh follows these basic tenets, but he also allows the men to question the exploratory process otherwise associated with devising and improvising a scene for performance. Within the first page of dialogue, Dave stops the story to ask, "Haven't we done that before?" to which John responds, "Well, I don't know!" (132). This first instance of a breakdown in the script leads the men to quibble over the questionable authenticity of the entire exercise in repetition and recollection. But eventually they come to the conclusion that they must simply continue with the chosen subject and "just use it" (132). As the scene continues, the men offer commentary suggesting changes or complimenting a particularly well-delivered line. In this way, the men act both as collaborative actors and directors. By providing critiques of each other, John and Dave try to take control of the past and mould it as they see fit. The actors gain agency over their own creative process and can manipulate it to suit their needs.

However, Walsh's creation problematizes the idea of constructed and regurgitated memory. Similar to Ricœur's statement, Dave and John see the fact that they are in control of the story and its outcome. There are major details which must be invented, and if this is the case then nothing can be "true" or "real," in a sense. They are unaware that one of the previous retellings may have been correct. But their hope for satisfaction stems from the possibility of an inspired performance where they will recognize the truth. But certainty and meaning fail to appear, and this collapse affords the characters some agency in acting out their dark desires. This opportunity leads to an invented truth around which they build their personal expectations, even if it means sacrificing one's own life.

In response to John's enforcement of strict repetition, Dave exhibits the behaviour of a child being caught and punished for doing something naughty. John, playing the parent, scolds Dave for his dalliance in focus and intent prompting him to a more truthful confession.

> **DAVE.** Have you started to fantasize about the time when we eventually reach the truth?
> **JOHN.** What?
> **DAVE.** I have.
> **JOHN.** When do you find the time to do that?
> **DAVE.** During.
> **JOHN.** What?
> **DAVE.** As we're ...
> **JOHN.** As we're telling the story?!
> **DAVE.** Only sometimes!
> **JOHN.** You're thinking about a moment of peace while we're supposed to be busy searching for what might get us there!?
> **DAVE.** Is that wrong?
> **JOHN.** Well, it's not very diligent, Dave! A strict man would say that it's shoddy work practice! Shouldn't you be concentrating wholly?
> **DAVE.** The brain wanders.

JOHN. Well, is it any wonder it's taking us all this time when you've got your sights on the prize! Stick to the details, Dave. Isn't that the problem with people?! They have no concern for "the now." (138)

The importance is placed on the process rather than the product. Only by fully giving over to the reality of the scene will Dave and John ever achieve "truth". The characters need to find truth through the ritualized reliving of collective memory, but this desire runs against John's obsession with living in the "now" because of the perpetual attention given to the past. The men search the past to respond correctly in the present which will lead to a reprieve in the future. But the men cannot see the fallacy inherent in their performance: while they may believe they are "getting closer to the truth", they can never be certain no matter how many times they re-tell the story (137).

In this way, the repetition does not create a sense of confidence within the men even as they perform their roles. The woman John supposedly murdered reminded him of someone for whom he held an immense hatred. Dave and John collaborate to complete the story and decide who should be the subject of their ire, but nothing is ever right. They both remember the basic outline of the story they tell. However, their memories splinter each time they attempt to recall the past in its entirety. The murdered woman becomes a surrogate[8] for an offense caused by someone earlier in John's life. But, again, the men are unable to fully conceive of the past because with each passing iteration the original continues to recede. Instead, they hope that by remaking the past with constructed tensions they can artificially infuse the present with the original meaning.

Rebecca Schneider, in her book *Performing Remains*, in relation to historical reenactments, says "if they repeat an event *just so*, getting the details as close as possible to fidelity, they will have touched time and time will have recurred" (Schneider 10). John and Dave believe wholeheartedly that their story will enable them to find that special something which is missing from their lives. Without the answer of what is "true" in their shared history, however, the men stagnate and

---

[8] I use the term "surrogate" in the way Joseph Roach does in *Cities of the Dead: Circum-Atlantic Performance* when he states, "In the life of a community, the process of surrogation does not begin or end but continues as actual or perceived vacancies occur in the network of relations that constitutes the social fabric" (2). John and Dave are the community, in this instance, and they install a new surrogate with each retelling.

flounder under the pressures of a world that by its very nature can never be repeated. John and Dave find it impossible to ever achieve their version of truth because they are unsure what constitutes reality; they now only know the performance, but the scenario is recognizably untrue because it is actively manipulated. This metaphor extends further as John and Dave rehearse their roles to clarify intentions and maintain the high stakes the scene demands. These invented notions of actual tension and fear perpetuate themselves through repetition. In other words, re-performing their invented history over and over imbues it with importance. The scene becomes more significant and true to the participants the more times it is enacted, even with minor variations.

The impossibility of perfectly, accurately, repeating a story or action does not, however, stifle the men's creative impulse to find their personal "truth". The inability to remember precise details, in fact, frees Dave and John from the limits of what they might consider reality. In an attempt to push beyond the innocuous repetition, when the men remember the events for the last full time in the play, John makes a drastic change to the way it has been previously done.

> **DAVE.** You decided there and then who she was to you. You decided you were looking at your ... ?
> *Dave stops and waits.*
> **JOHN.** My friend Dave.
> *Pause. Dave stunned. John too is a little surprised.*
> I decided I was looking at my friend Dave.
> (140)

The men have seemingly tried every other avenue, and now they find one possibility that has not been tested. The mechanism turns on itself, and the threat comes immediately into the room rather than on an unseen victim and scapegoat. Dave, who was just threatened directly and realistically for the first time, continues to question whether his guilt represents the true version, because that would mean the necessity to retell the story is finished. But John never commits to an answer, continuing his lack of certainty in finding reality in their actions. The stage direction states that, "*John lets go of Dave and Dave sits up, very anxious. John calmly puts down the gun and suddenly there's an ease to him*" (143). Before, it had been Dave who admitted to his lack of dedication to the process of living the scene, and now John has relaxed which upsets Dave. Refusing to believe that the truth cannot be had, Dave picks up the gun and forces it into John's hand and places it against his own forehead (144).

The physical implement provides the necessary catalyst for discovering purpose, meaning and truth. Dave resolves to continue trying to discover the truth behind the past events even when John has seemingly stopped. The final stage direction provides the most instructive note for these characters: "*We watch Dave continue. John then takes his hand away and Dave is left holding the gun against his own head as he talks frantically. John just sits back and looks at him for a moment. Nowhere to go, John takes the gun back off Dave and keeps it pointed at Dave's head*" (143-4). John looks for an escape and realizes he has no choice but to continue. He is complicit not by choice but by necessity. Recognizable rituals provide a stable sense of "reality", comfort and safety where the outside world represents the unknown and, what is more terrifying, other people who have crafted their own versions of history.

The realization that the men in *How These Desperate Men Talk* will eternally retell this story with varying details may seem dismal, but it is the way of surviving as a myth-maker. Stories transform along with the needs of the one doing the telling. As Joseph Roach notes of socially-created surrogates, "Improvised narratives of authenticity and priority may congeal into full-blown myths of legitimacy and origin" (Roach 3). The act of remembering and improvising becomes the history itself, no matter the "real" source. The men have created their own sense of being from a story that is (in all probability) completely fictitious and meant to endow meaning in an otherwise repetitive life. Diana Taylor's insight into repeated enactment confirms the eponymous men's greatest fears: "This ritual proves the opposite of confession, the opposite of testifying. It forces clients to enact painful stories that don't belong to them, rather than try to process their own pain or trauma" (Taylor 118). The stories they tell themselves do not necessarily correlate with a lived history but rather with something imagined. Each character brings past experience into their performance and expectations of the present; they dutifully serve their memory, even with its faults. In the same sense, encounters with another person's story cannot be avoided. This fact leads the characters in *How These Desperate Men Talk* to infinitely repeat their storytelling. The legitimacy of their myth has been proven through the idea that performance begets truth—but, in fact, it is the opposite. By re-enacting this history hundreds of times, the men have created a narrative which is simultaneously legitimate and purely self-constructed.

Works Cited

Austin, J.L. *How to Do Things with Words*. Oxford: Clarendon Press, 1962.

Bell, Catherine. *Ritual Theory, Ritual Practice*. Oxford: Oxford University Press, 1992.

De Certeau, Michel. *The Practice of Everyday Life*. Trans. Steven Rendall. Berkeley, CA: University of California Press, 1984.

Erll, Astrid and Ann Rigney, eds. "Introduction." *Mediation, Remediation, and the Dynamics of Cultural Memory*. Berlin: Walter De Gruyter, 2009.. 1-15.

Parks, Suzan-Lori. "Possession." *The America Play and Other Works*. New York: Theatre Communications Group, 1995: 3-5.

Postlewait, Thomas. "Self-Performing Voices: Mind, Memory, and Time in Beckett's Drama." *Twentieth Century Literature* 24.4 (Winter, 1978): 473-491. *JSTOR*.

Rappaport, Roy A. *Ecology, Meaning, and Religion*. Richmond, CA: North Atlantic, 1979.

Ricœur, Paul. *Memory, History, Forgetting*. Chicago: University of Chicago, 2004.

Roach, Joseph. *Cities of the Dead: Circum-Atlantic Performance*. New York: Columbia University Press, 1996.

Schechner, Richard. *Between Theatre and Anthropology*. Philadelphia: University of Pennsylvania Press, 1985.

Taylor, Diana. The Archive and the Repertoire: Performing Cultural Memory in the Americas. Durham: Duke University Press, 2003.

Walsh, Enda. *How These Desperate Men Talk. Enda Walsh: Plays One*. London: Nick Hern, 2011. 129-44.

9 | Real Versus Illusory in Enda Walsh's *The Walworth Farce* and *The New Electric Ballroom*

Tanya Dean

The 2009 Theatre Communications Group publication of Enda Walsh's two plays, *The New Electric Ballroom* and *The Walworth Farce*, is a double-sided edition; on one cover, a smiling woman in fifties garb is pictured riding jauntily on a bicycle. Flip to the other side, and a black-and-white photograph of a grimacing man flexing a mighty bicep is featured. In his *New York Times* review of *The New Electric Ballroom*, Charles Isherwood noted, "In both plays the bonds of family are kept pulled tight—to the point of strangulation, more or less—by the continual re-enactment of a shared mythology that has become a sort of sacred text, although in the case of the newer play, the tone is bleaker, and the family is female" (Isherwood). Both works exemplify Walsh's fascination with storytelling; *The New Electric Ballroom* explores the traditional oratorical mode of storytelling so often featured in Walsh's plays (*bedbound, The Small Things, Penelope*), whereas *The Walworth Farce* extends this tradition of storytelling into a self-conscious metatheatricality. Both modes of performance—storytelling and metatheatricality—are employed in delineating the theatricalist notion of the "Real" and the "Illusory". This binary consists of a world within (or without) the play that constitutes the theatrical incarnation of the "real world", which is highlighted by and contrasted to the "illusory world". Of course this is contrasted against the Real of the theatre itself with its seats and audience, and the Illusory of the playworld with its sets and actors. In this chapter, I intend to illustrate how Walsh employs these notions of the Real and the Illusory to create the hermetic playworlds and emotionally-stunted characters of *The New Electric Ballroom* and *The Walworth Farce*, and to examine the nightmarish quality of the characters' lives where story and performance overshadow all other aspects of existence.

In *The New Electric Ballroom* (first performed in 2008), three sisters relentlessly retell a shared story of betrayed love. For Clara and Breda (both in their sixties), the memory of how each of them pinned her hopes on the charismatic showband star, the "Roller Royle" in the 1950s, only to be disappointed, is grimly retreaded each day as proof of why they should sequester themselves against the world. For their younger sister, Ada (in her forties), who has grown up on a daily diet of their bitter screed, the story has become a ritual that both traps and protects her. In the anarchic *The Walworth Farce* (first performed in 2006), ex-pat Irishman Dinny and his young adult sons Blake and Sean spend their days compulsively enacting a play. This play both structures their lives and imprisons them; and it is Dinny who serves as playwright, director, lead actor, protagonist, and ultimately, warden. In his bizarre story, Dinny re-imagines himself as a rich Cork brain surgeon who ends up in a mortal conflict with his older brother about their mother's will, and stumbles through a series of unlikely events involving mistaken identities, two funerals and a poisoned chicken. The performance is Dinny's way of protecting his sons from the real world by obfuscating the true story of why he had to flee Cork. For both families, role-playing/performance is a way of exorcizing their bitterness towards their miserable circumstances and their resentment-infected love for each other. The difference is that the repeated storytelling in *The New Electric Ballroom* is an act of ekphrasis (the verbal depiction of visual representation), whereas *The Walworth Farce* employs a theatrical form of *mise-en-abyme*: the play-within-the-play.

The Walworth Farce delineates the boundaries of the play and the play-within-the-play through iconography. The frame of the play takes the form of a dingy squat in London's Walworth Road, but the hulking presence of a large, obviously fake cardboard coffin serves as a visual clue that this squalid council flat doubles as a performance site. Patrice Pavis said of the prop/scenery as object:

> The object is not reduced to a single meaning or level of apprehension. The same object is often utilitarian, symbolic or playful at different times and seen from different perspectives of aesthetic apprehension. It functions as a projectional Rorscharch test and encourages the audience's creativity. (Pavis 240)

Watching the characters interact with the cardboard coffin—a prop *qua* prop, a theatrical signifier for an imperfect theatrical signifier for a real artefact—makes it clear that Dinny and his sons are engaged in some kind of bizarre performance, and destabilizes the audience's notions of what is "real" onstage. The flat is almost skeletal in appearance—the stage directions described the walls as wooden frames that have been denuded of most of the plasterboard, like the exposed support structures of theatrical flats.

Even in the earliest moments of the production, Walsh layers in the metatheatrical doubling, writing a pre-show as a pre-show. The lights go up on the pre-performance preparations of the characters—getting into costume, checking their props, warming up—as they ready themselves for their daily ritual of the Farce. These preparations take the form of a dumb show—the characters do not speak until they are ready to begin their performance-within-a-performance. The first spoken line of the play is also the first line of the play-within-the-play.

> *DINNY takes a deep breath and exhales sharply.* He's ready.
> *DINNY holds the other end of the coffin with SEAN. He reaches to the light switch on the back wall and switches off the light in the living room as "An Irish Lullaby" [playing on the tape recorder] comes to an end.*
> *The room is thrown into darkness and silence. DINNY immediately turns the light back on.*
> **DINNY.** She was our mother, Paddy—
> *Suddenly the tape recorder blasts out the Irish traditional song "A Nation Once Again".*
> *The two of them startled.*
> Shite!
> *DINNY turns off the tape recorder. Again he takes a deep breath and exhales sharply. He then reaches back to the light switch and turns the lights off again. He immediately turns them back on.*
> *The Farce begins. The three speak in Cork City accents. The performance style resembles The Three Stooges.* (Walsh 7)

This cheap amateurish attempt at a black-out and lights-up via a domestic light switch and the malfunctioning of props like the tape-recorder, immediately disrupts the illusion of performance as reality by interrupting the first line of the play-within-the-play by a technical error. This calls to mind like the jarring buzz of the alarm that jolts Solange and Claire out of their ritualistic role-play in Jean Genet's 1947 *The Maids;* in many ways the artistic predecessor to *Walworth Farce*. Watching a character break from their character-as-a-character on a fumbled cue underscores what the garish costuming and ritual quality of the preparations have already indicated: that these characters are engaged in some kind of pantomime. (For the sake of clarity, I will delineate when I am referring to the characters as themselves, and when I am referring to the characters performing as characters; i.e. Sean and Sean-as-Paddy.)

By contrast, Walsh brings the audience into *The New Electric Ballroom* at an unspecified point in the narration, "*the atmosphere immediately taut and aggressive*" (Walsh 5). Clara is sitting, Breda (her face smeared with lipstick) stands in the corner facing the wall, Ada seems slightly out of breath. In *The New Electric Ballroom*, Breda and Clara are playing memories of their younger selves, but it is an act of narration rather than embodied performance (whereas in *The Walworth Farce*, Sean and Paddy adopt roles from a rotating cast of characters). Breda begins a monologue about the nature of speech as the currency and curse of humanity that she will repeat later in the play, signifying that this is an oft-repeated story. Ada's role appears to lie somewhere between director and prompter, as she prods the sisters into their lines. (More pragmatically, she also appears to be the breadwinner, the only one who will venture out into the world to her job at a fish-canning factory). Yet Ada, despite her comparative agency (and even aggression, at times), appears trapped by her sisters' memories. At first, the lines between the Real and the Illusory in *The New Electric Ballroom* are not clearly drawn, as the sisters' performance of bitter memory is less overtly theatrical than that of *The Walworth Farce*. Yet it is just as strictly regulated and enforced; it is through the sisters' language that the line between life and memory (Real and Illusory) becomes demarcated.

With *New Electric Ballroom* and *The Walworth Farce*, Walsh is toggling between levels of fictionality, such as those within Manfred Pfister's theory in *The Theory and Analysis of Drama* (219):

> a primary dramatic level, whose ontological status is characterized by the fictionality of dramatic presentation, contains within it a secondary dramatic level that introduces an additional fictional element.

Pfister offers two key incarnations of this stratification of fictional levels—the play-within-the-play and the dream inset. Within the Pfister model, the presence of a diegetic performance (the play-within-the-play) embedded in the production highlights the fiction of theatrical presentation as a mode of expression. When an audience is presented with actors playing characters who are playing characters, this doubled-performance draws attention to the artificiality of performance itself. Anne Ubserfeld observes that

> there is within the confines of the stage a privileged zone in which theatre speaks of itself (trestle stages, songs, choruses, speeches addressed to the audience). According to Freud, you know that when you dream that you are dreaming, the dream within another dream speaks the truth. Through a twofold denial, the dream of a dream produces truth. Likewise theatre-within-the-theatre does not convey reality but rather what is true, transforming the sign of illusion and identifying as illusion all that is mounted on stage. (Ubersfeld 27-8)

Both plays rely upon costume to differentiate between the Real and the Illusory. Exaggerated, grotesque costumes are the clearest signifier of the play-within-the-play (which, for ease of identification, I will refer to as the Farce), and much of the pre-show takes the form of the characters garbing themselves in their costumes—Dinny with his toupée, Blake in drag, Sean sporting a stuck-on moustache. This all takes place in relative silence, highlighting the nervous reverence in which the men hold the Farce as a ritual. This act of costuming visually differentiates clearly between the Real and the Illusory, the play and the play-within-the-play, even before the first line has been spoken. In *The New Electric Ballroom* (5), the costumes become ritual icons:

> On a wall, three different sets of clothes, hanging on separate hangers. A cashmere jumper and rara skirt; a 1950s' red blouse and a blue pleated skirt; and a glitzy show-business man's suit.

Clara and Breda don their outfits with solemn dignity as part of their daily observance. The glitzy suit, purportedly the only tangible memento of the mythic Roller Royle, hangs like a holy relic and carries a transformative power; when bumbling fishmonger Patsy (the only visitor in the sisters' home) is vigorously scrubbed in a nigh baptism by Clara and then prompted to don the Roller Royle's suit, he undergoes a startling metamorphosis, suddenly displaying an astonishing singing talent and a potent masculinity that had not hitherto been hinted at. This performance, whilst not quite a play-within-a-play, stands distinct from the previous narration; here for the first time, a new performance is offered (rather than a repeated telling of an old story), and it is a performance of startling virtuosity. That very virtuosity imparts a new and earth-shaking piece of information: Patsy is in fact the bastard child of Roller Royle and a Doris-day lookalike, conceived in the car-park of The New Electric Ballroom on the night of Clara and Breda's respective betrayals. This act of performative skill both retroactively rewrites the sisters' shared history, and provides the catalyst to finally alter Ada's role within the sororal cycle of storytelling.

Within *The Walworth Farce*, there is the Real of the disintegrating flat, which serves as the stage for the Illusory of the Farce. But there are also the larger unseen realms of London and Ireland. London and Cork are reimagined beyond the realms of the flat (and the stage) as both Real and Illusory: the Real geographic locations, and the Illusory in the form of skewed depictions of each city imagined by the characters. London is characterized by Sean-as-Paddy as a grim threatening place:

> A million tiny bedsits there are. Large carbuncles sprouting out from the ground. Massive flats. Deadly, pitiful places that even the rats have abandoned, the cockroaches have done cockroaching and all that's left is the London people ... To sum it up in pure Cork parlance ... the place is a hole. (Walsh 16)

By contrast, Cork is eulogized by Dinny-as-Dinny, in the inimitable manner of the homesick exile ex-pat, as a longed-for paradise. The Illusory imaginings are disrupted by the innocent entrance of Tesco checkout girl Hayley violating the hermetic world of the flat. Her embodiment of the Real London exposes by contrast the grubby, freakish quality of their lives.

The use of the convention of drag within *The Walworth Farce* provides an elementary *verfremdungseffekt*: by dint of placing a man onstage invoking femininity through performative gestures, we are forced to reassess the Real for which this blatant Illusory stands as a signifier. The physical presence of a male body onstage draws attention to the performative nature of gender, and so "femininity" is revealed as an act, Illusory. Within the performative world of the play-within-the-play in *The Walworth Farce*, Blake's drag performances as Blake-as-Maureen, Blake-as-Vera, and Blake-as-Eileen are bewigged, garish caricatures of femininity; either saintly maternal types or libidinous shrews. The only genuinely female figure that figures large in the boys' lives is also absent, the memory of the real Maureen, Dinny's wife, and Blake and Sean's mother, whom we hear is supposedly still living in Ireland. Yet even she is the fragmented icon of womanhood, remembered by the two brothers as purely a sense memory as part of their romanticized ideal of an Ireland they barely remember:

> **BLAKE.** When we came here as little kids you could still smell Ireland from our jumpers.
> **SEAN**. (*distantly*) Yeah.
> **BLAKE.** You could smell Mammy's cooking, couldn't you? It was roast chicken that last day and it was a lovely smell, hey Sean? And

> I think we might have come across on a boat ... (*prompting SEAN, smiling.*) Go on.
> *BLAKE holds SEAN's hand.*
> **SEAN**. (*Continuing*). And despite the sea and the wind, the smell of Mammy's cooking and that chicken was still stuck in the wool of our jumpers. (Walsh 21)

When a flesh-and-blood woman finally invades their hermetic, homosocial world, their inability to interact with her with any degree of social normalcy reveals how living in the story of the Farce to the exclusion of the outside Real world has stunted their development.

Invoking the performative tradition of drag highlights the theatricality of the play-within-the-play. Other performance styles are also embedded within the plays, highlighting the performativity of the Illusory. The most obvious is, of course, the use of farce within *The Walworth Farce*, as Walsh doubles up as playwright and *farceur*. In her work on the subject, *Farce*, Jessica Milner Davis says that

> structurally, as distinct from high comedy of manners and romantic comedy, farce-plots tend to be short and they are peopled not by complex, sympathetic characters, but by simplified comic types ... farce favors direct, visual, and physical jokes over rich, lyric dialogue (although words are not unimportant in farce and can be crucial to its quarrels, deceptions and misunderstandings), and it declares an open season for aggression, animal high spirits, self-indulgence and rudeness in general. (Milner Davis 2)

This exaggerated performance style (and the amateurishness of the performers) becomes an act of ostension, (or, to put it in Brechtian terms, a "gestus of showing"), highlighting its own metatheatricality.

The play opens with the Farce as a *mise-en-abyme*, which ably demonstrates the tropes of the genre. But there is a palpable note of apprehension thrumming in the background, which Sean seems particularly sensitive to. Although the Farce itself appears to be a presentation of anarchic fun, the tension seeping in from the Real ratchets up the implicit threat of the performance. Positioning the slapstick world of the Farce against the real-life pain of Sean highlights the ominous quality of this world: farce as a performance may be humorous, but farce as a way of life is nightmarish. This is brought home via the bleeding of violence from the Illusory of the Farce into the Real of Sean's life: Milner cautions that in farce,

> The acting must convince the audience that the action is psychologically believable, while reminding them that no-one is really getting hurt: a tricky balance to achieve. (Milner 5)

Dinny utilizes the classic slapstick trope beloved of cartoons, the frying pan as a weapon. However, while an animated cat or a *commedia dell'Arte* zanni can be smacked humorously in the face with a hefty frying pan and recover almost instantaneously, Walsh highlights the threat inherent in the men's lives by showing the consequences of this kind of cartoonish violence in the Real.

> *SEAN enters and immediately DINNY swings the frying pan across the back of SEAN's head. SEAN hits the floor fast.*
> *A long pause as DINNY and BLAKE look at SEAN on the floor.*
> *DINNY takes a cup of water and gargles a little. He then spits it out on SEAN's head.*
> (*To BLAKE, calmly.*) Get him up and sort him out. (Walsh 20)

The sickening thump of heavy iron against a human skull highlights the hellish quality of these men's lives, and the danger when the tropes of the Illusory begin to infect the Real.

Blake and Sean are at tipping point in their relationship with their father in *The Walworth Farce*: they continue to submit to the daily ritual of the Farce and dutifully perform his story for him. The father-son relationship is violent and controlling, but there is the suggestion of a familial affection between the brothers and Dinny. However both Sean and Blake each independently reveal their secret desire to escape the flat and the Farce, and no longer serve as the marionettes dancing to Dinny's manic manipulations. The story of the Farce is how Dinny controls his sons (and in his own twisted logic, keeps them safe). But the Farce is starting to unravel, and with it, Dinny's hold on the two boys. Blake reveals that where once the words of the story created a world of pictures in his mind that kept him happy, he is beginning to disintegrate mentally from the constant telling and retelling: "But all them pictures have stopped. I say his words and all I can see is the word. A lot of words piled on top of other words. There's no sense to my day "cause the sense isn't important any more. No pictures. No dreams. Words only" (Walsh 22). The word of God in their religion no longer has the power to create, instead standing impotently only as the word, a signifier divorced from the signified. Both sons are experiencing a crisis of faith. Sean understands even more than Blake that their Father's words are not only powerless, they are meaningless: "But none of these words are true" (Walsh 69). He reveals that his dedication to the Farce was out of hopeless loyalty, never belief; as a child, he witnessed Dinny murder the real-life Paddy and Vera with a kitchen knife. Finally revealed before his sons as a petty, impotent man, Dinny pleads with his son to keep the fantasy of the Farce going: "The telling of the story ...

it helps me, Sean ... we're making a routine that keeps our family safe. Isn't that what we've done here?" (Walsh 69). When this fails to persuade Sean to remain, Dinny plays his trump cards: he knows that Sean cannot abandon Blake, and that Sean is afraid of becoming like his father. If Sean kills Dinny to escape, he loses both Blake and his own identity.

The characters of *The New Electric Ballroom* are likewise ensnared in their repeated performance. As Patsy glumly sums it up, " ... in a town this size we've all got our roles to play and mine is to play a man of no great purpose ... " (Walsh 34). It becomes clear that whilst Breda and Clara endlessly re-enact their memory of that fateful night, it is not entirely by choice; they feel that they have been conscripted into their roles by the gossip of their small town.

> **BREDA.** Stamped by story, aren't we, Patsy?! So what chance any man or woman against the idle word? The idle word?! Sure, there's no such thing as the idle word. Branded, marked and scarred by talk. Boxed by words, Patsy. Those bitches in the cannery and the gossip rising above the machines. All talk of Clara and Breda and The New Electric and the Roller Royle and the broken hearts. Mocking talk all week turning the streets narrower around us. Them nasty words crashing about from Monday to Friday and locking that front door behind us. What chance for the broken-hearted and the fishmonger to keep clean when people have the making of us? No mystery, no surprise ... (Walsh 35)

Their performance calcifies their lives at their most painful moment, serving both as punishment and protection. The dividing lines between the Real and the Illusory are less immediately obvious in *The New Electric Ballroom*. Where *The Walworth Farce* employs exaggerated theatrical conventions to delimit the farce from the reality of the characters' lives, in *The New Electric Ballroom* the shift into memory/Illusory/performance is the subtle move from dialogue to soliloquy.

> Thus ... the soliloquy ... is an anti-realist convention that eliminates—or at least weakens—the restrictions imposed by the dramatic medium on the presentation of inner, psychological processes. It enables the dramatist to present an extreme form of subjectivization ..." (Pfister 222).

Unlike the *Walworth* men who escaped their past by fleeing to the anonymity of a large city, the sisters of *The New Electric Ballroom* have been trapped by their stories in the claustrophobia of a small-minded small town. Breda and Clara in particular resent the way in which the small-town gossip has objectified them. By shifting into soliloquy, they are given the chance to assert themselves as subjects and tell the stories on their own terms. The shift between the Real of their normal lives and the Illusory of their stories is a paradigmatic shift from the powerless role of character to the authoritative role of narrator.

In both *The Walworth Farce* and *The New Electric Ballroom*, the audience enter the playworld on a day when a new element enters to change the endlessly repeated, endlessly identical play-within-the-play. This new element raises the stakes of the performance—the play-within-the-play transitions from part of the characters' daily routine to a life-changing drama. In *The Walworth Farce*, the new element is in fact an encroachment of the Real (London) into the Illusory (the Farce). When checkout girl Hayley follows Sean home after he mistakenly picks up the wrong bag of shopping from Tesco's, her entry into the performance space of the flat marks her as alien from the world of the play-within-the-play, for she stands distinct from the three men as she is black, female and not Irish. Ben Brantley noted in his *New York Times* review, "It's an old device in drama, using an outsider to make us see with joltingly clear eyes characters we've been seduced by, but it's used to inspired effect here. Suddenly men we've been regarding as Larry, Curly and Moe are looking more like the flesh-eating yokels from the slasher flick "The Hills Have Eyes'" (Brantley). This new element— the first outsider ever to enter their home—means different things for all three men. For Sean, she both represents the freedom of the Real and the danger of the Illusory. His shy flirtation with her in the Tesco checkout line, which he relates to Blake out of Dinny's hearing, represented the chance for a life beyond the flat and the Farce. Her innocent suggestion that they could go to Brighton Beach together is the catalyst for Sean's nascent hopes of escape: "But her talking to me like that, Blake ... her just talking so nice to me ... it got me thinking more than ever ... it's right that us two leave" (Walsh 33). This terrifies Blake, who sees her as an unwelcome intruder who will destroy his family. Dinny views her only through the eye of a director and he appears to think that her being a real woman will lend authenticity to the play-within-the-play. He aggressively inducts her into the Farce, using her as an example for Blake to mimic her in an attempt to make his performance as the female characters more "authentic." Forcing the terrified girl to play the role of Maureen, Dinny considers how to make her fit into his "directorial vision" of the playworld ("You're black. What are we going to do about that, Maureen?"[Walsh, *Walworth Farce*, 56]). In one of the play's most discomfiting images, he colonizes her to better fit his character description, using moisturiser to whiten her face.

The new element in *The New Electric Ballroom* comes from an unexpected source; when the gormless Patsy reveals his parentage and his singing prowess, he seems to open up the opportunity for both himself and Ada to escape the roles they are locked in. The two tentatively, longingly begin to sketch out a new story for themselves. "... and I'm no longer sitting in the corner just watching but I'm centre stage with the lovely you now, Ada" (Walsh 39). But, much like her sisters, Ada's great romance crumbles before it even really begins, as Patsy runs away from their story on cold feet.

> **PATSY**. Christ! Already something's got a hold of me. In one breath all love is good and it keeps me and this love it fills me ... but with each step taken and a different love, a fragile love, a love blind, surely. I let go of your hand and walk away fast. And I want for the lover's walk and the lie-ins and the kisses and the sweet remembered details, the slow romance and the sudden lust of love, but my heart tells me that the risk is far too great. It's too great, Ada! (Walsh 44)

In *The Walworth Farce*, The new element also represents the potential to break the cycle of performance. Realizing that Hayley represents Sean's only chance for escape from their nightmarish lives, Blake locks Sean in the wardrobe, and then stabs Dinny. He meticulously coaches his father to deliver his final line to Blake-as-Maureen so that he dies in the Farce, clutching the acting trophy. Blake then directs Hayley to scream and unlock the wardrobe, so that the freed Sean mistakenly thinks that Hayley is about to be murdered by Blake. Sean stabs his brother, realizing too late what Blake has actually done. In his dying moments, Blake delivers his final line—"Now leave, love" (Walsh 84)—both as himself and Blake-as-Maureen, releasing Sean by ending the story. The conclusion of the play-within-the-play and the death of a sibling would seem to mark the end of the play. But rather than release Sean from the Illusory, instead it merely serves to act as catalyst for the beginning of a new story. Sean finds himself unable to follow Hayley out into the Real of London once the Farce has finished; instead, he recreates the events of the day as a one-man show, a new Farce, this time introducing the new character of Sean-as-Hayley. The lights go down on Sean with brown shoe polish on his face (to mimic Hayley's black skin), about to start a new cycle of performance to fill his days with endless repetition. Likewise in *New Electric Ballroom*, as a shocked Ada processes Patsy's sudden abandonment, Clara and Breda calmly set about inculcating her into their sisterhood of betrayed women, weaving a monologue for her and dressing her up in a costume, as the endlessly repeated cycle of storytelling begins again. Walsh is renowned for creating characters who must obsessively tell and re-tell their stories (*Misterman, bedbound, Ballyturk*); however, in the diptych of *The Walworth Farce* and *New Electric Ballroom*, the characters are not only trapped in their stories, they are addicted to their role as storyteller. In both plays, the opportunity to escape becomes simply finding a new story to tell.

Works Cited

Brantley, Ben. "Another Day, Another Play, for Rotten Old Dad." *The New York Times*. The New York Times, 18 Apr. 2008. Web. 13 Sept. 2013.

Davis, Jessica Milner. *Farce*. London: Methuen, 1978. Print.

Pavis, Patrice. *Dictionary of the Theatre : Terms, Concepts, and Analysis*. Trans. Christine Shantz. London: U of Toronto, 1998. Print.

Pfister, Manfred. *The Theory and Analysis of Drama*. Cambridge: Cambridge UP, 1988. Print.

Ubersfeld, Anne. *Reading Theatre*. Trans. Frank Collins. Toronto: U of Toronto, 1999. Print.

Walsh, Enda. *The New Electric Ballroom*; *The Walworth Farce*. New York: Theatre Communications Group, 2009. Print.

10| "Looking for martyrdom?": Enda Walsh and Steve McQueen's *Hunger*

Katarzyna Ojrzyńska

Awarded with a number of prestigious prizes including the Caméra d'Or at the Cannes International Film Festival, *Hunger* (2008) is largely the result of a fruitful collaboration between the British visual artist Steve McQueen and Enda Walsh, who wrote the script together. The film illustrates what Comer calls McQueen's continuing "ambition to show repressed histories ... in a very direct, physical way" (McQueen, interview by Comer), which is also visible in his later feature films *Shame* (2011) and *12 Years a Slave* (2013). A similar idea informs Enda Walsh's dramatic texts, such as *Chatroom* (2005), *The New Electric Ballroom* (2005), *The Walworth Farce* (2006) and *Penelope* (2010), which focus on "claustrophobic situations" and "the worlds characters create for themselves" (Walsh qtd. in Gompertz). Regardless of whether his plays are set in a hermetic domestic space, an empty swimming pool or a virtual chatroom, these places are the characters' personal prisons of their own making.

For McQueen, a visual artist who had earlier made a number of short art house films, scripting a feature film was a new challenge. He was ready to face it with the assistance of a writer who had some experience in this field and who would help him to articulate his ideas in a written form. As he admitted, his ideal partner in such an undertaking would be Samuel Beckett (Solomon). Since such a collaboration was not possible, for obvious reasons, McQueen eventually sought assistance from another Irish playwright, Enda Walsh, many of whose dramatic works are indebted to Beckett's Theatre of the Absurd. The subsequent partnership between a video artist and a writer proved to be fruitful. Walsh helped McQueen to achieve a perfect balance between the linear story and rich visual imagery and to endow the simple, three-part structure of the film with strong dramatic flavour.

Hunger focuses on the Irish dirty protest and the subsequent 1981 hunger strike in the Long Kesh/Maze prison, which intended to force the British government to re-introduce political status for republican prisoners. It is an event in Irish history which McQueen and Walsh attempt to depict from a novel, non-partisan point of view. As Walsh suggests, the former representations of the H-block conflict in Irish culture are rooted in the Irish tradition of storytelling, which frequently involves sentimentality and romanticizing (Kelly). He does not mention any specific examples, but this tendency can, for instance, be found in numerous Irish songs commemorating the 1981 hunger strike, such as Christy Moore's "The Boy from Tamlaghtduff" or "The People's Own MP," and Gerry O'Glacain's "The Roll of Honour." *Hunger*, by contrast, assumes a more detached perspective. The writing of the script was preceded by a period of thorough research into the Irish convicts' fight for political prisoner status. Walsh and McQueen visited Northern Ireland and "did a week of intense interviews with hunger strikers and prison officers" (McQueen, "Human Body" 24), around eighteen interviews in total (Walsh qtd. in Sierz). The accounts they gathered helped them to create a detailed, graphic depiction of prison life at that time, including perspectives from both sides of the sectarian divide.

Rather than providing the viewers with comprehensive social and political background for these events, the film underscores the visceral dimension of the extreme situation in which the characters find themselves. Raw physicality permeates the intense images of prison life. This is visible, for instance, in the film shots of the smashed knuckles of H-block prison officer Raymond or in the night scene in which one of the prisoners, Davey, secretly masturbates under his blanket, trying not to awaken his fellow inmate. A somewhat similar focus on the body can also be found in Walsh's plays. Their characters' psychological wounds and scars are given strong, corporal expression when they repetitively re-enact in a physical manner their own traumas and fantasies, which frequently rekindles their raw, brutal and painful emotions. Furthermore, Walsh's characters tend to use their stories, both those verbally articulated and those performed physically, as a means of resistance, an attempt to gain control over their lives and environment. A similar oppositional desire motivates the film's protagonist, who, as will be shown, uses his body as a tool of political and personal liberation.

Enda Walsh states that, together with McQueen, he wanted to create something that would be both "old and actual" (Kelly). On the one hand, as the playwright posits, the aim of the film is to show the environment of the Maze and its rules, which gives insight into the large-scale dysfunction in past relations between Ireland and Britain (Walsh, interview by Sierz). On the other hand, as McQueen further explains, putting *Hunger* in a very contemporary context, "What is interesting for me about this film is not just about what happened twenty-seven years ago, it's also about what's happening now, to a certain extent, with Guantánamo Bay and Abu Ghraib" ("Human Body" 25). One can surmise that for Walsh writing the film script was also a return to the contemporary political themes that he addressed in his short play *Lynddie's Gotta Gun* (2005), ironically dedicated to *"former US soldier Private Lynndie England"* (203), who was dishonorably discharged from the army and served a sentence for torturing and abusing Iraqi detainees at Abu Ghraib prison. The play approaches the issue of the war on terror in a grotesque fashion. Dressed up as a children's party clown, Lynndie is a mocking and, at the same time, menacing personification of American ridiculous incompetence and misconceived charity which informed their military operations in Iraq. In *Hunger* Walsh returns to the problem of the war on terror, but this time he explores it not so much through dark parody, but in a painfully direct and sombre way.

Hunger aims to address certain universal, human aspects that underlie the situation it depicts rather than taking sides in a specific political conflict. McQueen declares that, as an artist, he has "no answers to the bigger political questions" (qtd. in O'Hagan) and states: "I don't think *Hunger* is a political film, it's a human film" ("Human Body" 25), thus outlining the strategies he and Walsh followed while writing the script. What may shed further light on these strategies is Walsh's general preoccupation with form. When recently asked about the influence of Beckett on his dramatic works, he stated:

> Beckett's not a conscious influence ... but he taught us all two great things. One is that he helped free drama from any obligation to be sociological: the other is that he showed us the power of real time. I'm hugely attracted to that and don't really understand theatre that deals with action over several days. And, although I may have started out being preoccupied by language, I'm now obsessed by form. (qtd. in Billington)

Because of this concern with form rather than sociopolitical content, *Hunger* has garnered mixed responses. Emilie Pine, for instance, argues that the film fails in making a non-partisan point since it does not fully present the political context of the strike; for instance, it does not investigate the paramilitary activity of republican inmates (121). Furthermore, as she maintains, *Hunger* "is also, in a way, a misreading of the symbology of the protest and the hunger strike—by reading the prisoners' bodies in the light of their individual humanity, rather than their organization's ideology" (121). It is hard to deny that the film does not thoroughly examine some of the political aspects of the conflict, nor does it attempt to do so. Therefore, in order to better understand and appreciate Walsh and McQueen's script, it is also useful to look at it from different—personal and mystical—perspectives, which are often neglected by the critics who tend to centre predominantly on the Irish political and cultural contexts of the hunger strike. With this in mind, in my analysis I focus on the presentation of the protagonist, Bobby Sands, who initiated the second hunger strike in the Maze prison and was the first victim of the self-imposed starvation. I investigate three dimensions of his death, as depicted in *Hunger*, which I define as: the political, the personal and the mystical. Since, as has been mentioned, the political aspect of Sands's martyrdom has already been addressed by many critics and it does not offer a key to the full understanding of the film, the emphasis will mostly be on the two remaining dimensions which significantly complicate the moral evaluation of Sands's choices.

One of the leading Irish critics, Fintan O'Toole, considers Walsh and McQueen's attempt to present a balanced, depoliticized vision futile, since the film obscures the fact that many of the protesters were killers and that the prison officers murdered in the H-block conflict significantly outnumbered the casualties of the hunger strike. He further argues that McQueen romanticizes the image of the Maze inmates in *Hunger* by "essentially project[ing] himself into the persona of a hunger striker" who uses his body and its excrement as art materials. Although some merit can be found in these arguments, O'Toole seems to neglect some of the ways in which the authors of the script do not provide a simple evaluation of Sands's and the other strikers' deeds. Stressing the non-intellectual, visceral character of the prisoners' protests in the film, from which verbal expression has been almost totally eliminated, with the exception of one central scene, and focusing on human waste and body fluids, Walsh and McQueen explore the use of the abject and sacrificial bodies as a weapon, which strongly resonates in Irish republicanism. At the same time, by visually emphasizing repulsive physical details, the film perpetuates the colonialist perception of Ireland as England's Other. This perception is deeply grounded in binary oppositions: mind/body, purity/filth, order/chaos, with the British trying to civilize "Irish savages", subjecting them to forced washing, providing them with clothes which they refuse to wear, or using power hoses to clean the walls of the cells which are smeared with faeces. As Gary Crowdus observes,

> One might say that the film's principal protagonists are Bobby Sands, as the leader of the IRA hunger strikers, and Margaret Thatcher, the "Iron Lady," as the leader of the British Government. (McQueen 25)

While the latter's presence is limited to her disembodied, "strong and forceful and iconic" voice (McQueen 25), delivering a few excerpts from her political speeches, the former is mostly associated with the carnal sphere. He rejects entering the path of verbal negotiation and turns his body into a site of political resistance, which again fits into the above-mentioned colonialist dichotomy. The playwright-filmmaker team does not seek to elevate the Catholic inmates' political strife by providing them with strong religious motivation either; the characters use pages from the Bible to roll cigarettes (24), while the mass in the prison canteen, alive with conversations like a marketplace, is just an occasion to exchange "comms" and develop further political strategies rather than participating in spiritual experience (22-3). Still, as will be shown, although in the lives of the republican prisoners religious experience seems to have been replaced by political fervour, there is an element of mysticism to be found in the script.

In order to discover the complexity of *Hunger*, it is necessary to examine what McQueen calls "a three-act structure" of the film (McQueen 24), which he suggested to Walsh during the writing process (Walsh qtd. in Levy). The script consists of a series of scenes presenting the "no-wash" and "blanket" protests in the Maze, and the subsequent close examination of Bobby Sands's death in the hunger strike, divided by a lengthy dialogue. The conversation between the protagonist and a Catholic priest markedly differs from the remaining parts of the screenplay, in which the visceral aspects of life in the Maze prison in the early 1980s are explored. As McQueen explains, the key aim of *Hunger* is "to show what it was like to see, hear, smell, and touch in the H-block" (McQueen 23), which is most conspicuous in the first, expository part of his and Walsh's script. Two of the major sections of the screenplay can be described as almost silent. Walsh and McQueen mostly refrained from words and replaced them with a variety of sounds, such as "dust-bin lids crashing down against the concrete" (1, 79),[9] the sounds of birds (25) and the buzz of bluebottles (11-2), all forming the musical texture of the film. What seems unusual about *Hunger* is that verbal communication has been almost totally eliminated from it, which, as McQueen explains, was motivated by a wish to bring the viewers' other senses to the fore (McQueen 24). This strategy does not seem to be typical of Walsh's dramatic technique, which is predominantly based on his characters' preoccupation with storytelling and pointless, habitual talking. As Breda in *The New Electric Ballroom* puts it, "People talking just for the act of it. Words spinning to nothing. For no definable reason" (6). Yet, it is conspicuous that the stories Walsh's characters tell, for instance in *Disco Pigs* or *The New Electric Ballroom*, are often saturated not so much with intellectual sophistication, but with the memories or fantasies that are closely connected with specific sensory—aural, olfactory and tactile— forms of experience, which indicates the playwright's continuing preoccupation with bodily sensations.

The fragment of the film which visibly stands out is the central scene, entirely written by Walsh, in which Bobby Sands and Father Thomas Moran engage in, as Omar Assem El-Khairy notes, "a beautifully written ideological and theological chess match, which explores the political and strategic rationale behind the hunger strikes" (188) and in which the above-mentioned, three aspects of Sands's motivation are intricately interwoven. The dialogue, which is Walsh's most important contribution to the script, was skillfully brought to the fore by McQueen. With the two characters held in a medium-wide frame, it is perhaps the only time when the audience are supposed to carefully listen to a verbal exchange and analyze it. In order to create a natural situation in which the viewers would focus on the words of Walsh's dialogue, McQueen decided to make the scene very static and, therefore, filmed the majority of it in an unusual, seventeen-minutes-long, uninterrupted take. As the cinematographer Sean Bobbitt explains,

> Steve pointed out that when he's listening to two people talk, he doesn't stand up and walk around the room, looking at them from different angles—he sits in one place and listens. (qtd. in Oppenheimer 18)

---

[9] Republican women in Northern Ireland used to bang bin lids to warn their neighbours against approaching danger.

The static scene, in which Bobby Sands and Father Thomas Moran confront each other in an intellectual, verbal battle, strongly contrasts with the visual and aural strategies used in the rest of the screenplay and perfectly illustrates Walsh's talent for writing sharp and witty dialogues. The two major accusations with which Father Moran presents Sands and which touch upon the three basic aspects of the protagonist's motivation concern his pride and irrationality, due to his having lost touch with reality because of his too-long incarceration. The key questions here are whether the protagonist's self-imposed starvation should be considered in terms of a murder or a suicide, and whether it can be considered a self-sacrifice at all, or just an instance of excessive pride and self-conceit.

The serious conversation is preceded with a small talk, which mirrors the structure of the interviews Walsh and McQueen conducted with Irish ex-prisoners. Walsh describes these men as incredibly articulate and intense. As he explains, "When you talk to them ... you have a bit of banter beforehand but then you've got the meat of what you're talking about" (Sierz). Furthermore, as Jason Solomon notes, the structure of the scene, which presents the two characters in a slightly otherworldly situation, as if suspended in a void, is strongly reminiscent of Samuel Beckett's works, whose echoes critics have often found in Walsh's dramatic oeuvre. Compared by Solomon to Vladimir and Estragon from *Waiting for Godot*, Sands and Moran start their discussion with trivial, everyday issues only to arrive at crucial existential questions a moment later (Fassbender). The conversation opens with a friendly chat. The priest playfully mocks Sands, stating that, as a "Good talker, man of principle, leader of men," he would make "a fine priest" (42). This serves as a commentary on an earlier scene which depicts prisoners enjoying their time together in the canteen after the mass. Bobby remains at the centre of the inmates' attention: they approach him one by one to receive news, advice or support (23), as if they were to receive Holy Communion. This is just a prelude to one of the main arguments against Sands's resolution, which Father Thomas Moran, who is concerned with the "business of the [protagonist's] soul" (58), presents when he asks: "Looking for martyrdom?" The priest later develops this notion, stating: "I've listened to you eulogizing Wolf Tone, Connolly, MacSwiney ... all them boys ... Can't help thinking you're writing your name large for all them history books" (53-4). Sands instantly dismisses this accusation. However, he still seems to show some excessive pride and arrogance, the Greek *hubris*, when he suggests a possible comparison between himself and Christ—a divine figure setting a pattern for the future martyrs who, in the protagonist's view, should not only die for their beliefs, but above all be the agents of a far-reaching social change. Sands states:

> Jesus Christ had a backbone but them disciples, every disciple since ... you're just jumping in and out of the rhetoric and dead-end semantics. That's the sort of waffle you learn in the seminary, right Tom?! Well you need the revolutionary, you need the cultural/political soldier to give life pulse, to give life a direction. (56)

In this way, Sands presents himself as a warrior whose faith can change the world, since it is characterized by simplicity and directness, both of which the priest, with his ethical sophistication, lacks. Earlier, responding to Father Moran's doubts about the constructive character of his actions, Sands states, using typically Irish Nationalist rhetoric: "Aye, worst case scenario it might well mean all that ... but short term. Out of the ashes. ... Guaranteed there'll be a new generation of men and women even more resilient, more determined ... " (51). This strong conviction that Ireland will be reborn like a phoenix out of the ashes of its own people only underscores his self-assurance and lack of humility, when faced with ethical and intellectual counterarguments.

In this respect, Sands bears close resemblance to the protagonist of T. S. Eliot's *Murder in the Cathedral*, Thomas Becket, who on his path to martyrdom in an analogous fashion struggles with his own pride and conceit. The comparison between the two works is particularly worthwhile since their similarities extend to their core, tripartite structure in which the central scenes visibly stand apart from the rest. Explaining the protagonists' motivation, these scenes play the role of static centres—important moments when Sands and Becket explain the reasons behind their choice of passive action, understood as suffering, giving the viewer time for critical reflection upon their decisions.

In Eliot's poetic play, the scene in question is the Interlude, in which the protagonist, Thomas Becket, delivers a sermon on Christmas morning (the Feast of St Stephen, the first martyr) in 1170. The sermon is written in prose, which breaks the rhythmical structure of the remaining parts of the drama, which are composed in verse. This sermon also follows the four temptations which Becket undergoes—a situation analogous to the temptations of Christ, whose passion the death of a saintly martyr is supposed to imitate—and serves as an occasion for the protagonist to explain his resolutions and face his hubristic pride, doubts and desires which the tempters impersonate.

Most importantly, the Interlude sheds light on the issue of sainthood. In response to the last temptation, in which Becket is offered the glory of martyrdom, he lectures his congregation as follows:

> A martyrdom is always the design of God, for His love of men, to warn them and to lead them, to bring them back to His ways. It is never the design of man; for the true martyr is he who has become the instrument of God, who has lost his will in the will of God, and who no longer desires anything for himself. (Eliot 53)

A similar notion of becoming a tool in the hands of God recurs a number of times in the play, most significantly at the beginning, in the fragment in which Becket speaks about the women of Canterbury:

> They know and do not know, what it is to act or suffer.
> They know and do not know, that acting is suffering
> And suffering is action. Neither does the actor suffer
> Nor the patient act. But both are fixed
> In an eternal action, an eternal patience
> To which all must consent that it may be willed
> And which all must suffer that they may will it,
> That the pattern may subsist, for the pattern is the action
> And the suffering, that the wheel may turn and still
> Be forever still. (Eliot 22)

This excerpt addresses the key paradox in the play, that of passive action, in other words an action that consists in complete, voluntary surrender to the will of God. As Christopher Innes posits, "Indeed, the whole play is based on the paradox that "action is suffering / And suffering is action," derived from the Latin root of patience/passivity in the verb *patio*: to suffer" (268). Carol Straw explains this idea in relation to the early Christian martyrs: "The brave martyrs would astonish even the torturers themselves as "cruelty was overcome by patience." Suffering one's own death, not killing the enemy, won the cause" (43). In a number of ways Sands fits into this pattern; the only crucial departure from the above-mentioned Christian model concerns the unreligious nature of the cause the protagonist of the film is fighting for.

As regards the political dimension of his choice, Sands's decision has strong associations with the history of hunger strikes and self-sacrifice in Ireland. As Sweeney notes, the 1981 republican hunger strikes have frequently been perceived as "the re-enactment of the redeeming blood sacrifice of 1916" (Sweeney 342). In fact, what Richard Kearney calls the "redemptorist martyr cult of Irish nationalism" (35), which was visible, for instance, in Patrick Pearse's and Thomas MacDonagh's writings

(Kearney 36-7), strongly resonated in Irish history throughout the twentieth century.[10] Such references to Christ's sacrifice, which are the legacy of the Easter Rising,[11] are also present in McQueen and Walsh's script. They are visible in the similarity in appearance between the unkempt "blanket" and "no-wash" protesters and Christ, in the scenes when the warder Raymond soaks his hands with smashed and cut knuckles in warm water (5, 20-1), which alludes to Pontius Pilate washing his hands of Jesus's death, or in the bed sheet stained with the blood soaking out of the protagonist's bed sores (64), which is evocative of the Veil of Veronica. Furthermore, as depicted in their film, the 1981 hunger strike also alludes to the Irish pre-Christian notion of *troscad* (fasting). According to early medieval Brehon Law, "'fast[ing] against" [one's] debtor by taking up a place close to the debtor's dwelling and going on hunger strike" was a common tactic that could be "employed by the powerless against the powerful" (Sweeney 422). As George Sweeney further explains,

> If the defendant allowed the plaintiff to die of starvation near his dwelling he would not only have to compensate the plaintiff's kin but he would also be in a polluted state and would be fearful of the magical consequences that might result from the protestor's death. (422)

Sands makes a reference to the above-mentioned culture-specific notion of seeking justice through starvation when he insists that his death should not be seen as a suicide but as a murder (52). Another allusion to the history of Irish hunger strikes can be found when Father Moran lists the names of republican heroes whom Bobby has been eulogizing and mentions Terence MacSwiney, who died in an English prison during the Irish War of Independence in 1920, after seventy-four days of self-imposed starvation. All these references subtly locate the events depicted in the film in a broader Irish historical and sociopolitical context. As Martin Herbert states (77),

> Hunger ... is concerned with the physical corpus as the last line of defence, and with the external conditions that would drive a

---

[10] For more information concerning the hunger strikes that took place in Ireland after the Easter Rising and before 1981, consult Sweeney, "Self-Immolative".

[11] See, for instance, Pearse's poem "A Mother Speaks", which he wrote in prison before his execution.

person to its fundamental act: ... it involves throwing the body away, letting it degrade into nothingness, as a final act of defiance. (77)

Most evidently, the hunger strike is an act of defiance of English authorities and their punitive system which seems equally oppressive towards the warders as towards the prisoners. The key difference between the two groups is that the latter yield to the discipline which produces bodies that are obedient and useful for the system. This phenomenon is exemplified by the behaviour of Raymond, who tries to deal with the everyday tension and threat involved in his dehumanizing job by pedantically and dispassionately performing his daily rituals. These precise repetitions are indicative of Raymond's internalized discipline, which protects him against the stress and frustration associated with living in constant danger, but at the same time turns him into a cog in the penitentiary apparatus. Yet the apparatus of discipline depicted in *Hunger* seems highly deficient; it fails to provide those who obey with a sense of security, and it easily resorts to physical violence when other means of control prove futile. While Raymond surrenders to the disciplinary forces of his daily routine, the prisoners choose disobedience and transgress the imposed rules, taking recourse to the primal, the taboo and the abject. Tracing the corporeal deterioration of Sands, Walsh and McQueen show a body that in its self-destructive practice veers out of control and subverts the imposed ways of behaviour. Thus, they accentuate the protagonist's free agency.

Sands's determined stance does not mean that he has no doubts. To the contrary, as in the case of the encounter between Thomas Becket and the four tempters, the conversation with Father Moran is an occasion for him to confront his fears and uncertainties and fully verbalize his stance, as with Becket in his sermon. Although it is hard to perceive Sands as a model martyred saint, Walsh and McQueen endow his choice with a mystical flavour and numerous references to the established patterns of martyrdom, emphasizing the indomitable aspect of his character, which defines him as a defender of his personal faith. In this context, the scene of the conversation with the priest serves as an illustration of the protagonist's *psychomachia*. Traditionally, *psychomoachia* denotes a representation of spiritual struggle between virtues and vices; yet in the case of Sands's internal conflict the clear boundary between what is right and what is wrong has been blurred.

Trying to deter him from the ultimate sacrifice, Father Moran appeals to Sands's fatherly feelings to his son and asks him: "What does your heart say Bobby?" (56), to which the protagonist responds: "My life means everything to me. Freedom means everything," and later adds: "It's a time to keep your beliefs pure. You call it sectarian ... I call it faith. (*Slight pause*) I believe that a united Ireland is right and just" (57). Importantly, a moment earlier Moran questions the rationale behind the self-sacrifice, which he perceives as destructive to the Northern Irish community, as it will result in "many dead men, families torn apart, and the whole Republican Movement demoralized" (51). Criticizing the nationalist rhetoric of martyrdom, he argues that the Irish prisoners of the ongoing sectarian war have too long been kept in inhumane conditions and, as a consequence, they are "afraid of living" and "scared to say "stop"" (54). They have virtually lost touch with reality; they are single-mindedly, or even obsessively, following, as W.B. Yeats would put it, "one purpose alone," which in the film reaches beyond the narrowly-defined political objective.

In fact, referring at this point to the famous "Easter 1916" may be enlightening, since in his poem, written in response to the Easter Rising, Yeats addresses very similar issues to those problematized by Walsh and McQueen. In the last stanza, the poet warns that "Too long a sacrifice / Can make a stone of the heart" (194) and poses a crucial question in relation to the deeds of the revolutionaries, whose uprising was doomed to military failure from the very beginning: "Was it needless death after all?" (194). The image of the heart of stone is further reinforced in the third stanza, which starts with the following words:

> Hearts with one purpose alone
> Through summer and winter seem
> Enchanted to a stone
> To trouble the living stream. (194)

This excerpt is followed by a description of an animate, changeable landscape surrounding the stone, and the stanza finishes with a statement: "The stone's in the midst of all" (194). The symbolism of the stone seems very ambiguous. On the one hand, connoting changelessness, it stands for the concept of Irish independence and the lasting determination of Irish fighters. As such, it is also evocative of death, stone tombs and monuments, and thus alludes to the notion of commemoration, which is addressed at the end of the poem. On the other hand, the rebels' single-mindedness in following die-hard republican ideals could have deprived them of compassion and humanity, turning their hearts into stone. This idea also strongly resonates in the screenplay in the words of Father Moran, who describes Sands's decision in terms of "cold miscalculation" (52). As the priest suggests, the protagonist's determination has a somewhat dehumanizing effect on him. The question remains as to whether this should be viewed in negative, political terms or more positively, as an instance of Sands overcoming his earthly weaknesses.

Towards the end of the conversation, despite Moran's skepticism, Sands states that he trusts that, in the long run, he will cause a lasting change. Just as the death of the leaders of the Easter Rising did not bring any immediate effects, since the rebellion was quickly suppressed by the English, the protagonist's sacrifice is presented by him as planting a seed that will, in time, give fruit. Sands challenges the idea of transforming Irish society with religious resonance. Since for him Jesus was primarily a revolutionary, it may be useful to refer here to the rationalized definition of a miracle which George Bernard Shaw presents in *Saint Joan* in the words of the cynical, down-to-earth Archbishop:

> A miracle, my friend, is an event which creates faith. That is the purpose and nature of miracles. They may seem very wonderful to the people who witness them, and very simple to those who perform them. That does not matter: if they confirm or create faith they are true miracles. (70)

Although lacking the Archbishop's cynicism concerning the mystical aspect of miracles, the protagonist of *Hunger* similarly accentuates their social dimension. As a cultural/political soldier who will irrevocably change Irish history, Sands wishes to be, in a sense, a miracle-worker. In the script the protagonist seems successful in this respect, since his sacrifice causes an immediate reaction within the Catholic community. This reaction is conspicuous in the last scene, which clearly alludes to the idea of a saint's miraculous body, bringing spiritual rejuvenation to the believers. As it is stated in the screenplay, "The scene is very animated and graphic with the whole community out on the street: women banging dustbin lids on the street shouting, children standing around in groups scattered throughout the street and young men angrily chanting Bobby Sands' name" (80). However, it needs to be stressed that McQueen eventually decided to delete this fragment from the actual film, which ends with Sands's body being taken away by prison guards in complete silence and thereby avoids the possible political implications of the original ending.

On the one hand, his strife seems mostly oriented towards transforming the earthly order. And yet, Sands's struggle also involves a definite renouncement of the body and all temporal bonds. In fact, it can be claimed that the protagonist creates his own ideology, which, like a Celtic cross, combines pagan and Christian elements to suit his aims. Again, we are left with the questions of whether Sands's philosophy is evidence of his greatness or self-delusion and whether he should be perceived more as a defender of God-given freedom or a manipulator who appropriates various culturally-sanctioned patterns of martyrdom for his purpose, which is to influence the world's public opinion. Whereas Becket in Eliot's play summarizes his greatest moral dilemmas in the following way: "The last act is the greatest treason: / To do the right deed for the wrong reason" (46), Sands's problem lies in the fact that perhaps he is doing the wrong thing for the right reason, life being too precious a value to be sacrificed through self-imposed starvation for a socio-political purpose.

Sands concludes his conversation with Father Moran with a story from his childhood, which highlights yet another, personal dimension of his decision. In his youth, he was a keen cross-country runner. One time, running through the woods with other boys participating in athletic competitions in Derry, he found a seriously wounded foal. The only way to put an end to the animal's suffering was to kill it, yet none of his companions was able to take such a drastic step. It was only Sands who had enough courage to do "the right thing" (61)—to drown the foal in the stream. The story clearly shows that, in Sands's view, self-sacrifice is the only option left; it also underscores his sense of superiority. Apart from feeling personally responsible for the failure of the previous hunger strike, the protagonist seems to cherish a belief that he is the only person fit to take such a radical action. Still, it needs to be stressed that he is no cog in the IRA political machine. Sands's stubbornness, intransigence and endurance in the pursuit of his political goal are presented as his inborn features, which fuel his desire to transgress one's own weaknesses in a personal struggle with human limitations.

This idea is also communicated in the structure of the script, which can be compared to the diameter of a circle. The second part of the play mirrors the first one, which makes them similar to two radiuses of which a diameter is made. In Walsh and McQueen's script, the two sections separated by the static centre stand in clear opposition to each other. This contrast is based on the traditional body/soul dichotomy. The first section focuses on the communal engrossment of the prisoners in earthly and bodily issues, while the second depicts Sands's sixty-six days of starvation, which may be interpreted in terms of individual, spiritual liberation from the earthly confines into the unearthly, divine

(?) realm of freedom. It is a value which the protagonist holds in high regard, since his moral hierarchy seems to be grounded in the universal belief that "Free will separated men from beasts and inanimate creation" (Straw 44).

Although in metaphorical terms freedom is frequently associated with movement,[12] the protagonist's self-annihilation is paradoxically depicted in physical terms as a journey towards the final stasis. It can be seen as an instance of aligning oneself with the immovable world axis (*axis mundi*), which, according to Mircea Eliade, is the symbolic centre of the world—a point of connection which enables mortals to ascend to mythical (sacred) time, leaving profane reality behind. Eliade maintains that "every human being tends, even unconsciously, towards the Centre, and towards his own centre, where he can find integral reality—sacredness" (54). However, the thought of reaching absolute (sacred) reality "arouses an ambivalent feeling, of fear and of joy, of attraction and repulsion, etc." (51), which can be compared to the "terrible beauty" (Yeats 193) of Sands's sacrifice, as depicted in *Hunger*.

The idea of the immovable centre, understood as a point of mystical connection between the earthly and the divine, is also relevant to T. S. Eliot's exploration of the philosophy of a self-willed surrender through his use of wheel imagery and the symmetrical composition of his play. In *Murder in the Cathedral*, the wheel, apart from being a reference to the attribute of another martyr, Saint Catherine of Alexandria, as well as to the natural cycle of seasons, can be perceived as an allusion to Dante. According to Innes,

> The image of the wheel comes from Dante. Man liberates himself from bondage to the senses on the revolving rim ... by aligning his will with God as the unmoving axle, and so travelling down the spokes to the centre. And this forms the structure of the play. (466)

As has been stated, in *Hunger* the conversation scene between Sands and Father Moran occupies the middle, "divine" position and, not unlike the Interlude in *Murder in the Cathedral*, serves as "a reflective pause in the centre" (Innes 466). This is the moment when we are forced to ask ourselves if the protagonist's death can be seen in terms of passive surrender to English violence-- an act similar to Eliot's character Becket's wilful surrender to God's will and, consequently, his passive surrender to the assassins appointed by King Henry II.

---

[12] In the script this is most conspicuous in the images of running (77-78), and flying birds (25).

Furthermore, the composition of *Hunger* indicates that Sands is not entirely focused on the earthly order and that his actions may, in fact, be seen as an attempt to reach beyond the changeable realm of the senses.

The film suggests that the strikers' actions are oriented not only towards earthly, material outcomes, but also towards the world of ideas—individual spiritual centres which should not necessarily be seen in religious terms as synonymous with God, but may as well be identified with personal freedom, or Ireland's unification. In *Hunger* the above-mentioned concept is reinforced through the use of the symbolism that alludes to the notion of world axis. This is visible not only in the scene of conversation, which serves as the structural and dramatic centre of the film, but also in a number of images used in *Hunger*, such as a peculiar example of prison art—the image of a perfect spiral smeared with excrement on the wall of a cell by one of the inmates (8). Alluding to the Celtic symbol of the sun, the spiral may be seen as a visual illustration of a path to the static axis/centre. Together with the other elements I have discussed, this imagery suggests that through his struggle Sands transcends earthly temporality. Although in the conversation with Father Moran the protagonist does not fully verbalize the spiritual and mystical aspects of his decision, it is suggested in the composition of the script and reinforced by its rich imagery.

This progress from a cave-like prison into the world of ideas is presented in the screenplay mostly in visual terms. Hidden inside the labyrinthine structure of the Maze, the claustrophobic cells and murky corridors of the H-block, described in the script in the following way: "Colourless and everything dead and cold, it resembles a bunker almost" (10), are replaced with a bigger and brighter hospital room in the final section of the film. While the atmosphere of the first part is largely created through the use of dark, mostly brownish, earthy colours, shades of white and pastel blue dominate in the final section, which not only underscores the sterility of the prison hospital, but also denotes liberation from the bodily sphere with all its unclean aspects brought to the fore earlier in the film. The gravity of the images of brutal physical violence, excrement, urine and masturbation, showing human beings reduced to their most basic physical instincts, is replaced towards the end of the screenplay with images associated with lightness, weightlessness and purity: a floating dandelion pappus[13] or

---

[13] In the film the pappus was eventually replaced with a feather.

flying birds, with which Sands can be identified. The idea of the protagonist resembling a trapped bird which struggles for liberation is additionally highlighted when a white coffin-like cage is placed over his fragile body, which aims to protect it against the pressure exerted by the blankets (69). Furthermore, some of the shots in the second part of the film are taken from Sands's perspective, as in the case of him seeing his parents, whose image is blurred and out of focus (77), or when he cannot comprehend the words of a bearded man sitting next to him, but can only hear "the noise from the fluorescent light" (70). This highlights the mechanism of starvation and its effects on the way the protagonist experiences the world. Sands gradually loses touch with reality, which is presented in a physical, multisensory way. He finds himself unable to speak or to receive external stimuli. His senses become selective and weak, as he gradually progresses from the material, bodily world of sensory experience towards the realm of ideas, from the changeable rim of temporality towards the immoveable centre.

In *Hunger* Bobby Sands struggles for freedom—the value he cherishes as much as his own life. Yet, in his resistance he remains neither a perfect soldier nor a martyred saint, but a human being who does not fit into any idealized, flawless model. Undoubtedly, he is presented as an individualist who pursues his aims with great determination and perseverance. By positing Sands midway between a republican warrior and a Christian martyr, Walsh and McQueen hint at there being more to his sacrifice than just a political purpose. The presentation of his struggle suggests that his deed is not only an act of challenging English authority and order, but also an extreme attempt to transgress human limitations, to give witness to freedom, which he perceives as one of the highest God-given values, and to defy earthly materiality. *Hunger* is built around a clash of politics and spirituality, emotion and intellect. The way in which Walsh's words and McQueen's images complement each other underscores the human aspect of Sands's self-sacrifice, subtly hinting at a greater mystical design which informs it, without relying too overtly on the Catholic nationalist cult of martyrdom. By interlacing the political, personal and mystical aspects of his death, the film highlights the complexity of the protagonist's motivation and the choices he makes. It leaves the audience with the following questions: to what extent Sands's act is an instance of a perhaps misguided, boyish idealism, and whether he has achieved the desired freedom or remained trapped in a prison of his own making—in the belief that death through starvation is the only way out of the stalemate situation in which he has found himself.

Works Cited

Billington, Michael. "Enda Walsh: 'Pure Theatre Animal' Explores Solitude and the Void Below." *The Guardian* 18 Sept. 2014. Web. 17 Oct. 2014.

Eliot, Thomas Stearns. *Murder in the Cathedral.* London: Faber, 1976. Print.

Eliade, Mircea. *Images and Symbols: Studies in Religious Symbolism.* Trans. Philip Mairet. Princeton, NJ: Princeton UP, 1991. Print.

El-Khairy, Omar Assem. "Snowflakes on a Scarred Knuckle: The Biopolitics of the "War on Terror" through Steve McQueen's *Hunger* and Kathryn Bigelow's *The Hurt Locker.*" *Millennium—Journal of International Studies* 39. 1 (2010): 187-91. *SAGE Publications.* Web. 20 June 2011.

Fassbender, Michael. Interview by Jason Solomon. *Hunger.* Blast! Films, 2008. DVD.

Herbert, Martin. "Steve McQueen." *Art Review* 33 (2009): 74-9. *Wilson Web.* Web. 20 June 2011.

Hunger. Dir. Steve McQueen. Perf. Michael Fassbender, Stuart Graham and Liam Cunningham. Criterion, 2008. Film.

Innes, Christopher. *Modern British Drama: The Twentieth Century.* Cambridge: CUP, 2002. Print.

Kearney, Richard. "Myth and Martyrdom: Foundational Symbols in Irish Republicanism." *Navigations: Collected Irish Essays 1976-2006.* New York: Syracuse UP, 2006. 32-47. Print.

Levy, Emanuel. "Hunger: How Steve McQueen's Brilliant Film Was Made." *Emanuel Levy: Cinema 24/7.* Web. 21 July 2013.

McQueen, Steve. "The Human Body as Political Weapon: An Interview with Steve McQueen." Interview by Gary Crowdus. *Cineaste* 34.2 (2009): 22-5. *Wilson Web.* Web. 20 June 2011.

---. Interview by Stewart Comer. Walker Art Center. Youtube, 31 Jan. 2014. Web. 11 Apr. 2014.

---. Interview by Jason Solomon. *Hunger.* Blast! Films, 2008. DVD.

O'Hagan, Sean. "McQueen and Country." *The Guardian* 12 Oct. 2008. Web. 17 July 2013.

Oppenheimer, Joan. "Production Slate: Willful Resistance and Amped-Up Action." *Cinematographer* 90.4 (2009): 16-20. *Wilson Web.* Web. 20 June 2011.

O'Toole, Fintan. "*Hunger* Fails to Wrest the Narrative from the Hunger Strikers." *Irish Times* 22 Nov. 2008. Web. 24 Nov. 2008.

Pine, Emilie. "Embodied Memory: Performing the 1980-1 Hunger Strikes." *The Politics of Irish Memory: Performing Remembrance in Contemporary Irish Culture.* Basingstoke: Palgrave Macmillan, 2011. 100-26. Print.

Shaw, George Bernard. *Saint Joan.* London: Penguin, 1957. Print.

Straw, Carole. "'A Very Special Death': Christian Martyrdom in its Classical Context." *Sacrificing the Self: Perspectives on Martyrdom and Religion.* Ed. Margaret Cormack. Oxford: OUP, 2002. 39-57. Print.

Sweeney, George. "Irish Hunger Strikes and the Cult of Self-Sacrifice." *Journal of Contemporary History* 28.3 (1993): 421-37. *JSTOR*. Web. 14 Nov. 2013.

---. "Self-Immolative Martyrdom: Explaining the Irish Hungerstrike Tradition." *Studies: An Irish Quarterly Review* 93.371 (2004): 337-48. *JSTOR*. Web. 11 Apr. 2014.

Yeats, William Butler. "Easter 1916." *The Collected Poems of W. B. Yeats.* Ed. Richard J. Finneran. New York: Collier, 1989. 193-5. Print.

Walsh, Enda. Interview by Will Gompertz. *Culture Critic.* 12 Dec. 2008. Web. 11 Apr. 2014.

---. Interview by Garry Kelly. *The Garry Kelly Show.* Galway Bay FM. Youtube, 2 Dec. 2008. Web. 26 June 2013.

---. Interview by Alex Sierz. *TheatreVOICE.* Department of Theatre and Performance at the V&A, 3 Nov. 2008. Web. 26 June 2013.

---. *The New Electric Ballroom.* London: Nick Hern, 2008. Print.

Walsh, Enda and Steve McQueen. *The McQueen Project: Shooting Script.* 28 Sept. 2007. PDF File. *myPDFscripts.* Web. 21 June 2013.

11 | Dead Men Talking: Stagnation and Entrapment in Enda Walsh's *Penelope*

Audrey McNamara

Commissioned as part of a rewrite of the "Odyssey" by the Oberhausen Theatre, *Penelope* by Enda Walsh premiered at the theatre in Germany on 27ᵗʰ February 2010 directed by Tilman Knabe. Ironically, the decaying carcass of the Irish Celtic Tiger finds resonance in the empty swimming pool that has become home to Penelope's suitors in the eponymous play. Kevin Wallace in his article *Fintan O'Toole: Power Plays and the High Art/Low Art Discourse in the Narrative of Irish Theatre* argues that "... *Penelope* is a scathing critique of Irish capitalism, its megalomania, misogyny and myopia (126). The four male characters—all of whom bear Irish names, Burns, Dunne, Quinn and Fitz,—are portrayed as degenerate, egotistical specimens. As Wallace notes "the names of these characters resonate with those of controversial Irish businessmen and bankers who figured prominently in the media after the collapse of Celtic tiger (126). The silent but powerful presence of Penelope looms large in an elevated space above the swimming pool. CCTV enables her to watch the antics of the four men. The stage directions in describing the makings of a party, bottles of booze, snacks and a "helium-filled heart-shaped balloon bobbing above the table" (3) signal to a bygone "good life" reminiscent of the Celtic Tiger boom time. However, "the mass of junk" (3) under the table communicates a different story—signalling to the debris left in the wake of a society's excesses. The form the play adopts speaks to the very essence of classical Greek drama's depiction of excessive behaviour encompassing the formula of peripeteia (crisis), anagnorisis (recognition) and catharsis (cleansing). Worthen explains that

> Greek drama ... arises from an intense and economical
> relationship between ... a situation, usually at the point of climax
> as the play opens, ... a complex of characters each with distinctive
> goals and motives ..., a chorus used both as a character and a
> commentator ... and a series of incidents that precipitates a crisis.
> (17)

Signalling to this crisis and sitting centre stage, and central to the plot
as the harbinger of death, is "a large gleaming Taunton Deluxe
Barbecue". Gardening advertisements describe the barbecue "as top of
the range" and having "three cast iron burners at 4.3kw each with an
additional side burner at a lower 3kw" arguably one burner for each of
the four suitors. Each man has had a shared dream of the fate that waits
them. The Taunton Deluxe Barbeque is central to both this shared and
the gruesome end that awaits them. Quinn articulates the horror they
have all dreamt.

> The fire starts underneath the barbecue. It starts at the same time
> he steps from his boat onto the shore and looks up at the house
> here ... but he doesn't go to her but to us and to his knife ... he's in
> amongst us ripping apart our legs and we're scurrying around the
> floor like whinging bloodied slugs. He pulls Fitz aside. He fillets
> him ... he cuts him up. He shatters his old bones with his hands
> ... hacking up limbs and tossing innards aside ... Flesh is landing
> on the grill, the barbecue mocking us this final time ... He cracks
> open Fitz's chest, reaches in and takes his heart in his hand. (Slight
> pause.) And their eyes lock together now ... and he squeezes his
> heart slowly. Ever so slowly. (Pause) He's looking at one of us
> three, He's smiling. And we're next.

The verbalization of the dream sets the tone for the drama and becomes
the predominant thread in the fabric of Walsh's play. Nicholas Grene
argues that Irish drama ... has remained self-consciously aware of its
relation to the life of the nation and the state". (1) This essay explores
how *Penelope* demonstrates the way in which, as Rebellato contends
"the values of nation become dramatically uncoupled from those of the
state." (n.p.) Taking the definition of state as the political entity which
is supposed to safeguard the welfare of nation, Walsh's play displays the
catastrophic effects of how a single-minded desire, perpetrated by the
hubris of a few, to possess that which does not belong to them and
exposes the characters' hamartia or fatal flaw and creates a disastrous
outcome with far-reaching consequences. Fintan O'Toole, in reviewing
Walsh's newest play *Ballyturk* (2014), stated that:

> It's not accidental that Walsh wrote a brilliant play about the myth
> of Penelope, who weaves a shroud by day and unravels it by night.

> That is pretty much what Walsh himself does, weaving and unweaving the same metal cloth. (The Irish Times)

However, Walsh's play is much more than a mere story. Weaved through this Homeric tale is the thread of an Irish myth echoing shades of Lady Gregory's and W.B. Yeats's *Cathleen ní Houlihan,* albeit in a subverted form: Penelope, like Cathleen, is a woman waiting for heroic help to shape her destiny. The suitors in representing the trope of "too many strangers in the house" serve to ground the tale in an Irish narrative. The trope of "stranger" as defined by Grene is the person or persons who come from "without" (52). They enter a space that they do not belong to and cause the course of destiny to change. Grene argues that "these dramatic strangers were bound to be politically construed in the context of the time" (53). However, as the characters of the suitors demonstrate, it is a trope that continues to find resonance in modern Irish drama. Through the weaving of the frame of the Homeric tale and a nod to Irish mythology, Walsh transports the audience back and forth through time, always however, landing in a resonating Irish present over which the shadow of the dying Celtic Tiger hovers. Henry Merritt claims of *Cathleen ní Houlihan* that "'she was launched on a mythic life through the play's composition. Whatever allure she still possesses is that of death" (653). That same tension of a fatalistic suspense that is present in *Cathleen ní Houlihan* is replicated through Penelope's character in Walsh's play. The shared fate of the young men that answer Cathleen's call to arms, their impending deaths forebodes the fate of the suitors. However, the suitors are anti-heroes, dying not for the glorious salvation of their country, rather for destruction of an economy through their own greed and corruption. Quinn articulates the characters of the men when he states:

> We are all here to win and each second is a game! So let's play the game! We are all men of business! ... We are all the same type of men! Murray would sell his dead granny for a deal. He would have to find her grave first, "cause let's face it, he wouldn't have shown up at her funeral. He would ... sell her decaying, filthy arse because he loved money! We are all like that, Burns! (31)

Michael, in Gregory and Yeats's play, rejected money for glory while Quinn, Fitz, Dunne and Burns freely admit to their decadent, excessive lifestyle; they are parasites that fed on and played with a growing, burgeoning economy. In a subversion of the tale, Penelope arguably represents a modern day Cathleen. Portrayed as a young woman in her twenties, which is an anomaly in itself, as Penelope in Homer's tale, waited, with their son Telemachus, for twenty years for Odysseus's

return. Taking this into account and with reference to the early
twentieth century Irish play, this therefore, could suggest that Penelope
can be read as the Cathleen whom Patrick described as "a young girl
and she had the walk of a queen" (28); a "Cathleen" who attained youth
through the blood sacrifice of the young men who answered her call to
save her "four green fields". Merritt attributes that the change of the
"Old Woman into a young girl carries with it more than a few hints of
one specific change from age to youth: the change that occurs to a
vampire after an infusion of blood" (649). Penelope's youth in Walsh's
play is thus explained when she is read as a vampiric Cathleen ní
Houlihan, her character's ultimate purpose is to "suck the life from the
suitors". Penelope's silence throughout the play speaks volumes. This
transference of Penelope's silent voice in the Homeric tale to the
silencing of the voice of Cathleen, a silence that resonates an innate
disappointment of the results of a nation that fought so long and hard
for its freedom. This dramatic silence is also representative of a sadness
despite former heroics performed in its name, Ireland as nation has
turned in on itself and is creating destruction from within through the
greed and hubris of a powerful section of society, those who control the
nation's finances. The sentiment of Cathleen in the Gregory/Yeats play
"If anyone would give me help, he must give me his all" (25) resonates
as a silent wish throughout the drama in *Penelope*. It quickly becomes
obvious however, through the actions of the suitors that this will never
become a reality. Quinn attempts to unify them in action: " We sell our
love to her as we always do but today with the support of the others. It
is in our interest that someone at least wins her ... so we work together,
men" (21). This statement is very telling as it demonstrates that
heretofore they had not been supporting each other and, by the very
nature of the characters, and especially Quinn's character, there is no
way that words are going to change this. Indeed, as the drama plays out,
Quinn's hubris spoils their last chance just when Fitz seemed to be
making a connection with Penelope and the fate of all four suitors is
sealed by this fatal flaw in Quinn's character.

Fintan O'Toole maintains that "he (Walsh) gives us people who are
locked into stories they can neither escape nor end" (*The Irish Times*).
This certainly holds true in *Penelope*. Under the pretext of winning the
ethereal Penelope's hand in marriage, the four suitors wait like stagnant
pond life in the empty swimming pool that has become home: trapped
in a self-perpetuating grotesque cycle of inertia. Burns muses that "If
we leave, we leave to nowhere" (20). This enforced entrapment is both
ironic and detrimental as, in reality, they could leave at any time. Such

however is their collective need to win Penelope's hand, they lock themselves into a vicious competition that will not bode well for any of them. Walsh himself states in a recorded interview at the Steppenwolf Theatre Company that "'the heroes journey' within it [*Penelope*] actually, is these guys trying to clean up their fucked up lives , to try to ... sort of ... clean up everything they have left behind.' (*YouTube*) Bearing in mind their Irish names and that some of those names shadow those held accountable for the crash of the Irish economy in the first decade of the twenty first century, the play can be looked at in relation to the economic disaster perpetrated by the namesakes of these characters. Ondrej Pilny in his article *The Grotesque in the Plays of Enda Walsh* states that

> Penelope ... reflects prominent aspects of the Post-Celtic atmosphere. The protagonists names are based on those of prominent Irish business moguls, bankers and developers who were directly involved in the downfall of the Irish economy. (220)

In a note to this quote, Pilny qualifies this identification explaining that

> Quinn comes from Sean Quinn, a major shareholder in the Anglo-Irish Bank whose business has been destroyed by its collapse. Fitz's name is of Sean Fitzpatrick, the corrupt head of that same bank. Dunne is eponymous with Sean Dunne, a notorious property mogul, and Burns is most likely Johnny Burns of Burns Construction company. ... The attempted identification of Burns is mine. (224 fn)

However, it could be argued that the name "Burns" is in the mix to offset an overt link that would dilute the dramatic tone of the play and perhaps also to reflect a collective society *burned* by the actions of the main players in the Celtic Tiger. In the stage directions, Burns is described as "carrying himself subserviently" (3). This description is indicative of an underling and true to form, Burns is for the most part deferential to the other three. The stage directions also describe him acting *as a reluctant servant throughout* (5).

Burns mopping the blood of another suitor, Murray (who committed suicide), from the walls of the swimming pool could be interpreted as the position of one in the lower ranks left cleaning up the mess made by the "big boys" much as the Irish people were left to clear up the financial mess perpetrated by the main players in boom-time Ireland.[14]

---

14 The financial devastation resulting from the bank bail-out agreed by the late Fianna Fail Minister for Finance, Brian Lenihan, with the banks has

Murray's suicide also signifies another very serious result of the economic collapse. An article in the *Irish Independent* published in 2009 entitled "It's another financial -- suicide and the downturn" detailed a list of suicides directly attributed to the financial collapse. (Reilly & Sheehan) The blame, the article claims, can most certainly be attributed to the pressure applied by culpable financial institutions to hard-pressed business people. (Reilly & Sheehan) Jimmy Guerin, brother of the late, murdered journalist Veronica Guerin, asked "Have we lost all sense of decency that the banks are putting these people under such pressure that they felt they had to do this?" (Reilly & Sheehan) Quinn, by far the most evil of the suitors verifies this total lack of empathy when, in speaking about Murray to Burns

> ... I am speaking at him (Murray) so that he has no time to speak himself. I wear Murray down like an old rag! He's not Murray to me any more [sic], he's not even human. We share little pleasantries in the morning but I'm steering his moods, counting his words, building little corners and placing that little fucker in those corners! I might have just slit his throat but where's the sophistication in that, Burns? (30)

Stephen Donnelly in conversation with Patrick Honohan about Anglo Irish Bank stated that " ... the bank can do pretty much what it wants, that it can squeeze people, and the more it squeezes people, the more its share prices go up, which it believes is a good outcome."(n.p.) Quinn's attitude is indicative of that perceived attitude of the major financial institutions to the financial and indeed emotional problems of both businesses and families resulting from the collapse of the banks and their ability, with State support, to put pressure on their customers who are in financial difficulties.

Arguably, the inferences to the business world in Walsh's play are quite deliberate and by no means understated. Time and time again, the suitors talk about a plan to build a new company. Dunne describes them as "A group of men with a common ideology, a collective direction! That's what you're suggesting, Quinn! We're building a company right here!" (22) The dialogue, while each waiting for their turn to woo Penelope, is interspersed with references to trust and

---

had a resounding impact on the Irish taxpayer. The protection given to the banks and the bond holders has resulted in a multitude of extra and higher taxation for the PAYE sector resulting in a catastrophic loss of jobs and unprecedented repossessions of family homes.

honour and it becomes very obvious that each character is lacking a moral compass. Burns poses the question

> Has honour ever lived here?
> **DUNNE.** What are you talking about? We are men of integrity, Burns! I shit honour.
> **BURNS.** But will you ever return to reality?

Therein lies the crux of the fabric of the story; the men's existence in their own distorted vacuous sense of reality, a distortion that colours their judgement and stymies any thought of movement. In reference to escaping their situation Burns captures the mood of inertia and stagnation when he states that "We could row. But we've already sold our boats for beer" (21). The tropes of alcohol and excess point to the lack of direction possessed by the characters. Burns identifies their collective need to have "A reality closer to what the people of the world may ACTUALLY RECOGNISE" (38). However, this "reality" is not within their grasp as they are immersed in a stagnant pool of deception and decay that conveys their "myopic status" (McNamara 233). This myopathy does not preclude them from the awareness of their fast approaching impending doom and tells of their desperation to win the hand of Penelope in order to halt the inevitable. This is much the tale of the final weeks and days of the Celtic Tiger when the Anglo-Irish executives made a frantic effort to cover up the massive financial mess their books were in. The *Irish Independent's* report on the secret recordings made in Anglo-Irish Bank tells a tale of subterfuge, chicanery and fraud.

The audio recordings are from the banks' own internal telephone system and date from the heart of the financial crisis that brought the State to its knees in September 2008. Anglo itself was within days of complete meltdown—and in the years ahead would eat up €30bn of taxpayer money. Mr Bowe speaks about how the State had been asked for €7bn to bail out Anglo—but Anglo's negotiators knew all along this was not enough to save the bank. The plan was that once the State began the flow of money, it would be unable to stop. Mr Bowe is asked by Mr Fitzgerald how they came up with the figure of €7bn. He laughs as he is taped saying: "Just as Drummer (then CEO David Drumm) would say, picked it out of my arse" (Williams).

This sense of disregard and respect for anything outside themselves is mirrored through the characters in Walsh's play and Bowe's assertion is testament to Walsh's foresight for an evolving Irish financial disaster. The newspaper article, written some three years after *Penelope* was first written and performed, reflects the sense of selfishness and bloody-mindedness that Quinn, Dunne, Fitz and Burns display.

The story of the *Magic Porridge Pot* serves to strengthen the theme of excess and the devastating results thereafter. Dunne in stating that it was the only book he cared for as a child (9) initiates a dialogue between himself, Quinn and Fitz. Quinn maintains that it is "the only book there is" (9) clarifying in answer to Fitz's assertion that "There are others actually" (9) not one "that speaks so clearly of investment and growth or the fast development of an unstable economy. It needed that little girl to stay at home with the purpose of saying "Cook-pot-cook" and "Stop-pot-stop" (9). The main message of *The Magic Porridge Pot* points to the devastation that occurs when there is no one willing to take control or as the story goes "sleeps while the pot is still boiling". Quinn quite plainly states "What the pot needed was regulation" (9). This speaks directly to the overheating of the Irish economy. As Donovan and Murray maintain " ... the regulator failed to identify the underlying vulnerability of the Irish banks, let alone take vigorous action to defend them" (82). The over-riding analyses in the post-Celtic Tiger era was that there was "no keeper of the pot" as Dunne referred to the little girl. Indeed, as Donovan and Murphy argue "that by the time the crisis broke, the regulator had little substantive information on the extent and nature of the banks true exposure" (84).

Walsh's ending plays out in a grotesque, quasi-burlesque performance by Quinn featuring love matches from history, film and theatre. Pilny argues that "In the work of this bold inheritor (Walsh) of the comfortlessness and the puzzling grotesque of Romanticism: a measure of deliverance consists in the final triumph of theatricality" (Pilny 223). From Napoleon and Josephine, to Scarlett O'Hara and Rhett Butler, to Romeo and Juliet whose death scene plays into the beginning of the end for the suitors and penultimately the death scene of JFK (played by Burns' character) with Quinn as Jackie Kennedy. Quinn's final costume change has him dressed as Eros the Greek God of Love, and the pace at which this piece of theatricality is delivered crescendos to the murder of Quinn by the other three. His death signifies the complete dissolution of any notion of a civilized society and echoes the final roar to a whimper of the Celtic Tiger moguls as the realization that their carefully woven and falsely constructed fiscal inventions are all about to disappear into modern cyber space. The spectral omnipresent figure of Odysseus arguably finds resonance as an alternative to the European intervention of the Troika in the Irish financial meltdown. His imminent arrival in the play heralds the metaphorical death knell for those that caused the problems in the first place though Burns's final speech on the value of love and friendship seems to bring Penelope back to them. However, Burns's final line that "Love is saved" (51) proves to be premature as the prophesy of the shared dream of the barbeque bursting into flames becomes a reality. Odysseus has arrived and it is all over for the remaining suitors. Walsh's last stage directions *Blackout and The End* (51) create an irreversible sense of finality.

Between September 2007 and September 2008, the actions of the board of Anglo-Irish Bank were to have a detrimental effect on the future of the Irish economy. By September 29th 2008, the Irish Government initiated a bank guarantee, spear-headed by the late Brian Lenihan, Minister for Finance to the tune of €440 billion. The far-reaching disastrous effects of this guarantee resulted in a bailout for Ireland by the ECB in 2010. It is both ironic and fitting that a play which resonates so much of the Irish economic crisis should be premiered in a country that houses so many of the bond-holders that the ECB were determined should not be *burned* by Ireland's banking disaster.

Works Cited

Donnelly, Stephen. "In Conversation with Patrick Honohan about Anglo Irish Bank." N.p., 2 May 2014. Web. 31 Mar. 2015.

Donovan, Donal, and Antoin E. Murphy. *The Fall of the Celtic Tiger: Ireland and the Euro Debt Crisis*. Oxford: Oxford UP, 2013. Print.

"Enda Walsh Interview." Interview by Steppenwolf Theatre Company. *Youtube*. N.p., 19 June 2012. Web. 13 May 2015.

McNamara, Audrey. "The Seafarer: Male Pattern Blindness." *The Theatre of Conor McPherson: "right beside the Beyond"* Ed. Lilian Chambers and Eamonn Jordan. Dublin: Carysfort, 2012. 231-40. Print.

Merritt, Henry. ""Dead Many Times": "Cathleen Ni Houlihan," Yeats, Two Old Women, and a Vampire." *The Modern Language Review* 96.3 (2001): 644. Web.

O'Toole, Fintan. "Review: Ballyturk." *The Irish Times*, 16 Aug. 2014. Web. 31 Mar. 2015.

Pilný, Ondřej. "The Grotesque in the Plays of Enda Walsh." *Irish Studies Review* 21.2 (2013): 217-25. Web.

Rebellato, Dan. "From the State of the Nation to Globalisation: Shifting Agendas in Contemporary British Playwriting." Eds. Nadine Holdsworth and Mary Luckhurst. *A Concise Companion to Contemporary British and Irish Drama*. Malden, MA: Blackwell Pub., 2008.Print.

Reilly, Jerome, and Maeve Sheehan. "It's Another Financial- Suicide and the Downturn." *The Irish Independent* 15 Mar. 2009. Web. 13 May 2015.

Wallace, Kevin. "Fintan O'Toole: Power Plays" and the High Art/Low Art Discourse in the Narrative of Irish Theatre." *Ireland and Popular Culture*. Ed. Sylvie Mikowski. Oxford: Peter Lang, 2014. 115-28. Print.

Walsh, Enda. *Penelope*. Great Britain: Nick Hern, 2010. Print.

Williams, Paul. "Inside Anglo—The Secret Recordings." *The Irish Independent*. N.p., 24 June 2013. Web. 13 May 2015.

Worthen, William B. *The Wadsworth Anthology of Drama*. Boston, MA: Thomson/Wadsworth, 2004. Print.

12 | For *Once* and for all: Empathy and Mimesis in Enda Walsh's musical for the "people of the world"[15]

Mary P. Caulfield

As you enter the theatre, unknowing patrons to this theatre-turned-public house, the strident sounds of an "impromptu" Irish traditional music session immediately reveal the sacrosanct link between our characters and their music. This *seisiún* strives to be *"raw, chaotic and hugely positive"*—a quality that stands in stark contrast to the melancholy state of post-Celtic Tiger Dublin (during which, the stage adaptation is set) and likewise to that of *Once* protagonist "Guy" (Walsh, Hansard, and Irglová 9). Offering a type of counter-set to those of its more flamboyant Broadway neighbours—Bob Crowley's[16] North-side Dublin pub grown dusty and dim—is simple in design yet rich in the narrative that it hosts. Checker-floored and milk-stool furnished, this set is reminiscent of the urban battleground of Act 2 of Sean O'Casey's *Plough and the Stars* that delivered us from a pastoral representation of the macro-Nation to that of the individual Dubliner. In similar fashion, Enda Walsh's script (the stage adaptation of John Carney's 2007 film of the same name) renegotiates the time-honoured signs, symbols, and sexisms that masoned twentieth-century Ireland and thus serves as a revisionary national narrative not in terms of the political but rather as a reflection and soundtrack for the newly opened and integrated Ireland.

---

[15] Walsh, Enda, and Glen Hansard. *Once*. New York: Theatre Communications Group, 2013. 11. Print.

[16] Bob Crowley was "Once the Musical" set-designer.

Once, can be defined as a "book musical"–a musical that uses dance, dialogue, and song to tell a story that "has a serious plot in which every character contributes to the story" (Blood). The book musical reflects the late nineteenth century Modernist ideals regarding unity in that the director's role is intrinsic to unifying the "play's text, staging style, acting style, and design elements" (Blood). Stacy Ellen Wolf also defines this type of musical as integrated in which "dialogue, music, and dance" are used together "to invoke a (somewhat) believable setting of location and time, to tell a (somewhat) plausible story, and to develop (somewhat) realistic and psychologized characters" (Wolf 352). *Once's* protagonists are musicians. Because of this, music is integrated into *Once* in a way that blends both diegetic (when music is coming from a source inside the story space) and non-diegetic (music that comes from outside the story space) techniques. Walsh integrates the songs into the action of *Once* but also undermines the realism of the piece with the use of the chorus of actors on stage, the set, and fluid "diegetic" staging. Using folkloric texts, song, and story, Walsh creates an empathetic effect for his audience and thus carves out a place for the individual within the newly globalized Ireland. And, with eight Tony awards (including Best Book) this 2011 Musical places Irish theatre-makers (dir. by John Tiffany and musical direction by Martin Lowe) as forerunners into this rarely Irish chartered genre.[17]

On stage, mirrors of all shapes and sizes serve as backdrop to the curving bar counter (which also serves as a functioning bar for thirsty audience members during intermission). In the spirit of Walsh's prescribed "positivity" these mirrors offer a metaphorical suggestion that these archetypal lead characters—Guy and Girl—not only shape but also reflect our own lives' dramas. These mirrors reflect the characters, the audience, and thus the nation, making manifest this book musical's mimetic goals. While these mirrors serve as a clever mechanism to see our actor/musicians revel in their talents, the student of Irish theatre cannot ignore the implication of the impenetrable trope of self-reflection that haunts Irish theatre past and present. This idea made its debut with J.M. Synge's *Playboy of the Western World* (1907) when Synge's patricidal protagonist, Christy Mahon, takes his first good look at himself in a cracked mirror standing then forever as the allegorical

---

[17] For more information on the Irish Musical Theatre Repertoire see "Scenes from the Bigger Picture." *Scenes from the Bigger Picture*. 25 Nov. 2013. Web. 10 Feb. 2015.

figure of the critical gaze of the Irish theatre on its nation.[18] This mirrored set also invokes the original production of *Cabaret* (1966), which created a similar mimetic effect (the onstage representation of the "real world') for its audience. The large mirror in *Cabaret*'s case demanded that the audience feel a part of the cabaret but also reflect on the play's dark topic, the relationship between entertainment and politics: specifically, the Nazi's rise to power in 1931 Berlin—during which the play was set. In this sense *Once* not only invokes the themes and theories of Ireland's past but also reflects the global community present in Ireland as a result of high levels of immigration due to the European Union's enlargement in 2004 through 2007 (Ruhs and Quinn).

Once considers its audience as an integral part of its *mise-en-scène* and thus places it within the narrative. Millie Taylor's essay on *The Rocky Horror Show* states that its "audiences clearly feel an emotional connection and are drawn into an interaction" (Taylor 59). Taylor sees this quality as one of the reasons why audiences "respond to musicals" (Taylor 59). For *Once,* members are singing, drinking, and seeing themselves onstage, alongside, and across the table from the cast. In many ways this technique mimics the encouraged participation of the audience in *The Rocky Horror Show* and also taps into the inclusiveness of the Irish music tradition that invites the community to come together and share—often in a public house—the celebration of song. The invitation to drink on stage and the mirrored backdrop of the stage creates a participatory atmosphere where the audience takes centre-stage alongside the two young protagonists.

The plot of *Once* is not complex nor is it centred in the notorious Walsh aesthetic of dark disillusionment and dysfunction, but rather takes its cue from the 2006 film, which relies on the optimism of a young Czech woman and the desperation of a young Irish man. Walsh's process began in October of 2010 when John Tiffany approached him regarding this stage adaptation. Over two days in London, Walsh, Tiffany, and Lowe, "sat in that room in London with two very good actors and read John Carney's screenplay and sang Glen and Marketa's songs" (Walsh). Although some spectators will have knowledge of the film and thus bring their own experiences to the musical, this chapter does not intend to conduct a comparative analysis of both the play and the film but rather considers *Once* and its theatrical impulses as its own

---

[18] I refer here to Christopher Murray, *Twentieth-Century Irish Drama: Mirror Up to Nation*. Syracuse: Syracuse UP, 2000. Print.

work with its own performance history. Walsh himself declared that, "the story of *Once* existed in movie form but needed its own stage style and also its own specific stage language and pace." While Carney's indie film met success in spite of its modest budget, Walsh said that "Our sensibilities were always to retain the heart of the piece, but you know, it needs a language and it needs a more sort of physical narrative" (Lunden). He continues, "Because if you were to place [the film] onstage it would just evaporate. We know that, as theatre-makers" (Lunden).

After the cast improvises a series of traditional Irish ballads such as, "Raglan Road" and "Red Haired Mary", the lights dim and lead character Guy sings "Leave" (the musical maintains the songs written for the film by Glen Hansard and Marketa Irglová). This song laments the fractured relationship of "Guy" and his newly emigrated "Ex-girlfriend'—a character that appears as part of the chorus onstage and is named for how she stands in relation to Guy. As Guy demands we "Leave", "Girl" who is a newly welcomed Czech émigré, ironically arrives. Walsh then instructs:

> *He's finished. He quietly takes the strap off the guitar and slowly lowers the guitar to the ground. He turns to leave the stage. Then from the shadows:* **GIRL**. That song you play—is it yours? (Walsh, Hansard, and Irglová 9)

The audience is immediately thrust into the intimate conversation between two strangers; we meet them as they meet each other. As Guy ends his song, Girl simultaneously appears as an apparition reminiscent of an 18th-century *aisling* and thus, the narrative of *Once* begins.

The *aisling* or dream vision poem relied on the promise of a beautiful woman who appeared in dream-like fashion to the male Irish poet who was busy contemplating Ireland's oppressive state awaiting redemption. "He", in a state somewhere between sleep and waking, questions her form and asks if she is a woman from the epic tradition such as Deirdre or Helen of Troy. "She" then laments the current state of the Irish people and then predicts the future reversal of their misfortune. This poetic form developed out of an earlier, non-political genre—the French *reverdie*—in which the poet meets a beautiful, otherworldly woman who represents the spring season, the bounty of nature, and love. Built in part on the great tradition of 18th-century Irish poetry, the rhetoric of the Irish Nationalist movement was forged on the figure of woman (appearing as either mother, maiden or crone) as the symbol of hope and inspiration to the predominately-masculine hegemony of Irish liberation. The pre-eminent theatrical rendering of this dream-woman appeared in 1902 with Augusta Gregory's and W. B. Yeats's *Cathleen ní Houlihan*. In this play Cathleen ní Houlihan first appears as an old woman who, through conspicuously nationalist metaphor, inspires the young men of Ireland to sacrifice their lives for "her" who thus represents an independent and autonomous Irish state. After she succeeds, she is transformed to a young woman with "the walk of a Queen" (Yeats and Gregory 9). This lyrical poetry is still also hugely popular in the repertoire of Irish folk singing (Ó Ceaurúill). It is no wonder then that "She" once again appears at the end of a song on Walsh's stage however, this time, she is not of Irish blood but that of the new population of women in Ireland, the Czech young mother.

Girl may not be concerned with national endeavours but certainly laments the melancholy music of her new "friend" Guy, she says, "Let's go? We are in a music shop all alone and you sing very good songs—why are you giving up on your music?" (Walsh, Hansard, and Irglová 11). It is here that Guy and Girl start to sing the widely acclaimed song from both the film and the musical, "Falling Slowly". Guy however, cannot finish the entire song. Guy says, "There's no point to it anymore. It's got me nowhere" (11). These few lines encapsulate the drama of the next two hours. *Once* relies on the age-old tale of Guy meets Girl, Guy and Girl fall in love, yet Guy and Girl do not live happily ever after, at least not together. And, in this way, *Once* shares the unsettling aftertaste of the majority of Enda Walsh's repertoire. In almost tragic Greek fashion, his characters know what happiness means for them however, achieving it may be a self-imposed impossibility. Here Walsh demonstrates a resistance to the Broadway musical form that demands the classic comic "hetero-normative" ending of marriage and "happily ever after" (Wolf 353). Stacy Wolf concludes that most musicals, specifically those integrated musicals which take their cue from those of the 1940s and 1950s, include "Two principals, one male and one female [who are] introduced early in the show by solos that convey through music how they are opposites who will eventually unite" (353). While Girl is not forced into the marriage rite with protagonist Guy (as the normative musical theatre formula would demand) she is left to reconcile a broken relationship with a never-seen estranged husband. This is an unusual precedent for the musical theatre stage, which is often dismissed because of its conservative policing of gender roles: male as hero, female as damsel-in-distress. While Walsh at times subscribes to the behaviours prescribed for female protagonists, Girl as hero to Guy yet (reluctantly) dismissive of his attempts at a romantic relationship, challenges such demands.

While the drama primarily involves Guy (by day a vacuum repairman) and Girl, the scenes between these two are observed, interrupted, and commented upon (via music) by an Ancient Grecian inspired chorus that literally surrounds them, sitting against the walls of the stage throughout most of the performance. Charles McNulty of the *LA Times* says:

> There's nothing artificial about this convention here because music is woven into the fabric of the characters' lives. It's both their communal bond and their private outlet for feelings that lie too deep to share over a pint. (McNulty)

The Chorus rarely ever *exeunt* and more than that, they are the orchestra, the community, and the public house patrons. Because of the mirror device the audience too can be seen as part of this chorus. The audience is ever present and its reactions are also always informing the production. The songs the actors create as characters form the play's *libretto*. This "knowing" and these deliberate vocal expressions help to create a bond not only between the musical's characters but also creates empathy and connection with the musical's audience. The audience then doubles as this extended chorus as we are encouraged to watch, react, drink with, and sing with, these characters. Millie Taylor's article that discusses the mimetic and empathetic effect of *The Rocky Horror Show* states, "Empathy involves emotional identification with the characters in the story and in the plot" (Taylor 63). Taylor here cites Klaus R. Scherer's and Marcel R. Zentner's study on music and empathy:

> [and] even if we are not directly affected by the consequences of the event [...] we may evaluate the injustice or unreasonableness in exactly the same fashion as the person that is directly concerned and react equally with anger or irritation. (qtd. in Taylor, 63)

Taylor suggests that:

> The voice extends the physical presence of the singer and impacts on, and alters, the physical space of the listener. There is a vibratory connection between bodies, a vibration that joins audience and performer in an acoustic and corporeal time and space. (64)

Taylor calls this the "vocal touch" (64). In this way then *Once's* songs are not to be taken for granted as musically melodramatic moments but serve as testament to the integral part music plays in these characters' lives and thus our lives and empathetic relationship to the play's characters and situations. Girl says, "Now how will I pay you? Bach, Bartók, Brahms, Mozart? Something of my own?" (Walsh, Hansard, and Irglová 14-15). Music is the currency in this pub, the only notes these "patrons" have in excess. Girl begins to play Mendelssohn's "Song Without Words".[19] Like Girl, the audience struggles to understand what Guy is thinking and feeling. Soon after they meet Girl asks, "Is it always me who has to start the conversation?" (11).

> **GUY.** (*responds*): Well you seem more up for it than I do.
> **GIRL.** It's not even my language this English.
> **GUY.** You speak it well.
> **GIRL.** I have an accent.
> **GUY.** We all have accents.
> **GIRL.** We are people of the world. (11)

Girl can provide the music but awaits the lyrics that may come as a result of Guy continuing the "conversation".

While Walsh's script improvises on the essential Irish themes and images that were invoked from Irish folklore, Walsh places the immigrant women of the (then) newly opened European Union on familiar territory to that of early 20th-century Irish nationalist iconicity in which women serve as inspirers and catalysts for male action. Walsh says, "Really the key to that was the "Girl" character, who on page one became the driving force, the idiosyncratic swagger of the piece, the person who would change everything" (Walsh).

Suitably and serendipitously, Czech nationalist folklore also looks to a young, beautiful woman for its fortuitous "future". Walsh's story summons the wisdom of the legendary Libuše, the Czech granddaughter of Father Čech, the progenitor of the Czech tribe (Murphy). Libuše became the leader of her people in her father's place and ruled from the castle at Vyšehrad on the Vltava River. Libuše was prone to both prophecy and rumination. She thus became (in)famous for her divination and wise decisions. Girl likewise sees her divine place in Guy's life, she says, "It was my destiny to meet you today—to listen to your beautiful story—to hear of your fabulous fixing" (Walsh, Hansard, and Irglová 11). The fixing she refers to is of her hoover, which, after hearing Guy's song and learning of his day job *"somehow a vacuum cleaner has appeared right beside her"* (11). While this hoover was an

---

[19] Mendelssohn spent some time in Dublin and many of his most popular and admired works were inspired by the rolling landscapes of the (then) British Isles.

integral part of the 2006 film, it plays a smaller role in Walsh's book and perhaps stands as a tribute to both Carney's film and Walsh's more surreal and illusionary work. Similarities are prevalent throughout Czech Nationalist ideals (during the 19th century Czech revival after centuries of Austrian Rule) and those of Ireland at its time of nation-formation. Libuše ultimately yields to the promise of an appointed Duke husband and relinquishes her control of the Prague state. Walsh suggests that *Once's* characters are "transformed by a young woman who seems more "stopped" than they are. She changes lives—but she can't start to change her own" (Walsh). Girl chooses duty and family in Dublin versus love and music in New York. One cannot help but see the dichotomy between the emigrated Irish ex-girlfriend and the newly immigrated Czech "girl" as a theatrical reaction to the state of immigration in Ireland in 2008.

Luke Gibbons insists on "the transformative capacity of culture in Irish society" and "its power to give rise to what was not there before" (Gibbons 8). Gibbons argues that, "Cultural representations do not simply come after the event, "reflecting" experience or embellishing it with aesthetic form, but significantly alter and shape the ways we make sense of our lives" (8). In 2011, making sense of a new economy, making sense of a mass of immigration into and from Ireland, making sense of what Ireland has become culturally, politically, economically, and traditionally was at the core of every conversation. Girl asks Guy:

> **GIRL.** Do you enjoy being Irish?
> **GUY.** Seriously?
> **GIRL.** I'm always serious—I'm Czech. Are you enjoying your life right now?
> **GUY.** Sorry, what?! ... (Walsh, Hansard, and Irglová 11)

Once relies on both the individual and the communal in the sense that there is onstage a merging of cultures through the budding friendship and romance of both Guy and Girl. After a brief practice session at the local music store that is owned by Billy, the proud "Northsider" (13) and friend to Girl, Guy and Girl walk awkwardly to Girl's house:

> **GUY.** Oh look I burnt you some songs! (*He hands her a CD*)
> **GIRL.** Oh great!
> **GUY.** The quality's not all that but ... well if you ever fancy listening to ...
> **GIRL.** I will—I want to.
> **GUY.** Thanks for being interested by the way.
> **GIRL.** Sure.
> (*A long pause. He really doesn't want to say good-bye. Then:*)

Do you want to come in for a cup of tea? (25)

Walsh's stage directions suggest a real-time sense of time and space. We discover as they discover their feelings for one another. They enter Girl's "flat" and "*A new lighting state: the Girl and the Guy enter a whirlwind of a scene ... They speak in English, but Czech is shown on surtitles behind them*" (25). The chorus members are now revealed as Girl's flat-mates. In contrast to Guy's "Da's" house, that they visited earlier, the atmosphere inside Girl's home is boisterous, vibrant, and bawdy as they discuss the latest happenings of the *RTÉ I* soap opera *Fair City*, their "passion" and the free means by which they learn English. Andrej yells, "She's a liar—the woman is evil!" Réza retorts, "You understand nothing! Don't you live in the world?! This is the real world, Andrej!" (26). While we laugh at the irony and melodramatic tone, we are reminded once again of this "real world" that Walsh keeps alluding to as Girl did once before, we are in fact amongst "people of the world". Girl's flat-mates, Andrej, Réza, Baruška (Girl's mother), and Švec—like Billy—are named and by contrast thus emphasize the universal in our protagonists archetypal status as "Girl" and "Guy".

Girl yells: "Speak English!" and the surtitles disappear (26). The conversation about *Fair City* continues with each line of dialogue more spirited than the next. Finally Andrej says: "(*Noticing the Guy*): Who are you?" **Guy:** "No one." Guy reveals his sense of self and realizes his place within this new world. After hearing Guy's accent, Andrej who is dressed in a Tesco uniform, proudly mentions his interview for an area manager position, Réza states she is "looking for an Irish husband", and Švec in "*fierce Dublin accent*" asks Guy, "Fancy a pint in McCoy's later, yeah bud?" "What d'you mean you're pregnant?! Jaysus dats awful news!" "I'm keepin'da baby! I want to keep da baby!" (26-27). He is dressed in a green shiny tracksuit and slim white trainers and clearly takes his lessons from *Fair City* as well. In this mimetically comical moment the personal side of mass immigration is revealed in place of the social-political and statistical.

During this visit Guy meets Ivanka, Girl's daughter. While born in the Czech Republic she will be raised in Ireland. Her father, and Girl's husband, still remains back in the Czech Republic. Guy and Ivanka then "*shake hands and a remarkably robust and energetic*" Baruška shouts, "ZPIVAT!" (26-27). Immediately the flat-mates, including Ivanka, erupt into a Czech folk-song (former lullaby) that was re-written by Hansard and Irglová for the musical (not included in the original film soundtrack) called, "Ej Pada, Pada Rosicka". Walsh's stage directions state, "*Andrej and* Réza *dance on the table throughout. The flat is going wild. The Guy is standing back smiling*" (26-27). Guy witnesses and reacts to this demonstration of Czech pride. While Walsh's work and typically existential aesthetic is often compared to that of Samuel Beckett, this impromptu song and dance channels Brian Friel's *Dancing at Lughnasa* (1990). Friel's non-musical play remembers the story of five sisters and their horrific impoverishment in Ireland's summer of 1936. Fintan O'Toole's response to *Dancing* states that:

> The play's most vibrant moments—the wild dance in the first act— are moments of surrender by the sisters to the force of music, the urge of the dance, a force at once joyous and tyrannical, a dance of grief and liberation. (O'Toole 214)

While these "vibrant moments" are characteristic of most musicals with Walsh's "dance" we witness an integral exchange of culture and ideals, the established currency of *Once* and an assertion of this Czech family's own authoritative space within the newly multi-national Ireland. While at times *Once's* form subscribes to that of an integrated musical its tone is reminiscent of Friel's *Dancing*—the music, songs and dances are diegetic reactions to the emotional, political, and social contemplations and frustrations of the play's characters.

In Stacy Ellen Wolf's article "In Defense of Pleasure" she argues for the legitimacy of musical theatre discourse and its place within theatre history, scholarship, and pedagogy. She states,

> Conductor and musical theatre scholar Lehman Engel noted that in a musical, a three-minute song equals what, in a non-musical play, would be fifteen minutes of dialogue. This exceedingly condensed form of communication, from the point of view of the character, allows her to express herself and often takes her to a new place by the end of the song. (qtd. in Wolf 53)

With this potency in mind, while Walsh did not write the songs his characters "did". In that sense he must consider it as part of his narrative, as part of the story he wishes to tell. These songs then must speak to him as they speak to those singing them.

Throughout, Walsh negotiates the universal and the individual, the macro and the micro. After Guy leaves, Girl says to her mother (Baruška):

> **GIRL.** His life's stopped. But he has a good heart.
> **BARUŠKA.** And you? (*slight pause*) You're not stopped, too? (A pause.) Your man—he left you here ... (slight pause)—now you can start over.
> **GIRL.** Don't say that—

BARUŠKA. It's true.
GIRL. It's not a simple thing, Mama!
BARUŠKA. I know ... (Walsh, Hansard, and Irglová 30)

Girl and her daughter go to bed and Girl sings "If You Want Me"

I can't tell dreams from truth
For it's been so long since I have seen you
I can hardly remember your face anymore ... (31)

As Girl's song ends Guy's song immediately begins, entitled "Broken-Hearted Hoover Fixer Sucker Guy." Our protagonists are finally separate and alone for the first time and these songs sung juxtaposed reveal their synonymy in spite of their distance. These sung moments also serve as soliloquies during which we get to learn more about Guy and Girl as they reveal their emotional vulnerabilities. Girl longs for her estranged husband while Guy laments his unfaithful and recently emigrated ex-girlfriend. Taylor suggests that moments like these, "allow the audience to identify more strongly with them for several reasons. More time is spent with this character alone, so more identification is possible" (Taylor 65). The audience then is privy to the deeper thoughts and emotions of these characters—the song and lyrics that are too powerful and revealing to sing to one another.

In her article, "Integration and Distance in Musical Theatre: the Case of *Sweeney Todd*" Millie Taylor argues that the term "'integration" and the concept of "the integrated musical" are generally taken to imply that songs, dances and narrative work towards the same dramatic end (Taylor 75). When song is not enough for Girl to reveal her deepest emotional impulses, she turns to spoken language—that of Girl's native Czech. Guy asks: "So what's the Czech for, "Do you still love him?" Guy is referring to Girl's husband. Girl responds, "Ty ho este miluješ?" Then Guy, "So ... Ty ho este miluješ?" The stage directions read *"A pause. In Czech she answers:"* "Miluji těbe." The audience reads the surtitles in English this time. Girl said, "I love you". This moment is reminiscent of Friel's *Translations* when Maire and Yolland express their love for each other—she (as implied) in "Irish" and he in English—yet in spite of that they understand one another. In her own language Girl is able to reveal to Guy just how she feels. In English, she covers, deflects and remains prisoner to her absentee husband. Walsh in his article discussing *Once* that he wrote for Broadway.com says,

> I am a slave to all story, whether dark or light, and my instincts were pulling me towards this delicate love story, which I felt would really lighten my soul—would somehow reaffirm for me the

potential of the individual to do some good.

Girl encourages Guy to conquer his sadness and ultimately his fear. Her manner is direct and absent of hyperbole:

> So we are going to make a demonstration tape of these songs—me and you—with good musicians—and we send this tape around the world and a fat man with a fat cigar will pick you up for his record company and you will go to New York and you make something of yourself, ok?!" (Walsh, Hansard, and Irglová 33).

Guy has no choice but to reply, "Ok ... ". With that Girl insists that Guy wears a suit that she gives him (Andrej's "lucky interview suit") and they head to the Bank Manager (as he's called throughout) to ask for the 2,000 euro they need to make the album. Guy asks Girl where she gets her energy from and she replies, "I'm a young mother. We are a special breed" (33). Girl is *aisling*, maiden, and mother.

As they leave for the bank Walsh finds an opportunity to tell a story, a meta-narrative, colorfully spoken in Czech (although actually in English) with surtitles for the Czech. This story speaks to Guy's fears and perhaps a universally shared fear. The story begins "Once upon a time there was a little man who lived in a little house in a little city and he had a little job in a little office" (34). This little man goes on to dream of a wonderful life full of adventures but when he finds the courage to leave his little house he saw the world as a place to "torture and crush him! Love was there to tease him and break him!" (34). This man then takes off his new clothes and returns to his bed never to dream of anything again." (34). Baruška's moral of the story (said to Guy) is "Those who live in fear ... die miserably in their graves" (34). Guy "*shocked to his core*" asks Girl, "So what did she say?" Girl responds, "Good luck" (34-5). Walsh begins his story with the clichéd "Once upon a time ..." indeed improvising on the musical's title and thus offering us a story within a story, recognizing both in form and function how this piece of theatre serves as a story for anyone who has ever "dared".

Girl's self-assurance and faith in Guy's talents inspires even the nameless Bank Manager to realize his dreams. Bank Manager, described as "*a prim man from County Cork*" at first reveals his reluctance as Guy starts the conversation saying he only holds an account with the Post Office as his "da says postmen are a lot more honest than bank managers" (35). Walsh is of course alluding to the contemporaneously tenuous relationship between the individual and the Banks. Girl sensing this conversation is going in the wrong direction asks the Bank Manager, "Are you proud to be Irish?" (35). The Bank

Manager evades this question at first but when provoked answers he's proud of "Our Culture" (36). Girl takes this opportunity to prophesy. She says:

> And yet on this little rock in the middle of the ocean you make men and women who for centuries can speak and sing of what it is to be a person. Yeats, Swift, Wilde, Beckett, Joyce, Van Morrison, Enya, the fantastic people who gave the world Riverdance! But it is people like you! People who invest in Irish culture who also make the culture, sir! You are responsible for showing the world that Ireland is still here! Ireland is open for business! (36)

Girl here is eerily redolent of Libuše whose visions rendered

> a large city, whose glories shall reach the heavens! I see a spot above the river, where the brook Brušnice makes a bend. ... There you will build a castle and call it Praha. ... It will be a noble one, respected by all the world.[20] (Murphy)

As Libuše stood as progenitor of a great Czech Republic, Girl envisions a great cultural renaissance in Ireland with Guy and his music at the heart of it. Bank Manager reluctantly listens to Guy's song "Say It To Me Now" and in return sings his own song, "Abandoned in Bandon," the lyrics of which tell the story of the broken heart and dreams of a young boy who only wishes to get to County Clare. The Bank Manager seeks to revise his story as well and here Walsh offers another glimpse into his lightened heart with this Bank Manager turned symbol of a financial and cultural revision for Ireland. Ultimately Bank Manager is inspired to loan them 2,000 euro. He also joins the band of merry rebels comprised of Billy, the music shop owner, Andrej, Švec, and of course Guy and Girl. Here we return to the Irish tradition of music and story telling which, a hundred years ago inspired a grass roots rebellion of national proportions. Billy is at first skeptical of the Cork-born Bank Manager both because of his roots and because he represents the "very people who are threatening to steal these premises offa me if I don't start making sales" however, he concedes for the sake of "this musical odyssey" (Walsh, Hansard, and Irglová 43-4). Together these mismatched musical rebels—comprised of both Irish and Czech—unite not against the colonial yoke but rather for the state of "chassis'[21] that

---

[20] *Praha* is Czech for "threshold". For more on Libuše and Czech nationalism see Jirasek, Alois, and Marie K. Holecek.; *Old Czech Legends*. London: Forest, 1992. Print.

[21] This refers to the final line of Sean O'Casey's *Juno and the Paycock* 1924). Captain Boyle: "Th" whole worl's in a terrible state o" chassis."

the Irish government and banks have left its people living in and the failed promise of an EU dream come true. This theme also penetrates Walsh's *Penelope* (2010) in which his stage hosts this doomed scenario regarding Ireland's bankers and misguided capitalists. This time however, through the metaphorically opportunist efforts of four men eager to woo Penelope in the absence of her husband who is away at war.

Emigration has been declared as "one of the most traumatic elements of the Irish collapse" (Carter). According to Alan Barrett, of the Economic Social and Research Institute:

> For all the years from independence to the Celtic Tiger of the 1990s, people born in Ireland could never assume that they would work in Ireland. That changed with the Celtic Tiger, but has now reversed again. (qtd. in Carter)

Guy does leave for New York. It seems the only answer for a promising future in music. Girl stays in Dublin, and hopes to make her story a part of the newly global Ireland. Her husband has called and said he wants to work things out and that he is coming to live with her. Guy protests:

> You've turned love around for me and you've done it in five days. And yeah I wrote these songs at another time for another girl, but when I sing it's for us, I think—it's you I see in the songs ... (Walsh, Hansard, and Irglová 58)

Girl refuses to hear this because it "can't be about that!" (58). Guy realizes the integral part Girl has played in "finishing his songs" and unstopping his life. Girl helps Guy realize his dreams; however, she chooses duty to her family and refuses her own self-confessed love. Guy had no lyrics and no story before Girl. She inspired him to realize his dreams yet she will stay behind to try and finish her own story.

Guy does leave with his demo CD and with this heart "travelling" (58). After some time in New York and "in a new lighting scheme" Billy and Andrej deliver Girl her beloved piano that she could only practice on as it stood unaffordable in Billy's shop. This is a gift from Guy and the musical ends with both Girl and Guy singing "Falling Slowly". This time Guy is able to finish the song with his dreams realized. While the universal is prevalent in our principle characters' names, and the traditional tropes of Irish theatre and iconicity inform the onstage representations, there is something much more personal and empathetic at *Once's* core which privileges the potential within the individual—the power of the individual to "do some good" (Walsh). In a final moment, Andrej and Švec remark about Dublin's beauty. Andrej says "million times heartbroken and Dublin keeps on going. You've got to love Dublin for dreaming" (60). While Walsh's theatre often suggests that we live solitary lives, at times hermetic lives, *Once* asks how we recreate a community that is full of disparate peoples in an increasingly dystopic time. In this sense then the distance between this musical's narrative and the narratives of our own "Once upon a time" is proximate.

Works Cited

Blood, Melanie. "Musical Theatre Part I." *Musical1.html*. SUNY Geneseo, n.d. Web. 24 Apr. 2015.

Carter, Helen. "Celtic Tiger at Bay: A New Generation of Migrants Crosses Irish Sea." *The Guardian*. The Guardian, 8 Mar. 2012. Web. 5 Mar. 2015.

Ó Cearúill, Pádraig. "Eoghán Rua Ó Suilleabháin: A True Exponent of the Bardic Legacy." *Barra Ó Donnabháin Symposium 2007*. Glucksman Ireland House NYU, 2007. Web. 31 Mar. 2015.

"Celtic Tiger at Bay: A New Generation of Migrants Crosses Irish Sea." N.p., n.d. Web.

Gibbons, Luke. *Transformations in Irish Culture*. Notre Dame, IN: U of Notre Dame, in Association with Field Day, 1996. Print.

Lunden, Jeff. "'Once' And Again: A Love Story Gets A Second Life." *NPR*. NPR, 6 Dec. 2011. Web. 22 Jan. 2015.

McNulty, Charles. "Simplicity Supplies Emotional Eloquence to Pub Musical "Once'" *Los Angeles Times*. Los Angeles Times, 18 July 2014. Web. 22 Jan. 2015.

O'Toole, Fintan. "Marking Time: From Making History to Dancing at Lughnasa." *The Achievement of Brian Friel*. Ed. Anthony J. Peacock. Gerrards Cross: Colin Smythe, 1993. 202-14. Print.

Ruhs, Martin, and Emma Quinn. "Ireland: From Rapid Immigration to Recession." *Migrationpolicy.org*. N.p., 01 Sept. 2009. Web. 24 Apr. 2015.

Taylor, Millie. "?Don't Dream It, Be It?: Exploring Signification, Empathy and Mimesis in Relation to." *Studies in Musical Theatre* 1.1 (2006): 57-71. Web.

Taylor, Millie. "Integration and Distance in Musical Theatre: The Case of." *Contemporary Theatre Review* 19.1 (2009): 74-86. Web.

Walsh, Enda.
"Tony Nominee Enda Walsh on How Writing Once Lightened His Soul." *Broadway.com*. N.p., 22 May 2012. Web. 22 Jan. 2015.

Wolf, S. ""WE'LL ALWAYS BE BOSOM BUDDIES": Female Duets and the Queering of Broadway Musical Theater." *GLQ: A Journal of Lesbian and Gay Studies* 12.3 (2006): 351-76. Web.

Wolf, Stacy Ellen. "In Defense of Pleasure: Musical Theatre History in the Liberal Arts [A Manifesto]." *Theatre Topics* 17.1 (2007): 51-60. Web.

Yeats, William Butler, and Augusta Gregory. "Cathleen Ni Houlihan."
    (1903): 9. *Aughty.org*. Web. 24 Apr. 2015.

13 | *Ballyturk:* Theatre and Event

Michelle C. Paull

Stephen Rea points out, "I think it will be an evening of pure theatre, it won't be *about* something, and it will *be* something" (Rea 2014). Enda Walsh's *Ballyturk* rages through huge human emotions of love, identity, and death but his audience would be forgiven for not realizing it was "about" any of these topics. Though we are taken into an intensely sombre and reflective examination of all these topics, such is the level of playful comedy, inflected by the theatrical style of Jacques Lecoq (with whom Mikel Murfi trained) and Phillipe Gaulier[22], that the audience is led through a joyous encounter with these subjects, rather than left to consider them at the level of language and intellect typical of the stage. The play is a theatrical spectacle, almost a circus event, featuring intense narrative interludes. Walsh himself felt that the play would strike the audience "kinetically ... People will be going "What is that?" and trying to decipher it" (Walsh). Walsh's use of "kinetically" is revealing, since the play is comprised of energising moments of action and events, which affect the audience as much at the level of their body as their mind. *Ballyturk* is a complex theatrical entertainment, an imaginative space for the audience to wonder at, ponder upon and marvel in, but also offers a dramatic staging of profound philosophical human questions accessed through comic theatrical techniques laced with mordant humour. The play is also structured like a musical composition, developing to moments of sheer theatrical intensity and

---

[22] Jacques Lecoq and Phillipe Gaulier are both European physical theatre practitioners whose approach to performance includes clowning and physical comedy and communication through the body. Mikel Murfi trained as a performer at the Lecoq Theatre School in Paris.

emotional engagement, then quietening to a peaceful reflective mood, as well as in its own use of music as a kind of aural counterpoint to the action throughout.

British and Irish critics of the play seem at a loss to know how to discuss the play. Both at the Galway premiere in July 2014, and after the London opening at the National Theatre in September 2014, there was a critical struggle to define the parameters of the play, or to explain its energy and vibrancy—other than as a theatrical tour de force. Described as "deliciously strange" or even "pickled in its own absurdity" (Hitchins 2014), the play eluded its descriptors, who, despite the strangeness of much of Walsh's previous work, including *The New Electric Ballroom* and *The Walworth Farce*, still seem surprised by *Ballyturk's* rejection of naturalist representation. Michael Billington, reviewing the play at its Galway premiere, noted in *The Guardian* for example, "I was less struck by the play's philosophy than by its sheer physical and verbal exuberance ... imagine *Under Milkwood* interpreted by Buster Keaton and you get the picture" (Billington 2014). In *The Irish Times*, Fintan O'Toole creates his own imaginative moment of strangeness, as he conjures a combination of literary and philosophical figures who could potentially have been involved in the play's creation, to give a sense of its overtly literary and theatrical context:

> So Jean-Paul Sartre, Samuel Beckett and Flann O'Brien are jointly commissioned to write a sketch for The Morecambe & Wise Show.[23] Over a bottle of absinthe they concoct something like Enda Walsh's Ballyturk. (O'Toole, 2014)

O'Toole neatly identifies the genres which the play alludes to—philosophy, existentialism and the fictionally surreal—but the result in Walsh is not simply comically entertaining as in the vein of Morecambe & Wise; the form is an intrinsic part of the examination of the existential and philosophical principles in the play. Walsh uses each strand as a means to offer the audience an encounter with the theme via different sensory means. To watch a Walsh play requires an engagement of the body and the mind and the sheer physical skill of the actors will create a sense of watching the thrill of the piece.

---

[23] The Morecambe and Wise Show was a British tv comedy show of the 1980s, featuring two middle-aged men who formed a straight-man and his hapless friend in a series of sketches and domestic and tv show settings.

Walsh himself sees the origin of the play in a question about dying, raised by his six year old daughter, when she marvelled that everyone living carries on their existence with the knowledge that they are dying. In an interview with Benedict Nightingale, Walsh commented that he began to think about the point at which we realize our own inevitable demise and saw it as a moment marking the end of innocence, when we recognize that we cannot live forever and are mortally doomed (Nightingale 2014). Throughout the play this sense of the inevitability of death lurks in the background and the play is about "two childish characters who are ultimately confronted with an end of innocence" (O'Riordan 2014).

The play's plot is straightforward—very little actually happens. This is not a play about events but about stories. Two men are living in a sparsely furnished room, without any windows or visible signs of escape and are visited by a third man who tells them one of them has to make the decision to come with him to meet their "death"—or as Matt Wolf says "to join him in whatever world lies beyond the hermetically sealed space ... " (Wolf 2014). The play is set in no recognizable place, though the musical soundtrack, which counterpoints the action throughout, is made up of 1980s British pop tunes, so a sense of recent modernity is suggested.

The opening of the play will be familiar to those who have seen Walsh's *The Walworth Farce*, the play with which this piece has most in common from Walsh's previous works and Walsh seems to be carrying over Dinny's question from that play "For what are we without our stories?" (Walsh, 2008) into a new context. The play opens in darkness, music plays—the 1980s pop tracks intercut the action throughout the play, sometimes ironic, sometimes mad-cap, sometimes solemn, but always offering a melodic commentary on the action. The first scene is the most terrifying for an actor—alone in the middle of the stage, spotlighted by one harsh white spotlight beaming harsh bright light in the most Brechtian manner. This is Cillian Murphy as "1" wearing a 1970s tank top and a red hurling helmet. We hear him speaking *in medias res* as if we have shone a light on him in the middle of a speech in performance—which of course we have. He looks vulnerable and scared, the tone of his monologue is pleading and anxious—it seems he is uncomfortable about being on stage. There is a strong meta-theatrical dynamic in the early stages of the play; music plays, the actors self-consciously begin to dress and make-up for their parts, we are clearly being given a well-rehearsed experience. Character 2 is later seen filing through a collection of old 45s, covered only in their white sleeves as if the decorated artistic cardboard cover would only be a distraction to the main tasks of getting to the music. The audience thus sees 2 selecting the soundtrack of the production and this sight of 2 sorting through the records suggests he knows what he is looking for, as if he might have put on this production before.

There are no windows in the room but the stage directions stress that from the visual image of the inside, *"There is something unquestionably rural about this dwelling"* (Walsh 5). The room revealed as all the lights come on is a sparsely furnished 1970s space with basic cupboards and all the furniture deliberately pushed to the sides of the room. A cuckoo clock fixed to the wall on the left, a series of images of indefinable faces, animal and map shapes drawn in black chalk on the grey concrete wall at the back of the stage as if the back wall is a vast whiteboard. A chair and table are placed down right of the stage and a fold-up bed just behind this, which comically folds into the wall at discrete moments in the play. There are red balloons on the floor, as if left over from, or preparing for, a party. The environment is like that of a more inviting Beckettian landscape, though there are no visible windows or doors and this could easily be *Endgame* with the two men hermetically sealed inside the room.

The meta-theatrical nature of the piece continues throughout and as an audience we are reminded that we are witnesses to the process of storytelling. The tales we will hear might make little sense, since we have no concept of where Ballyturk is as a place to give the story a context. As a result we are constantly forced to engage with the question of identity—even the character who is talking to us on stage remains unnamed, a number only in the script, giving us no clue as to his origin, background or personality. We also wonder who it is that 1 is addressing, who, or where, is the on-stage audience for this story; why we are hearing a fragment of the story of "him" (Walsh 5) and the account of another man's memory of a visit to a woman called "Marie Reynolds", and why the figure of "Larry Aspen" is carrying a knife.

The sense of Brechtian distance is maintained through the manner of the storytelling in the play—the memory of another woman is told through the memory of 1 as the storyteller on stage. The status of the story is paramount—who are these people we are hearing about and what is their relationship to the speaker? It is only as the word "nothing" is uttered that the audience ironically hears something from the dark space surrounding the speaker, the comically banal noise of crisps being eaten, which alerts us to the fact that the speaker has his own audience. The whole stage lights up to reveal No 2 "a man in his mid –forties" (Mikel Murfi) in the room with 1, who is possibly listening to the story—but may not be. No 1's story is not explained or commented upon as a story in its own right, 2 simply stands next to 1 and folds up his crisp packet—as the character of 2 is in the process of getting dressed when we see him. He is covered from head to toe in white talcum powder and wearing only underpants and socks and he appears to be preparing for a performance. As in *The Walworth Farce*, the audience knows that they are about to be treated to a performance— but of what, and for what reason, remains unclear.

The first exchange between the men addresses their performative roles in an openly self-conscious way. A simultaneous sense of emotional detachment is created for the audience watching these "performers" rehearse or present a well-worn scenario. 2 immediately characterizes that the start of his performance was a failure—the sound of the crisp eating that we heard should clearly not have happened and there is a feeling that something was not quite right with the men's agreed routine:

> **2.** I probably should have dressed
> **1.** (*cold*) I don't think that would have helped.
> **2.** It caught me off-guard.
> **1.** It happens sometimes.
> 1 looks down at the knife he is holding. (Walsh 6-7)

The characters could be alluding to the representational nature of their appearance on stage. This potential awareness of their own role-play works to complicate their innocence about their own situation later in the play, when they appear to be surprised by the turn of the plot.

This sense of a previously rehearsed narrative being played out, and not as successfully at this "performance", because of 2's tardy lack of preparedness, is underlined by 1's gesture as he walks away with the knife in his hand, "*inexplicably*" (Walsh 7) the stage directions tell us, hopping twice like a rabbit and miming stabbing someone before throwing the knife back in the drawer in fright.

The significance of these actions and their suggestion of a previously performed existence on stage is proleptic. The logical connection between the characters' gestures is not evident until after an extensive interlude of comic physical theatre virtuosity—of which this hopping rabbit imitation seems to be a part. Instead, the audience perceives Cillian Murphy's hopping as a piece of comic business in its own right, which at that moment does not make sense except as part of the comic turn of the piece and only later will recognize it as a disturbing link between repeated events in the wider narrative of the play.

A madcap series of episodes follow where 1 sees and captures a fly, which has been buzzing around in the room, and hides it in the cuckoo clock on the left hand wall of the stage without showing it to 2. No 1 now comically has a secret from 2—who is busy sorting through his record collection and doesn't notice 1's capture of the fly. 1 seems to feel guilty, but also a little gleeful about his secret horde. Again this visual moment is highly comic, but the scene is also proleptic and poignant, as it marks the first metaphorical connection between 1 and the theme of death in the play. The fly is suggestive of decay and is linked to death, since it is usually the first visitor to the human body after death. While this comic episode is thus visually engaging, it also allows a suggestive aura of death to hover over the action. Conversely the fly links the room we see on stage with the world beyond the stage wall, like a poetic symbol it means more than one thing. The fly also functions to suggest life outside the room—it must have come from somewhere, yet there are no windows or doors visible in the room.

This kind of symbolic suggestiveness in the play allows the audience to read the play poetically and to link together the symbols and metaphors as a means of creating connections between disparate moments where the themes are individually played out. 1 secretly hiding the fly in the cuckoo clock creates several comic moments between him and 2, when he tries to prevent No 2 opening the clock and thus releasing the fly. These moments of comic business work well within themselves to entertain the audience. But, the fly also works to provide a unifying symbol between 1 and 3 later in the play, since it links the theme of death between them and draws together their stage stories. 3 finds the fly stamped flat on the floor after it has eventually been released by 2, who had killed it, bends down and picks up the fly and is able to "resurrect" it—the audience hears the buzzing of the insect after 3 lifts the corpse from the floor. The sense of the mystical and the inexplicable surrounding 3 is thus pointed through the fly. The insect is a means of linking the themes of the real and the unreal, life and death, while also uniting the men with their looming nemesis—3. The resurrection of the fly further allows 3 a natural transition into his verbal pondering on the nature of life and death, drawing together the sense of a physical body and a cerebral reflection on the human awareness of death as a counterpoint to the comic episodes.

A Chaplinesque slapstick routine is played out to lead up to this reflective moment. To the accompaniment of ABC's "The Look of Love", the men present a frenetic and farcical "getting dressed" routine, with each going to get clothes and shoes from separate wardrobes. 1 is faced with a tumble of *"dozens of shoes"* (Walsh 9) falling out on top of him, while 2 tries on *"a succession of jumpers and cardigans very fast"* (Walsh 9), finally deciding upon a *"Brand new"* yellow jumper, still in its cellophane wrapper. The pair proceed to a fast-paced "breakfast" routine, running to and fro from the kitchen with bowls, milk and "Variety" cereal packets, *"eating each other's cereals every other mouthful"* (Walsh 9). After breakfast 2 removes 1's clothes and gets him to take a *"woefully weak"* (Walsh 9) shower in their rudimentary conditions. 2 simultaneously carries out an exercise routine and practices his golf swing, before 1 emerges from the shower sporting a Star Wars beach towel, to be covered in talcum powder being fired at him from washing-up bottles by 2. Such dynamic comic encounters can be enjoyed visually for their skilful virtuosity, but they also enact at a furious pace our attempts to fill the hours of the day with endless activity. In much the same way that Beckett would fill the performance with verbal exchanges, Walsh's characters fill their stage time with active routines. Their flight into action presents us with a sense of humanity as the busy fool, constantly having to "do" in order to prove that we can "be".

The pace and intensity of the life the men live is depicted throughout the first section of the play, where the performers continue an impressive series of physically challenging "acts" of jumping against walls, dancing together and telling the stories of the men and women whom we presume are from Ballyturk. The sense of strangeness and alienation is clear—we listen to 1 and 2 telling us stories about the people, but we simply don't know the status or veracity of these narratives. They are not presented to the audience in comfortable or reflective manner; instead 1 is often pressed back into the harsh spotlight to orate the stories at a frantic pace with 2 behind him, apparently forcing him to carry on with telling the tales –which often seems against his will. The sheer difficulty of telling the story of a life is enacted here, the complexity and struggle to represent the story correctly, or to give an accurate account of who we are or who we know is painful, partial and random. And it is here that the significance of 1 earlier comic bunny-hops functions as a metaphorical link is made between the telling of stories, the men in the room and the topic of death through the comic notion of rabbit sibling murder. 1 carries on his story:

> **1.** Our bunny—the creamy-white one- hopped across the road
> —the busy road—
> **2.** Already foreboding.

1. I know, right!
2. Was he struck by a car!?
1. He wasn't no.
2. Was it a truck?
1. No
2. Was he very nearly struck by a vehicle?
1. No he wasn't at all. He made it unharmed to the other side of the road—whereupon his brother pulled a knife on him and pushed it into his head. Out of nowhere, no reasoning at all, no history.
2. Well that's family for ya. (Walsh 12)

The sense of random violence, the inexplicable nature of existence, the surreal situation of the rabbits discussed as if they were human beings, conjures a world which is difficult to make sense of with reason and logic. Instead the audience accrues a series of atmospheres and emotional uncertainties, which give a clear sense of the fragility and the random nature of existence through such humorous yet bleak tales of incipient danger and betrayal.

Walsh's drama instead fills human silence with sounds and activity. *Ballyturk* enacts existence lived at a manic pace, packed with mundane activities, carried out at a furious rate. Both 1 and 2 populate their day with an intensity of energy, drive and activity. The play suggests that we push away thoughts of mortality and the banality of our human existence by packing every second full of activity, which functions to numb the mind. When 1 and 2 consume their food at a break-neck pace, choose their clothes from the plethora of options from the wardrobe spilling its contents on to the floor or pick their breakfasts from the Variety pack of cereals, the excess of selective opportunities is demonstrated. Such maximum choice creates an excess of options, overloads the senses, exhausts thought processes and is suggestive of all the excess of contemporary capitalism epitomized by the over-abundance of choice in our Internet age. *Ballyturk* suggests human feeling is numbed and quashed by surfeit not by absence as in a Beckett play. In *Ballyturk*, "the feverish dialogue, the breakneck pacing, the menacing and turbulent atmospheres" (Wallenberg 22) are all part of the evocation of the human spirit on its path to inevitable destruction: in Walsh's work intensity activity is seen to offer spurious protection and security delivering humanity from having to acknowledge the inevitable fact of its own demise. As Mikel Murfi says "The people in his [Walsh's] plays are always that heightened version of what we recognize as ourselves" (Wallenberg 22). In a comment that might as easily be about Pinter's plays as those of Walsh, the playwright says "My characters talk and talk and talk .... But it's not what they're talking about that matters. It's what they avoid talking about. That's where the real drama is" (Wallenberg 24). Both 1 and 2 talk in surfeit. Beckett's characters struggle to fill the time, but Walsh's characters instead are struggling to have time to fit everything in, constantly battling against all there is to do and say.

For what Walsh himself has talked about is "the complete ... inability for these words to, actually, really mean the big stuff." (Wallenberg 24) Instead of words, his plays emerge from "an image and the atmosphere surrounding it". Words cannot accomplish complete expression of the issues raised; we still need something other than dialogue and discussion. It is as if Walsh feels that the audience needs a visceral experience of concepts we are too adept at eliding in language, and the play is an attempt to allow a sensation of something, a feeling of life, an intimation of death, the fleeting nature of existence, none of which can be defined, but can nevertheless be felt. It is this rejection of the domination of the word that is at the core of Walsh's theatre. *Ballyturk* conveys emotion, anxiety and tension about something—even if is not always clear what that "thing" is specifically. The vibrant and visceral theatricality of the play is what creates the reflective and quiet consideration in the mind of the audience afterwards.

The arrival of the third character "3" can be seen as metaphor for the impact of death upon life, arriving unexpectedly, bringing chaos and inevitable change. The play suggests this catastrophic impact through its collapse of theatrical convention and undermining any expectation of dramatic safety from the audience by deconstructing the genre of the play. While 1 & 2 are in the midst of acting out the story of Ferdy and Marnie, the notion of what theatre and storytelling is itself becomes the nature of the drama. As 1 asks 2 "Are you listening ... ?" (Walsh 35) a sound of ripping and tearing fills the auditorium " *Suddenly a huge hydraulic noise—the sound of cracking ... we watch the back wall slowly tear away from the two side walls ... the wallpaper rips- the power cables spark aggressively- water pipes buckle and spray water"* (Walsh 35).

The crumbling edifice here suggests that even anarchic theatre story-telling, such as is being attempted in this play, remains an inadequate theatrical means of conveying human experience on stage. Every convention and stage tradition is inadequate—what is representational cannot be real, and as such is foredoomed to failure in any attempt to convey big human questions. In this section of the play such theatrical inadequacy of form is pointed through the literal breakdown of the theatrical edifice of the physical stage space. The secure stage box shape which traditionally provides the geographical framework for storytelling, crumbles before our eyes. Until now the fourth wall has been maintained in the play, but now the third has toppled in a way the audience wasn't expecting. It is as if the whole context for storytelling on stage is being deconstructed. Yet despite the anxiety and danger of this collapse, what is revealed beyond this traditional theatre space behind the wall however, is not a dangerous place of threat and distrust, but instead a vista of colour and tranquillity. There is a life outside of the space of the theatre and dramatic representation—and it may even be more beautiful and attractive than the stage space and a playwright's imagination inside, since the view is one that is infinitely more attractive than the room we have seen inside so far *"What is revealed is a beautiful blue light—onto a small hill of green perfect grass"* (36). The play may suggest here that theatre is good, it is entertaining and even meaningful, but it is not life, and life could be better.

That the audience is supposed to find this vision compelling and attractive is clear—the music thunders to a climax and positioned at the top of the hill, louche and relaxed, like the entrance of a rock star at his concert, stands 3, dressed in a black suit and casually smoking, a kind of Mick Jagger made dramatic. The music rises to a crescendo so loudly that 1 and 2 have to cover their ears—clearly the star of the show has arrived. 3 is apologizing for smoking "'Terrible habit"—ironic perhaps that this Mephistophelian devil figure should be conducting a peroration on a "coffin nail". The surprising and bizarre nature of his appearance in the piece is also ironically alluded to in his first speech when he discusses the relative importance of his right hand compared to his left—an extended pun on the truism "the left hand doesn't know what the right hand is doing", which would resonate with the audience at this moment in the production, since we have all been taken by surprise at the sudden drastic change in what is happening on stage. Walsh in this way has a playful dialogue with his audience about the nature of performance, their own expectations of narrative progression and theatrical genre; Walsh does not want his audience to relax into the world of the madcap genre which has been extended to them as the structure of the play so far. They must not think that they have now understood the style of the play entirely and can sink into a display from two skilled actors who will entertain them with the physical feats of jaw-dropping athleticism. The entrance and change of tone with the arrival of 3 makes it clear that gone now is the theatre of 1 jumping from the floor on to the tops of wardrobes or orating frenzied accounts of the people of Ballyturk (if that is who they are) at vast speed and with perfect diction. Walsh is trying to convey that his stage is not only about spectacle, it is about silence and serious moments of reflection upon deeply emotive themes of human existence.

The key to Walsh's theatre is that it is not restricted to any one genre, sensory style or intellectual approach. Instead, it is a theatre which constantly reflects upon its own medium as well as its message and transforms itself into a style and genre that is seen to fit the content. Such shifts of dramatic style alert the audience to the disjunction between the apparently ordinary nature of the discussion and the wider resonance of the events being shown. A quite reflective and thoughtful moment might be suggested by a speech for example, when 3 considers the length of a fly's life span "I wonder do they know how brief their life will be?" (Walsh 42) which refers not only to the consciousness of a fly, but is directed out at the audience, offering a theatrical moment to consider a possible link between the thought process of an insect and a similar human evasion of consciousness about the fragility of human existence and the sense of our own comparative brevity in the world. This is underpinned when shortly afterwards such a link to human experience is emphasized by 3, when he offers a similar quietly intoned reflection on the human reluctance to consider our own inevitable demise. He discusses a man waking up in the morning every day and carrying his memories of every similar morning with him as he goes about his daily existence:

> Only occasionally he's conscious that life is beginning and ending to the beat of time—that millions of others are walking in the exact same moment that he is— are travelling with the same purpose but singular histories—but travelling nonetheless with the same basic need—to keep on living ... A lifetime—of packing his life with experiences, some of which will change him greatly and others with no more consequence than wasting a little more of his life. (Walsh 45)

Only after this reflection upon the desire to live and the human capacity to ignore this drive, is the question of life and death raised in a practical form for the audience. The play now has a specifically structured moment of the "live" choice between life and death, which the audience is forced to experience as part of the drama. The audience is not given the luxury of evading an emotional engagement with the topic, either by rational explanation or by ignoring the thought. 3 says he will give 1 and 2 the choice of which one of them will go outside the room to meet him and die: "I give you a choice as to which one of you will step outside, walk the twelve seconds to me and die" (Walsh 46).

For the audience, there is now no escaping this moment of consciousness that death can be but a moment away. Instead we are forced to engage with an aspect of human existence that we would prefer to shy away from: one day we will face our own moment of death and the moment itself will come upon us as a surprise, just as it does to 1 and 2 and as it has to us as the witness to their moment of choice.

Again the audience's expectations of stage drama are circumvented. We might struggle to accept the alternative that the men have been offered as a legitimate part of the drama. Both of the characters appeared safe, if trapped, in this room, and have now had their security removed yet there is no doubt that this is definitely a "real" choice for them in the structure of the play's plot. It is as if the actors have been faced with the revelation of a fatal disease, and cannot believe, while they are at this moment of wellness, that they will ever die. After offering the men this choice 3's entry music is played again and he leaves the stage the same way he arrived—through the collapsed third wall. The room then seals up and everything is as it was at the start— except for the knowledge that this choice is hanging over the two men, waiting to be made. As the pop song "Situation" is ironically played, a moment of Beckettian repetition occurs—2 goes back to begin his frantic exercising, while 1 climbs on the exercise bike, pedalling at a manic pace as if riding in flight to escape the horrifying choice to be made. Both men then exchange activities, hoping that what has failed for one might work for the other, frantically trying to evading conscious thought through activity.

The men have attempted to go back to what they did before the arrival of 3, but everything has changed. 2 tries to force 1 to go back to his storytelling, but 1 is now scared to return to the memories and stories of other people, since he now realizes they might be memories of a life he had forgotten, not figures of his imagination. 3 has told him "Everything you imagined is real'[24] and now the sense of what is true and what is false, what is real or imagined has disturbed his equilibrium, he cannot function as a storyteller any more,

> 2 grabs 1 and throws him into the spotlight.
> **2.** Do it!

---

[24] This dialogue is from the National Theatre stage production—the text says "everything you imagined—it is" (Walsh 44) but perhaps the stage dialogue was felt to make the point more directly.

Then—

> I'm too scared to talk.
> Then don't.
> *1 pulls back the lever and the space is lit back up.*
> Go on.
> *A pause.*
> **1.** Bits and pieces of the almost forgotten—pictures I had thought were stolen from Ballyturk—where before they could never have been mine—now that man's face is knittin" them all together. (Walsh 49)

3 has made the words that 1 has been uttering repeatedly, coalesce. Suddenly 1 has begun to associate all that he had imagined as a fiction with real people and to realize that his stories are in fact evidence that he may have had a life before the room, and before 2's creation of this world, through what 1 had thought was the imaginative repetition of stories. The sense of narrative cohesion and identity is fractured for the audience, the philosophical question of whether we are living a recognized reality or merely actors in another person's narrative has been made manifest. An explanation for human existence is never forthcoming, even at the moment of our own demise. The eternal human metaphysical question—why are we here?—cannot be answered in the play any more than it is in reality. The reason for 1 being isolated in this room, being kept here away from people is never made clear. Has this been some elaborate torture? Has he been kept here for his own safety? Is the whole of his existence an imaginative dream? Perhaps 1 has been kept in the room against his will and discovers only now, at the moment of his death, that the reality which he thought was based on imagination was actually life, and that all that he imagined was fiction, is real. 1 thinks back to the first day of his arrival in the room and offers a kind of reflection of each human being looking back on their life and wondering where it has gone and how it has been spent, "There must have been more thoughts on that first day I spent here?... everything's eaten by the now—by what we build, by what we've become" (Walsh 54).

1 offers this poignant evocation of the eternal rush of the "now", picking up on the endless activity we have seen in the play and its representation of the desire to cover the present with endless activity, to reassure ourselves that we are alive and that we are significant.

But instead of leaving the audience to feel despondent and despairing about the nature of death there is instead a sense of the unity and ethereal companionship of joining the realm of the dead:

You walk from this room and your spirit, past and present, wraps
with the spirit of billions of others, and it's this that invisibly holds
up this planet of ours in space—in brilliant openness—in freedom.
You walk away quietly. (Walsh 56)

The play allows us to imagine death as something that could be
welcomed or seen as liberation from the endless demands and frenetic
nature of human existence. Instead this sense of escape and liberation
from a life of care, responsibility and action is presented as a journey of
development, "And it must be happiness that you feel—and what you
are walking towards is forgotten—or if remembered it holds no fear this
'death'" (Walsh 56).

Placing death in quotation marks in this way marks the way we hold
the word as a concept, something that we cannot know since by its very
nature we have not experienced it and when we do so, we will be past
the point of language to express its condition. The play is trying to
represent death and its emotions. "Death" creates an anxiety that we
can only leave in quotation marks, because it holds no reality for us—it
is an imagined concept, a signifier without a signified for us until the
moment we experience it. Instead, *Ballyturk* attempts to convey what
the moment of death must be like. Perhaps a human life is experienced
as a mere 12 seconds in the life of the world; the human race has existed
for such a short space of time that an individual human existence must
be as if it were but 12 seconds in the life of the universe.

In a quasi-religious sense but without any mention of a deity, the
play suggests the beauty and release of death as itself a kind of ritual
and transition, which we all make and through which we achieve a unity
with all those who have gone before, and whose spirits or bodies make
up the universe in mystical and philosophical sense. This sense of a
mystical engagement with the concept of death is reinforced in the play
by the manner of the exit to this moment of death or transition. As
before, the back wall of the stage collapses but there is no music or
creaking noises this time, instead " *it is the imagined quiet elemental
sounds of the Earth heard from our troposphere—of winds, oceans,
nature and of us"* (Walsh 56).

As the wall opens to reveal the grassy plane and 3 waiting for
whichever of the men in the room have decided to go, this time—
perhaps echoing Beckett's leaf appearing on the tree in the second act of
Waiting for Godot, marigolds have grown on the grass outside, and the
vista before us is expansive and beautiful, inviting and attractive. The
stage directions tell us that "the evening light is beautiful out there"
(56). Both the destination and the journey are in this sense full of

wonder; both life and death are presented as part of a universal pattern, which has resonance and significance beyond human intellectual understanding, "You're a lived person and in those 12 seconds you are a part of the world—you've stared at life and walked in it and it's all the life you need. It's real. It's real life" (Walsh 57).

The play here offers a sense that all living is the important thing: however fleeting, however oppressed, however restricted—life is important in and of itself. In this sense Walsh's work forms a kind of anti-existentialism—it is not nihilism or bleakness which will be the end of us all, repetition and frenetic routine does pass the time but it does not define us.

Yet, of course, there is a complication. 2 is now left alone in his "*cell*" (Walsh 57) as the stage directions tell us. He faces the rest of his life in isolation in an enclosed space and without the support of another's imagination. Death brings loneliness to us all. But in a possible Beckettian evocation of the power of duality, suddenly from the side of the stage comes a knocking. The small door which has been papered over, unseen until now is gradually broken through and a seven year old girl enters, as if she were posted through the letter box of a house.

At first there might be a sense of relief on the part of the audience that 2 will no longer be isolated. But then the anxious questions arise about what she is doing there. Has 3 sent 2 another person to look after because he felt sorry for him, in a kind of "Bride of Frankenstein" moment? Will 2 look after the child until a point in the future where 3 returns to collect his charge, just as he did with 1? Will this scenario play out again, twice? How will the change from a male to female charge affect the stage dynamic—and is there a chance that this relationship could develop into one that will lead to the creation of more children in the room itself?

Such contradictory emotions of hope and companionship, of repetition and entrapment cannot be explained in language and dialogue, so Walsh uses music to try to capture the complexity of these mixed feelings. There is a sense of hope in continuity, life goes on—but what sort of life is being experienced in this room we have seen? Walsh leaves no easy explanations. As Colm Tóibín puts it,

> The drama comes from the conflict between our hope that this is leading somewhere and Walsh's refusal to allow it to lead to anywhere obvious or comforting or easily transcendent.

The resolution of this scenario will not be provided for the audience by the playwright, the audience needs to work through explanations unaided.

Stephen Rea, who played No 3, suggests "I have a feeling we are all living in Ballyturk, whether we like it or not" (Rea 2014). The play may be about our own environments or our own moment of psychological development, and may lead to a personal reflection of the sound of time's wing-ed chariot. The audience may reflect upon the need to "live with one another and be with one another and be sort of happy and exist and carry on" (Walsh 2014) or the play may more simply strike the audience as a tour de force of comic physical theatre where we understand and respond to the play's humour and emotion, even though we cannot make sense of the narrative. Many possible interpretations work for the play and none are exclusively correct. For Mikel Murfi *Ballyturk* has a kind of lyrical universality, which will see it adapting to its own geographical environment and the personal consciousness of the audience responding to the work at any given production "it [*Ballyturk*] will place itself within the psyche of whoever is seeing it, wherever they are looking at it, wherever they are making productions of it" (Murfi 2014). If the play is about friendship, identity and death it is also about our inability to capture, define or express these experiences as well as a rejection of the need to define in any absolute form, style or language.

To engage with a Walsh play we need to be a different kind of audience. We must have more varied expectations of what we want our theatre to do for us. This play uses farce, Brechtian, Beckettian, Pinteresque, absurdist and comic theatre tropes to try to engage our attention. All these forms are seen as eloquent to a limited extent— because they also indicate their own vacuity as theatrical forms and a fundamental inability to comprehensively express their subject on their own. *Ballyturk* both expresses theatre's wonder and excitement, and its failure to define and enclose, just as the play itself has been unwilling to contain its own narrative to a specific area or to offer the audience a definitive conclusion about characters, names or themes. The play refuses identity and final definition—and it is fitting that it does so. To look for the rational, cerebral representations or explanation of themes would be an anathema to Walsh's theatre; his is the theatre of emotion, experienced both in the mind and in the sensual self.

Works Cited

Walsh, Enda. *Ballyturk*. London: Nick Hern Books, 2014. Print

---. *The Walworth Farce*. London: Nick Hern, 2008. Print.

Wallenberg, Christopher. "Small rooms full of words", *American Theatre Magazine* March (2010): 22-25 *Academic Search Premier*. Web. 11 Nov. 2014

Reviews

Billington, Michael. Rev. of *Ballytur*k by Enda Walsh, *The Guardian* 27 July: 2014 http://www.theguardian.com/stage/2014/jul/21/ballyturk-review-cillian-murphy-enda-walsh Web.

Hitchens, Henry. Rev. of *Ballyturk* by Enda Walsh, *Evening Standard*, 17 Sept. 2014: 23. Print.

Nightingale, Benedict. "A woman said my play was terrifying but I was a lovely boy", *The Times* 4 Sept. 2014: 8. Print.

O'Riordan, Alan. "Ballyturk to take Dublin and Cork audiences by storm", *Irish Examiner*, 4 Aug. 2014. http://ballyturk.com/2014/08/05/ballyturk-to-take-dublin-and-cork-audiences-by-storm-irish-examiner/ Web.

O'Toole, Fintan. Rev. of *Ballyturk* Irish Times, 8 Aug. 2014 Web. http://ballyturk.com/2014/08/18/review-fintan-otoole-irish-times/

Woolf, Matt. "Trapped Irishmen and Anarchic Britains", *International New York Times*, 25 Sept. 2014. http://www.nytimes.com/2014/09/26/arts/international/on-the-london-stage-ballyturk-the-wolf-from-the-door-and-the-comedy-of-errors.html?_r=0 Web.

Programme

Tóibín Colm . C. "Desire and Mystery", *Ballyturk* National Theatre programme, London September 2014. Print.

Website

"Ballyturk@Galway International Arts Festival." Interview by Landmark Productions and The Galway International Arts Festival. Youtube. N.p., 8 July 2014. Web. 13 May 2015. <https/::www.youtube.com:watch%3Fv=vwWGPWh1pjA>.

Rea, Stephen Ballyturk@Galway International Arts Festival YouTube. 8 July. 2014 . Web. 6 Sept. 2014 https://www.youtube.com/watch?v=vwWGPWh1pjA

Walsh, Enda *Ballyturk@Galway International Arts Festival* YouTube. 8 July. 2014 6 Sept.2014. https://www.youtube.com/watch?v=vwWGPWh1pjA

14| On Directing and Performing the Theatre of Enda Walsh

Mikel Murfi

I started working formally with Enda in or around 2004-5 when he sent me a play called *The Walworth Farce*, asking me would I "have a read", with a view to directing it. What a day *that* was!

We had known one another for some years previously. I had met him *originally* when he was working with The Dublin Youth Theatre. In the meantime he had moved to Cork and was working with Corcadorca and I was aware of and had been keeping in touch with the work he was making there including *Disco Pigs*. We were amongst a bunch of people at the time who were a new generation of theatre practitioners in Ireland many of whom were generating work that was moving away from drama that was text-based in any traditional sense. We were now exploring the form of theatre, the malleability of text in a theatre setting and engineering a physical strand to our work. It was an exciting time.

When Druid and Garry Hynes got a hold of Enda's *The Walworth Farce* they came looking for a director. That turned out to be me and that's when our collaborative work began in earnest. Enda is a theatre-maker like no other. He is radical in his approach to form, technique and text. With Walsh there are no limitations. When he wrote *The Walworth Farce,* one of his stated aims was to create a work that would "kill the actors" by which he meant, to provide actors with a work that would push them to physical and psychological limits. The very idea of writing to challenge the actors in this way is already such an inclusive (and slightly terrifying) idea. And it highlights a particular thing about his work. Namely that the work as proposed, will undoubtedly produce a theatre experience that will leave its audience reeling. It also produces another effect. The plays themselves become organisms. And they are *voracious* organisms. An actor who feels he or she is beginning to understand or have within their control a piece of Walsh work will encounter this organism that effectively says "You think that's all that's in me? I am more, I *want* more." No matter how much energy you expend, the play's muscularity, the speed with which it asks you to think, the types of energies it asks you to put at its disposal become all consuming. You give it all you have—it will demand, nay, *roar* for more. It's a thrilling experience.

I say this from mid-rehearsal on *Ballyturk*, Enda's new work for The Galway International Arts Festival in a co-production with Landmark Productions. We're in week three of rehearsals and it's a precarious, delicate time. I've worked as a director and actor and movement director with Enda and the work is always intense, in a very calm way. At present we're meeting this play full on. It is beginning to show itself to us and it's making some big demands. Enda is directing the piece himself, I'm acting (trying) with Cillian Murphy and Stephen Rea. And it's astonishing to me how he arrives into the room prepared to direct something that he has written but to which he can apply such a keen objectivity. It's only when the play is up and running on the floor of the rehearsal room that it begins this strange journey from page to stage and Enda is at times near oblivious to the fact that he wrote the work. His ability to now, in the rehearsal room, see this play as a beast with all these moving parts, is pretty astonishing. It means that we can shape the piece, see how it functions, now that it's in the hands of actors. We can feel it, it has started talking itself back to us. We work fairly loosely and freely until the conversation between the practitioners and the play begins to get louder in the room and, if it's necessary, then Enda puts on his writing hat to make small adjustments. Ultimately this work is for public consumption so, with an eye on that, we're testing the accessibility of the piece. We're testing our own validity within it. I'm a firm believer that the creative team are there to allow a play "pass though" them to an audience. I'm not interested in us putting a stamp all over a work. Hamlet is a play where we should see the story of the young prince played out—I've no interest whatsoever in seeing Whoever deliver *his* Hamlet as is so often the case. Our job is ever so slightly contradictory. We have to get to the core of the piece and then get out of the way and let it pass through us so an audience can interpret it for themselves, without spoon-feeding them.

But back to the beginning: *the writing*. Enda writes very quickly once he starts. A play will germinate, gestate for some time in his head but when it's ready to emerge it does so very quickly and very intensively. I think audiences get to experience that rush when they see an Enda Walsh play. He is the quickest writer I know to embed himself in the audience's subconscious. And once he's in, he keeps digging, deeper and deeper. He can develop anxieties and tensions within 20 seconds of the lights going up. He will keep a grip on those less known, dark regions of the psyche right through the play and often for days after. There's a curious thing too about his language—'Walsh English". I think part of the reason he's able to discombobulate an audience so immediately is because his form and technique as a writer are wholly his. His version of English is a kind of patois. We think we're at a play written in English but the nature of his sentence structure, his specificity of word choice, is a theatrical trick of the mind that means we are always in Walsh World as opposed to hearing what *we* think is a language spoken by many of us. It is *not* a language we know. It is a language he is able to teach us quickly and comprehensively and through which he can access our subconscious, wherein lies the most potentially disturbing and revelatory ideas. It's very important that I say here that the remarkable thing about Enda's writing is that it's not showy. Live, in the theatre, you're not necessarily aware of, or admiring in the moment, the brilliance of the writing. The writing forms part of a whole and is such that it finds its place in and amongst all the other production elements. We have the effect of knowing or seemingly understanding, while not really being in control. We are limited by what we can process in real time and that has a startling spinoff: we can never predict where we're going.

Having directed *The Walworth Farce* and *Penelope*, having been in *The New Electric Ballroom, Lyndie's Got a Gun,* movement directed on *Misterman* and performing now in *Ballyturk,* I marvel at how Enda is continuously able to write himself into bigger ideas, to constantly mine his form of theatre, to crack open our sense of self. He contends that the work is not there to be a mirror of who we are but rather to bash bin lids and crash ideas against one another to break open other avenues in the mind.

People often find Walsh's work bleak or dark but I find it uplifting and life enhancing. The characters are usually confined somehow and the pressure of "situation" builds to untenable levels. The energy and fragility in those liminal spaces of the mind, where we can meet the parts of ourselves that we don't wholly know, are being tramped through, in big Walsh boots and yet he can often reach these places with startling delicacy.

And the *theatricality* of it all! Walsh plays can only happen in a theatre. Other writers' work could easily be transposed into TV drama or radio plays or even film contexts but Enda's plays are purely theatrical, they only make sense in a theatre context. They're written with the "pure context" of theatre in mind and that in itself is a measure of their worth. Academics can pore over and interpret and feel well pleased in their analysis of Enda's plays and dissertations and theses will continue to be written and that can't be helped I'm afraid but the work ultimately is written to be experienced.

I must sound like a fan. But I have to say that when you read and play these works you are in a constant state of questioning, a constant state of shapeshifting, a constant state of wonder—to get to make theatre with these constants is pretty humbling. You won't meet greater challenges.

I like Enda too for his utter decisiveness. In preview situations he is fearless. He is not precious. I've asked for text to stay in a production because it's so beautifully written or disturbing or hilarious or all three (combined!) but he will cut wholesale because he knows the kinetic energy of a particular sequence is being hampered by his text. In earlier published versions of *The Walworth Farce* for instance, there is a whole subplot of the "Farce" that we cut in previews because it was holding up our momentum. In that sequence Mr Cotter asks Dinny to recite some poetry and the improvised poem, that Dinny, in a moment of panic extemporizes, titled *Because you Are Dead Mammy,* is one of my favourite poems of all time. But it had to go. Cut in preview. As a writer and then director of his own work he sees quicker than anyone something that no longer needs to be said because the actors can play it. Nothing is safe. There is no pretentiousness ... if it's not serving the moment, it goes. There are a number of reasons why this will happen with Enda. Firstly nothing must get in the way of the progression and drive that the piece must have. Secondly and very importantly Enda is so aware that there are *two* subtexts in operation in live theatre, particularly his own plays: that of the text and that of which is never spoken but can be seen. He is so keenly aware that if you put actors' minds and bodies under the pressure of a situation that those lies that they are trying to suppress or those emotions that the characters leave unspoken, that these will out in the actors' bodies leaving the audience to deal with subtext that is now multifaceted. He is aware enough to know that this can happen and to write so that the space for these other *non-verbal* dialogues can occur in performance.

It's December 2014. *Ballyturk* has taken to the stage in Galway, Dublin, Cork and London. Now, we have a new thing to talk about. The reaction across the board was that audiences were thrilled by what they saw and yet were wholly content that they didn't fully *understand* what they saw—that they were moved immeasurably but couldn't define why. *Ballyturk* is unknowable. The form now accommodates something by way of further excavation in Enda's writing—namely that the theatrical experience and Enda's trust that the kinetic potential in staged ideas will evolve rapidly and efficaciously in the complicity between performers and audiences. That like an art work which has certain abstracts—he trusts that the theatre-going collective can absorb the abstract and intuitively respond without needing to be led by the nose. It is rare when a writer is so consistent at generating this type of response in an audience and even rarer to do so with ever growing trust in theatre as a performance medium, that requires the audience to involve themselves in the "world" generated by a production. It is raw, disconcerting, thrilling. It's this glee in testing the limits of what language can do, the places it can take us in our minds, the reassuring of us that we are incredibly flexible in our imaginations to the act of being, that make Enda unique amongst his peers.

15 | We Laugh A Lot When Mum's Away: The Production and Reception of *The Walworth Farce* in Turkey[25]

Nursen Gömceli

The Walworth Farce (2006) was the first play to introduce Enda Walsh to Turkish theatregoers, with almost thirty performances staged in both the metropolitan cities and in small towns since its first production in Istanbul in 2011 by Tiyatro Gerçek.[26] An Istanbul-based private theatre company, Tiyatro Gerçek was established in 2008 with the principle of staging theatrical portraits (monologues and one-man shows) of nationally and internationally well-known figures. This has led to them producing Gordon Smith's *Van Gogh*, Irving Stone's *Clarence Darrow for the Defense* (*Savunma*) and a collage from the poetry and prose of the Turkish poet Cemal Süreya, *Keep the Change*[27] (*Üstü Kalsın*) (*Tiyatro Gerçek*, "Oyunlar"). Having established a reputation for such plays that give prominence to a single actor in a narrative-based performance, Enda Walsh's *The Walworth Farce*, which includes frenetic action and demands precision ensemble playing posed a new challenge and different direction for the company. The aim of this paper

[25] I would like to express my deep gratitude to Hakan Gerçek for his genuine interest and support of this research, without which this paper would not have been managed to be written. I am also grateful to the Antalya Foundation for Supporting the University (AÜDV), who generously supported me during my research stay at NUIG for my research on Enda Walsh and his drama.

[26] The "ç" in Tiyatro Gerçek is pronounced like the "ch" /tʃ/ in "chat".

[27] All translations from Turkish into English in the present essay are my own.

will be to examine the production and reception of *The Walworth Farce* in Turkey through an analysis of its translation, promotional materials and reviews, following a similar analytical model to that proposed by Huber (2012).

In other non-English-speaking countries where *The Walworth Farce* was staged in translation the original title was preserved like in the Polish version, for instance, where the title was "*Farsa z Walworth*" (*Teatr Wybrzeze*), and in the Catalan staging, "*La Farsa de Walworth*" (*Temporada Alta*) but in the Turkish production a new title was given to Walsh's play , "*Annem Yokken Çok Güleriz*", which can be translated into English as "*We Laugh A Lot When Mum's Away*". This Turkish title at once draws attention to the absence of a mother figure in the piece but also emphasizes the fun and entertainment that can be had when mother is away. In Turkish culture, the mother is ascribed the role of "home-maker". She is the parent that keeps the family together and is seen as the chief controlling power in the upbringing of the children. Moreover, the mother figure, as the "home-maker", is symbolically conflated with the concept of homeland in the nationalist discourse, thus for the Turkish people homeland is synonymous with "motherland" ('*anavatan*'). The mother is equated not only with concepts of peace, order and stability but also the sacred in both the public and private spheres. Consequently, the Turkish title for the play, in its gendered approach, suggests a home that might prove very entertaining but one that is out of order in the absence of its controlling power and all the values this power represents.

A close look at the poster, which can be accepted as a significant document of reception preceding the actual reception process (Huber 86), might support this observation. On the poster, which at first glance bears a resemblance to the original poster used by Druid in its 2006 production of *The Walworth Farce*, the three major characters Dinny, Blake and Sean are seen in a frame in their stage costumes reflective of their images in the play, and a tattered wallpaper design is used as a background to the frame. At the front of frame, Dinny (Hakan Gerçek) is sitting dressed in a red jacket and a patterned shirt, a dominant and imposing character—a father figure, while Blake (Bülent Şakrak) and Sean (İlker Ayrık), as the children, are in the background, standing side by side behind Dinny. Blake appears in his cross-dressed state, with a patterned skirt, sleeveless orange top and a wig, while Sean is wearing a short-sleeved grey t-shirt, with his fake moustache hanging around his neck and his bald-head prosthetic displayed. So, at a surface glance these characters seem to inhabit a world of fun existing in a male-dominated private sphere. However, a closer look at the postures, the facial expression of each of the characters and their eyes reflect a very notable state of desolation and a deep sadness, which tells us that not everything is right in this sphere wherein the mother is absent.

Another significant element on the poster is a tag line placed to the left on the bottom, which poses a question central to the play, probably adapted from Dinny's line, "What are we ... if we are not our stories?" In the Turkish version on the poster, this line appears as "Can we exist without our stories?" with the phrase "our stories" given prominence through the use of a much bigger font size. This might have intentionally been given as such, with the purpose of attracting audiences to the storytelling aspect of the play since the oral tradition of storytelling, (just as in Ireland), has a long history in Turkey, "go[ing] back to the dawn of Turkish history in Central Asia more than fifteen centuries ago" (Halman). Oral literature in the Turkish culture developed and evolved not only during the nomadic era, when the Turks immigrated from Central Asia into Asia Minor, but also in the later centuries in the Seljuks Anatolia and the Ottoman Empire, where a "synthesis" of "the autochthonous legacy of the Turks and the rich material they amassed from the Asian (mainly Chinese and Indian) tradition, from the Islamic lore, from the Middle East, Byzantium, the Balkans, and the rest of Europe" developed through their contact to these cultures and turned into "a prevalent form of entertainment and enlightenment" (Halman). As Halman, the recently deceased Professor of English and Turkish literature and cultural historian explains, "in a society where the rate of literacy remained below ten percent until the mid-1920s, oral narratives played a major role in cultural transmission" and was revealed not only as an "imaginative resource" of Turkish society but also enabled the survival of its folk culture, through the vast number of greatly diverse stories (Halman). Today, oral narrative in the form of anecdotes and short tales is still part of everyday speech, particularly in the rural parts of the country. The tag line on the poster in its emphasis on "our stories" does not only reference Turkish tradition but also serves to stress the "Irishness" of the play, with the Irish being known for their equally strong storytelling tradition. Storytelling as performance is thus identified as something common to both cultures and invites Turkish audiences to experience the strange (Irish-ness) through the familiar (oral tradition).

Another striking point that could be mentioned with respect to the Turkish production of *The Walworth Farce* is the strategy employed by Tiyatro Gerçek to prepare their audiences for the play prior to its performance, which can be accepted as a kind of familiarization process. Before the performances, the audiences were given an informative brochure providing some equations explaining what the play is about and clarifying who is playing whom and the relationship between the characters in order to help the audience "understand the play better" (Gerçek, "Re: Annem Yokken"). In an e-mail correspondence with Hakan Gerçek, he explains that this was a method they regarded as essential for the understanding of the play, since they thought it would be difficult for the audience to follow the plotline in a structure where the acting style is based on multiple role playing with quick changes from one character into the other in a fast pace throughout the play, adding that it was a challenge even for the actors to work out the script ("Re: Annem Yokken"). The equation devised for this purpose reads as follows:

> We Laugh A Lot When Mum's Away" [The Walworth Farce] = 1 father + 2 sons + 3 women + 2 more men + 2 coffins + 1 shop assistant + 1 chicken and its smell = 3 % reality + 4 % love + 47 % lie + 46 % violence". (Tiyatro Gerçek, "AYÇG İçin Denklemler")

At this stage, it should be pointed out that even though the company staging the play seriously saw this formula as a kind of solution towards making the plot more understandable for its audiences, the equation itself adds another playful dimension rather than adding clarity. The equation funnily reflects not only the insane logic of the play but also ridicules the idea of being able to simplify a complex play and theatrical act in measurable terms. After giving a brief synopsis of the play, the brochure introduces *The Walworth Farce* as "a vibrant black comedy" which "tells the story of violence in a style to which we are not so accustomed", by which the element of farce in the depiction of violence must have been intended to be signalled, since the Turkish theatregoers' expectations of a theatrical performance are largely shaped by the conventions of realist drama. With such emphasis on violence combined with the image of the male characters on the poster, the production not only associates violence with male behaviour but also presents to the audience a picture of masculinity, which in return invites a discussion on gender roles. The reference to the absence of the mother in the title, the presence of a male dressed as a female behind a very masculine looking father figure on the poster, and the synopsis foregrounding violence as intrinsic to the play, all contribute to promote conversation on gender roles among the audience. Further details about the play on the brochure present it as a narrative of those "who feel trapped in the world", "have lost their stories" and are "lowly-paid workers", which prepares the audience for the world and characters of the drama, or in other words, the social and cultural background they will encounter on stage (*Tiyatro Gerçek*, "Annem Yokken").

At this point, one can look at what the audiences have made out of these brochures and posters as "paratexts" (Huber 86) that are devised to help them develop an idea about the play before seeing the actual performance on stage, and to what extent these paratexts have fulfilled their function. Most audience reviews of *The Walworth Farce* in Turkey, which can be accessed on webpages like *Tiyatro Dünyası* (*The Theatre World*) and the interactive web pages like *İTÜ* Sözlük (*Dictionary of Istanbul Technical University*) and *Ekşi Sözlük* (*The Sour Dictionary*) widely used by university students, reveal that the brochures were indeed helpful in grasping which performer was playing which character(s) and the relationship between these characters, whereas some commentaries state that it was difficult to follow the play despite the introductory brochures delivered before the performance, displaying the fact that it was a challenging play for the audience to follow and comprehend. A third view regarding the brochures claims that the distribution of such informative guides in itself served to obfuscate and distance the audience from the play even before they encountered it on stage.

From the online reviews we also learn that the poster, the title and the advertising of the play influenced audience reception. These reviews reveal that the poster was primarily received in comic terms, due to the humorous depiction of the two actors, İlker Ayrık (Sean) and Bülent Şakrak (Blake). This reception of the show as a light piece was furthered by the advertisements that promoted the play as "black comedy", something repeated also in the brochures. The playgoers thus expected to see a broad comedy with much laughter and entertainment. It is observed in the audience reviews that the very prominent title on the poster of *"We Laugh A Lot When Mum's Away"* was most influential in such expectations on the part of the audiences, which shows that the strategy employed by the producers had been successful. In his reply to the inquiry of the author of the present essay about the background to the production of Enda Walsh's *The Walworth Farce* in Turkey, Hakan Gerçek conveys the idea that the title of the play was deliberately recreated as *"We Laugh A Lot When Mum's Away"* to attract the theatregoers to the play. He explains:

We thought of several names for the play. Staging the play, which is quite intricate to understand in any case, with its title directly translated from the original would have made it very difficult for us to draw audiences. We wanted to have a name that would surprise the audiences and so gave this name to the play following Mehmet Ergen's [the translator] suggestion. ... I think it's been better like this, because mine, Bülent and İlker's pictures on the poster together with the title "We Laugh A Lot When Mum's Away" created in the theatregoers the feeling that they would laugh a lot and have a good time, but they were struck by surprise at the performance. ("Re: Annem Yokken")

Some related audience commentaries in the previously mentioned online platforms above confirm what the actor divulges to us: "Don't be fooled by the description of the play as a comedy. There was very little laughter throughout the play" (*Tiyatro Dünyası*, entry 2); "the friend who got the tickets had thought that we would laugh a lot since the play was said to be a comedy so we went to see it with this expectation, but even if we didn't laugh, I liked the play" (*Tiyatro Dünyası*, entry 3); "because of the title of the play, I thought it was a comedy and didn't feel very excited about it, but it was priceless to reach the *finale* almost in tears" (*Ekşi Sözlük*, entry 9); "the play has an unusual story. It might lead you to expect a very funny play if you focus only on its title and go to the performance with no idea about its genre and storyline. But it can't be said that it makes you laugh" (*İTÜ Sözlük*, entry 1). One other commentary exposing the audience's perplexity about the play's title incongruous with its actual story focuses attention also on the poster:

I suppose I'd prepared myself for a more laughter-filled play, depending on the already known images of the actors. Yet if I had looked at the picture on the poster a little bit more carefully, it would have told me the truth about the play. The picture on the poster is in fact a complete summary of the play! The costumes, postures might seem funny to you, but try looking at the faces of the actors! Is there anything funny about them? One should see the sadness within the surface comedy. (Ben Oyun İzledim)

In the online theatre magazines announcing the opening of the play, where it is introduced both in its Turkish title and the original title in parentheses, distinct reference is made to Enda Walsh's Irish background, thus introducing the playwright to Turkish playgoers in the context of the Irish dramatic tradition. Moreover, emphasis is made on the play's history as an award winning play at the Edinburgh Fringe Festival and its international standing. Based on the information given about the play on Tiyatro Gerçek's own homepage, these sources describe *The Walworth Farce* as a "strange funny play", a "dark comedy", an "interesting narrative" which tells "the story of a father and his two sons, who had to leave their homeland Ireland in order to leave behind a past which is not an easy one to face, and who take shelter in London and produce a new past for themselves in order to get away from their own" (*Tiyatro Online*; *Mimesis*; *Tiyatro Dünyası*). Although emigration is mentioned here in the blurb in relation to the plot the Tiyatro Gerçek production curiously did not attempt to foreground the theme of emigration in their performances. Emigration is not mentioned in any of the paratexts and no attempt was made to relate the production to the Turkish emigrant experience, for example trying to make a correlation between the Irish in Britain and the Turkish in Germany. The interpretation of the play was more interested in the existential qualities of the piece rather than the cultural or political aspects.

In an interview with the actors and the director, Mehmet Birkiye, who was the person behind the idea of staging *The Walworth Farce* and who soon became the director of the Turkish production of the play, he interprets *The Walworth Farce* as "an amusing theatrical play on man's problem of existence" which "brings two different styles, farce and tragedy, together in one text by intertwining but without intermixing the two." Emphasizing the elements of farce and tragedy as combined but still kept apart from each other, Birkiye further comments on the expected effect of the play on the audience: "Everyone will leave the theatre hall in a befuddled state, because thinking makes one dizzy!" (Memiş, "Bu Oyundan Herkes").

This dimension of the play as "challenging" for the spectators was an aspect that worried Hakan Gerçek when he first read the text, he explains, since he was to provide the platform for the staging of the play as the owner of the theatre company and would take a part in it, acting the role of Dinny. He writes:

> I got extremely worried when I first read the play. It's a highly complex and intricate text. What I found attractive about the play, however, were its two specific features: firstly, its content and secondly the high demands it makes of the actors who must deliver a very strong performance. I thought with good actors we could communicate the text much better, as well. ("Re: Annem Yokken")

Hakan Gerçek goes on to state that he was very conscious of the fact that Turkish theatregoers were not ready yet for a play like *The Walworth Farce*, with such a complicated story and such a very energetic and demanding acting style that is hard to follow:

> If you consider that the original script would be difficult to

comprehend even for the society in which it was produced, it was quite clear to me, to tell the truth, that it would be very hard to understand and would not be appreciated in our society, where people are habituated into [expecting] the easy. It was complex enough even for us during the rehearsals. But to me, the important thing was to put a challenging text like this on stage for the first time in Turkey and to force the audiences to come. ("Re: Annem Yokken")

Indeed, when we consider how most plays in the repertoire of the Turkish state theatres and those produced by the private theatre companies are predominantly presented in a realist style, it is no surprise that *The Walworth Farce* would prove highly challenging to Turkish audiences. The online reception of *We Laugh A Lot When Mum's Away* (*The Walworth Farce*) disclose that the most prominent features of the play which contest the realist mode, like the complexity of the plot, the play-within-a-play structure, the multiple-role casting, the quick changes from one character into the other, the extremely fast pace, are of primary concern in the discussions about the play's intricacy. For example, on the online interactive platforms, like *Tiyatro Dünyası, Ekşi Sözlük* and *ITÜ Sözlük*, they describe it as a play which "demands much effort and energy" (*Tiyatro Dünyası*, entry 1), "is highly difficult for both the actors and the spectators" (*Tiyatro Dünyası*, entry 3), "makes you cudgel your brains, and think" (*Tiyatro Dünyası*, entry 7), "requires patience to understand" (*Tiyatro Dünyası*, entry 17), and "is difficult to digest" (*İTÜ Sözlük*, entry 5). One other audience commentary clearly exposing the mind-set of an audience associating theatre and drama with the realist tradition observes: "Nothing happened in the play until the girl [Hayley] entered the stage" (*Ekşi Sözlük*, entry 8). As Patrick Lonergan states in his review of *The Walworth Farce*, with Hayley in Act II, Enda Walsh brings the element of "realism" into the play, primarily because she is a "normal person" (*Irish Times*, 14). Correspondingly, for the Turkish theatregoers more comfortable with theatrical realism it was only in the second act that the play "begins to make sense" (*Ekşi Sözlük*, entry 2), or "all the pieces of the puzzle fall into place" (*Ekşi Sözlük*, entry 3) as the *expected* "normality" enters into the play, making it easier for the Turkish audience to comprehend what has been happening on stage.

Any reference to the "events taking place on stage" in research into the production history and the reception of an Irish play in a Turkish context inevitably invites us also to consider certain aspects regarding the text, like the content and language of that specific play, as it is through its translation that the play under discussion reaches its audiences. However, since the Turkish translation of *The Walworth Farce*, provided by Mehmet Ergen, still remains unpublished at the time of writing this, a comparative textual analysis of the English and Turkish texts is not possible. Nonetheless, the knowledge that Hakan Gerçek imparts to us does help shed some light on the issues of language and content and what elements of adaptation were considered for the Turkish production of Enda Walsh's play. In this respect, the author of this essay posed the following questions in an e-mail addressed to the actor: "Do you think the play narrating the story of an Irish family emigrating from Ireland to England has been interpreted by the Turkish audiences as a story to which they could relate?"; "Regarding the language and content, would you say your production remained entirely faithful to the original or did you feel the need to make certain changes to the play according to the expectations of the Turkish audiences?"; "The language in the original play bears a heavy accent associated with the region of Cork in Ireland. Parallel to this, did you consider performing the play in an accentuated language also in your production?" (Gömceli, "Annem Yokken"). While the first question above has remained unanswered (as already mentioned), Gerçek did divulge in his reply to the succeeding two questions that they largely remained faithful to the original in their production, chiefly because it was a complex text. He explains:

> With such texts [foreign plays], an adaptation could certainly lead to a better understanding of the play. Yet, for this text, this would have been difficult because of the storyline of the play ... For Turkey, what we could have done with this text could be to locate the play onto an east-west axis. But in this case it would have been necessary to use the eastern accent, which we didn't think would be a good idea because of the delicate balance in our country.

Another question addressed to the actor with regard to the content is about the character Hayley, whose racial identity as a black girl is used as an element to introduce the theme of racial discrimination almost in a provocative way with Dinny's smearing her face with a moisturizing cream in the scene where he forces her to be a part of his play, but insists that she should have a white face for the role. Considering the fact that Turkey is not a country with a history of anti-black racism, the question directed at Hakan Gerçek in this regard asks if there has been an alteration to this scene with respect to the character's identity as a black girl and the dialogues in her part (Gömceli, "Annem Yokken"). In reply Gerçek explains that the director of the play, Mehmet Birkiye, tried to bring a solution to this situation by changing Hayley into an Indian character, so her costume and colour were much more evocative of an Indian girl ("Re: Annem Yokken"). Gerçek makes no particular reference for their reason for choosing the Indian identity for Hayley but it could be surmised that through such conversion, the producers may have aimed at creating among the audience the effect of a character that would be immediately identified as foreign and strange among the group of white Irish characters on stage. As for the query about any changes in the dialogues particularly between Hayley and Dinny in the Turkish production of the play, no explanation in this regard was provided by the actor in his reply to the author, but a scene from one of the company's productions available on *YouTube* shows that in that particular scene where Dinny forces Hayley to play the role of his wife Maureen, the dialogues and action stick to the original (Feyizm). Hence it can be concluded that in the Turkish production of *The Walworth Farce*, where the play has been introduced with a title very different from the original in its translation, Tiyatro Gerçek has otherwise largely endeavoured to remain faithful to the original script in both form and content.

The Walworth Farce in Turkey proved of great interest to theatregoers in the cities and towns where it was staged. As I have tried to show within the scope of this essay, most audience reviews in Turkey are of the perspecive that Enda Walsh's *The Walworth Farce (Annem Yokken Çok Güleriz/ We Laugh A Lot When Mum's Away)* is a very challenging play due to its highly complex and perplexing plotline that demands a particular unfamiliar acting style leading to the adoption of a critical attitude in the audience toward what transpires on stage. Yet almost all the reviews concur in the opinion that the actors delivered exceptional performances deserving of a standing ovation. This view was confirmed and validated by the presentation of "Best Actor of the Year Award" to the actors Hakan Gerçek, Bülent Şakrak and İlker Ayrık at the prestigious 16th Sadri Alışık Theatre and Cinema Awards in 2011 (*Milliyet*).

Like the online audience reviews, theatre critics have praised the play for its great capacity for performance. With regard to the staging methods employed in the Turkish production, one commentary points out that it can be observed that "every dimension of the play has been processed with great care", and that "even in its Turkish, the flowery style peculiar to Hiberno-English can be felt" (Yüksel, *Annem Yokken Çok Güleriz*). The interpretation of the play with respect to its content, however, has been manifold. One view is that it is a play "about the story of violence", which people frequently resort to in order to sustain the institutions they regard as benevolent yet can never openly confess that they have done so (Memiş, "Bu Oyundan Herkes"). Another interpretation holds the view that like Harold Pinter, Enda Walsh gives us the message that just like the outside world, our safe and secure homes, too, have potential risks for us (Akmen). Ayşegül Yüksel, a leading theatre critic and scholar in British drama, however, believes that the play carries the tradition of patricide in Irish drama as observed in J. M. Synge's *The Playboy of the Western World* (1907) as well as in Martin Mc Donagh's *The Beauty Queen of Leenane* (1996) into the 2000s by displaying the unbearable dimensions of parental oppression in a tragic farce ("Annem Yokken"). On the whole, all the theatre critics whose views about *The Walworth Farce* and its Turkish production have been presented in this work describe the play as "one of the most ambitious plays of the season" (Kaya) which should be "on the "must-see" list" of all theatregoers (Akmen).

As a concluding remark, following perhaps a humorous commentary by a spectator who puts forth that the audience "should undergo training first" (*Tiyatro Dünyası*, entry 4) for a better understanding of the play, it could be said that the 2011 production of *The Walworth Farce* for Turkish audiences has similarly functioned as a training of sorts for future Enda Walsh plays. Looking at the reviews his play has received from Turkish theatregoers and critics, it is clear that *The Walworth Farce* has placed Enda Walsh in a prominent position from which he will continue to be closely observed.

Works Cited

Akmen, Üstün. Rev. of *The Walworth Farce*, by Enda Walsh. *Tiyatro Online* 15 May 2011. Web. 10 Nov. 2014.
    <http://www.tiyatrogercek.com/basin.asp?icr=7>.

Ben Oyun İzledim. "'Annem Yokken Çok Güleriz" Ama Aslında Hiç Komik Değiliz!" *Ben Oyun İzledim*. 13 April 2011. Web. 12 Nov.
    2014.<http://www.benoyunizledim.com/annemyokkencokguleriz.html>

Ekşi Sözlük. "Annem Yokken Çok Güleriz." Ekşi Sözlük Teknoloji, n. d.
    Web. 26 Oct. 2014. <https://eksisozluk.com/annem-yokken-cok-guleriz--2606333>.

Feyizm. "Annem Yokken Çok Güleriz." Online video clip. *You Tube*. You Tube, 17 Feb.2012. Web. 11 Oct. 2014. <
    http://www.youtube.com/watch?v=Pd8_BvML64w>.

Gerçek, Hakan. "Re: Annem Yokken Çok Güleriz." Message to the author.
    13 Sep. 2014.E-Mail.

Gömceli, Nursen. "Annem Yokken Çok Güleriz." Message to Hakan Gerçek.
    31 Aug. 2014.E-Mail.

Halman, Talat Sait. "The Heart of the Turkish Tale." *Turkish Cultural Foundation*. TurkishCultural Foundation, 2015.Web. 2 March 2015.<http://www.turkishculture.org/literature/literature/-126.htm>.

Huber, Werner. "Contemporary Irish Theatre in German-Speaking Countries." *Irish Drama: Local and Global Perspectives*. Eds. Nicholas Grene and Patrick Lonergan. Dublin: Carysfort. 2012. 81-91.

İTÜ Sözlük. "Annem Yokken Çok Güleriz." İTÜ Sözlük, n. d. Web. 26 Oct. 2014.<https://www.itusozluk.com/goster.php/annem+yokken+%E7ok+g%FCleriz>.

Kaya, Yaşam. Rev. of *The Walworth Farce*, by Enda Walsh. *Tiyatro Online* 22 March 2011. Web. 10 Nov. 2014 <http://www.tiyatrogercek.com/ _haber.asp?durum=detay&hb=31>.

Lonergan, Patrick. Rev. of *The Walworth Farce*, by Enda Walsh. *Irish Times* 22 March 2006:14. Print.

Memiş, Betül. "Bu Oyundan Herkes Sarhoş Çıkacak". *Habertürk* 12 Jan. 2011. Web. 10 Nov. 2014. <http://m.haberturk.com/kultur-sanat/haber/590654-bu-oyundan-herkes-sarhos-cikacak>.

Milliyet. "Sinema ve Tiyatronun Onur Gecesi." Milliyet.com.tr, 2014. Web. 7 Nov. 2014.<http://www.milliyet.com.tr/sinema-ve-tiyatronun-onur-gecesi-sahnesanatlari-1382463/>.

Mimesis. "Tiyatro Gerçek'ten Annem Yokken Çok Güleriz." Mimesis, 17 Sep. 2010. Web. 23 Oct. 2014. <http://mimesis-dergi.org/2010/09/tiyatrogercekten-annem-yokken-cok-guleriz/>.*Teatr Wybrzeze*. "Spektakle Farsa Z Walworth." Teatr Wybrzeze, n. d. Web. 5 Nov. 2014.< http://www.teatrwybrzeze.pl/spektakle/farsa-z-walworth>.

Temporada Alta. "Programacio La farsa de Walworth." Temporada Alta, 2014. Web. 11Nov. 2014. <http://www.temporada-alta.net/ca/programacio/270-la-farsa-de-walworth.html>.

Tiyatro Dünyası. "Annem Yokken Çok Güleriz." Tiyatro Dünyası, n.d. Web. 10 Nov. 2014.<http://www.tiyatrodunyasi.com/tiyatro_detay.asp?oyunid=415>.

Tiyatro Gerçek. "Oyunlar." Tiyatro Gerçek, 2010. Web. 18 Feb. 2015. <http://www.tiyatrogercek.com/oyun.asp?oyn=138#>.

---. "Annem Yokken Çok Güleriz İçin Denklemler." Tiyatro Gerçek, 2010. Web. 11 Nov. 2014. <http://www.tiyatrogercek.com/haber.asp?durum=detay&hb=25>.

---. "Annem Yokken Çok Güleriz." Tiyatro Gerçek, 2010. Web. 12 Nov. 2014.<http://www.tiyatrogercek.com/oyun.asp?oyn=132>.

Tiyatronline. "Tiyatro Gerçek'in Yeni Oyunu Annem Yokken Çok Güleriz Tüm Hızıyla Sahnelenmeye Devam Ediyor." Tiyatronline, 22 March 2011. Web. 8 Nov. 2014. <http://www.tiyatronline.com/haberler/haber/1137/tiyatrogercek-in-yeni-oyunu-annem-yokken-cok-guleriz-sahnelenmeye-tum-hiziyla-devam-ediyor.html>.

Yüksel, Ayşegül. "Annem Yokken Çok Güleriz." Rev. of *The Walworth Farce*, by EndaWalsh. *Tiyatro Eleştirmenleri Birliği* 6 Dec. 2011. Web. 10 Nov. 2014.<http://tiyatroelestirmenleribirligi.org/elestiri-yazilari/117-annem-yokken-cok-guleriz>.

16| Sculpting the Spaces of Enda Walsh's Theatre: Sabine Dargent in Conversation

Siobhán O'Gorman

Foreword

Sabine Dargent is a French scenographer who has been working in Ireland since the late 1990s. Prior to this, she worked in Paris with Théâtre de Châtillon, L'épée de Bois, TGV, Sylvain Maurice, and architect Maurice Bachet. The experience of physical theatre that Dargent garnered from working with French companies has remained central to her conception of performance design. In Ireland, Dargent also began by designing for physical theatre companies such as Blue Raincoat, and shortly after she did a few shows for Belfast-based company, Aisling Ghéar. She then moved on to designing sets and costumes in theatre for young audiences with TEAM Educational Theatre Company, including Michael West's *Jack Fell Down* and Frances Kay's *Burning Dreams*, both directed by Martin Murphy in 1999. Later, she designed *Senses* (2002) a dance piece co-produced by Maiden Voyages and Liz Roche's company Rex Levitas, as well as Sophocles' *Antigone*, adapted and directed by Conall Morrison for Storytellers Theatre (2003).

In 2003, Dargent won the ESB/*Irish Times* Award for Best Set Design for Morrison's version of Ibsen's *Ghosts*, produced at and by the Lyric Theatre, Belfast. She went on to build a portfolio of cutting-edge design work with a variety of companies and directors. Dargent won the *Irish Times* Theatre Award for Best Set Design again in 2006, for two shows: *Hysteria* by Terry Johnston, and the first play by Enda Walsh on which she worked, *The Walworth Farce*, produced at and by the

Druid Theatre in Galway. The opportunity to work on Walsh's play came about through the development of a working relationship with Mikel Murfi with whom Dargent shared a background in physical theatre. Dargent went on to design Druid's productions of Walsh's *The New Electric Ballroom* (2008) and *Penelope* (2010). The following conversation reveals much about the collaborative ways in which Dargent, Walsh and Murfi sculpted the spaces of Walsh's theatre.[28]

Siobhán O'Gorman: I'd like to know about your process from receiving a script to sketches, model boxes and the stages of that process—both in general and for the three Enda Walsh plays you have designed.

Sabine Dargent: Generally, my main approach is usually painting. I make books because I need to see the chronology of my thoughts. I do books where I mix painting and other textures. It's sometimes quite difficult for other people to read these books. And I mix in pieces of text.

SO'G: From the play?

SD: Not only; there are parallel things happening. I'm just trying to understand this myself. If it's theatre, I begin by reading the text, to understand the story. This seems basic but to understand the story, to understand the spatial movement, and I document all my influences. Sometimes, not always, I also need to understand the writer. I need to read the stage directions, and decide if they are important for me or not. But I always find stage directions really interesting. And the evolution of them is really interesting because sometimes they are really busy at the beginning and after that they disappear. So there is that part, text. This is followed by me painting, trying to sense what is important and it's quite abstract at the beginning. I'm going from abstract to more solid but trying to merge everything in the beginning.

SO'G: Gradually sculpting the vision?

SD: Yeah, and the execution works like a funnel. At the beginning you have the text, image, themes or whatever is the starting point. You have your own impressions, your drawings and all that. Also the practicalities of it: Where is it? Which space is it in? How much money

---

[28] This is an edited version of a longer interview in which Dargent explains in more detail her background, training, inspirations and processes as a scenographer—in addition to the transition from working in France to working in Ireland. Those wishing to access the more extensive version should contact the interviewer on siobhanmogorman@gmail.com.

do you have? Which actors? Most of all, which director, and what is his vision? I will try to understand this. I'll know what I want to say but I also have to consider what the director wants to say. Communication between the director and the designer is very important. So, to go back to the process, it's book, model box, plan, how it will be done, and after you build it. The way it's usually done here is that you have the performing space on one side and you have the audience space on the other, and it has to be designed quickly. And that's not the way I've been trained—I've been trained that everything is worked out together—so that's quite tough. Regarding Enda's work specifically, when I read that [points to *The Walworth Farce*], I couldn't understand what was happening. It's fascinating because when you read it, it's really complicated. I mean, for me, I thought it was really complicated. I think what Mikel Murfi did was to divide the story. Just to explain that, because they are doing theatre *in* the theatre, Mikel divided Enda's play into the world of the *play*, you know *The Walworth Farce*, and the theatre story *in it*.

SO'G: He isolated the moments of metatheatre?

SD: Yeah, because the way that play works is that you don't know where you are as a spectator, so you are lost. And that's what's really exciting in one way in the theatre, you know, you have this abundance of words and all that. And then you just arrive to something really pure. And what is mad is that when we started to workshop it, when Mikel started to workshop it, he just drew on the floor, which is described in a really realistic way. I mean, you *need* to see three different spaces, which is tricky. But he did that on the floor and when he did that, it was unbelievable, it was so much clearer for me. And for Mikel. And I think for everybody. It was just so much clearer because we could *see* it. That's why I think Enda's work is actually very visual.

SO'G: I can see clearly how you sculpted your vision of the set out of the stage directions. What informed your decisions on the costumes?

SD: I think the term "stuck in the seventies" also appears in the stage directions. *That* was central to the whole design. One thing that struck me about *The Walworth Farce* when I read it was that in a way it seemed like a vision for cinema. You see three things at the same time. So I felt I was *forced* to do it in a certain way. When I was looking at the description I was thinking about the sight-line. You can't physically have a partition in the middle and see everything. I mean, it's not possible. If you imagine the theatre, and the edge of the theatre and you have walls cutting through the space, the guy who's here doesn't see there. There were different things at play. There was the fact that it was "stuck in the seventies." I then started to visually associate the lines of this weirdly-shaped seventies shelf, and the structure of the beams structuring the wall underneath the plaster. I said to them—or we said together, I can't remember exactly—that we needed to have some of those walls gone. To see what was under the surface of the walls suited the period, and the practicality. We had that conversation with Mikel about the need for the sight-line to be clear, and Enda rewrote to help the design. So when one of the sons is breaking the wall, this was inserted to explain the design, to help the design. It was not in there before, when I first read the text. That was really interesting because I think that is what theatre is about.

SO'G: That kind of collaboration?

SD: Whether it starts with a text, or whatever it is, there is often that very strong collaboration between directing and writing. And that's what makes it powerful ...

SO'G: And designing ...

SD: Yeah.

SO'G: So how did you bring your work with other Irish companies to bear on your work with Walsh and with Druid?

SD: I find it really difficult to differentiate my influences. But what I would like to say in this context is that, certainly, what is important is that I'm *not* Irish. And Enda's work is very Irish, in one way, even though sometimes it's set somewhere else. I mean, it's very interesting because he's living abroad but he's using Ireland as a tool to transmit his idea. The fact that he knows Ireland so well means there is a part of humanity that he knows so well. He can use that. In one way it doesn't matter if it's in Ireland or elsewhere. I think his work is speaking about much more than that. It seems to me that Enda's work is speaking mostly about the problem of communication, loneliness—and his work progressing. When I saw *Ballyturk*, that's what it was also speaking about, and about what is beyond us. That show is really funny and crazy but I also think it's very existential.

SO'G: In general, how do you approach working with other co-creators of scenography—for example, directors and writers—and how did this kind of collaboration play out across the three plays? Was it, in each case, the three of you working together from very early on?

SD: Mostly, we started at the same time. If Mikel was directing, I would have started probably about the same time I guess. And sometimes we'd need the three of us but most of the time, I would meet with Mikel, and he would meet with Enda because that's the way it usually happens. In one way, you need the director to be at the centre of the production process.

SO'G: In texts of both *The Walworth Farce* and *Penelope*, compared with the text of *The New Electric Ballroom*, Walsh seems to take a very directorial approach to setting the scene. In both, there are a few pages of stage directions right at the beginning. How do you find this as a designer?

SD: I find that extremely interesting. Enda's work is very visual. I know people say it's very wordy, but I think it's maybe more visual.

SO'G: As a designer, did you find these directions helpful?

SD: Yeah, because I think it's really born from what he wanted to say. Do you know what I mean? Like, they're not just decorative. They're really an expression.

SO'G: They are very clear and very defined. Right down to the six cans of Heineken in *The Walworth Farce*, these are quite exacting stage directions. So I was interested in how you might negotiate this as a designer? Do you feel it impacts on your freedom as a designer?

SD: I think it doesn't interfere with my freedom because whatever the frame is, you always have freedom. No, it didn't bother me.

SO'G: In the text of *The New Electric Ballroom*, we just get a kitchen/living room space with some '50s clothing hanging on the wall and a sponge cake on the counter. Did you feel you had more work to do in designing this work?

SD: Perhaps I had more freedom there, but I didn't really notice at the time. Every time I design, I try to understand the world. I think probably *The Walworth Farce* was the most constrained one. There was a lot of constraint because it's *so* physical. It's a tiny set, like, it's tiny, tiny. It looks bigger because I played a lot with perception. But I don't really think about how much freedom I have when I am working. I know Enda's directions and descriptions are really important. And then there's the responsibility you have when it's a new play. You need to be really clear about the work.

SO'G: Did you feel a responsibility to be very faithful to the worlds Walsh has created?

SD: Absolutely, because you give a frame and a kind of body language to the play—and also because I have admiration for his work. I think he's a fantastic writer.

SO'G: I want to get a bit more specific in relation to these three works. In *Penelope*, we have this group of men down in an empty swimming pool. And in *The Walworth Farce*, we have these three men sharing this dilapidated flat. In each case, I think, there's a sense of a very cluttered space—and dilapidated I think in both cases as well. Whereas, when I look back at your design for *The New Electric Ballroom*—Ada, Clara and Breda exist in a much cleaner space. This made me think about gender across the plays. And then you have the food items as well. We have sausages in both *The Walworth Farce* and *Penelope*. Then we have the cake in *The New Electric Ballroom*. Could you talk about the scenographies of these works, and the ways in which you and Walsh have directly and indirectly collaborated in conjuring them, in relation to gender?

SD: What is strange is that you make an association between *The Walworth Farce* and *Penelope*. For me, because *The Walworth Farce* and *The New Electric Ballroom* are sister plays, I associate both of them, and this informed the design. And also what is massively important for me is that Mikel Murfi directed *The Walworth Farce*, and Enda Walsh directed *The New Electric Ballroom*. So, I was with two different directors. And *The New Electric Ballroom*, Enda being the writer *and* the director, was a new experience for me. And that was fascinating—absolutely fascinating. Regarding the gender stuff, yes, this was really important. *The Walworth Farce* was a challenge regarding the movement, seeing everything as I said. For me, visually, *The New Electric Ballroom* was a completely different challenge. It was more *designed*. I think it's so much about love, *The New Electric Ballroom*, for me it had to be quite precious, metaphorical. But at the same time not obviously precious. There was that grey of the tiles, and I put some sparkle in the grey. It was just kind of an undertone. It was very reserved. I think the play is very reserved. So that's what I tried to do. And the *New Electric* has movement through lights: the monotony of life and the huge shift given by love, or hope of love, opening up the sky like a sunset after a grey day. In one way, it's actually quite a masculine space, because it's like a warehouse but that's what Enda gave.

SO'G: This must have been through directing because it's not there in the published text. I was going to ask about the big metal doors, and where that idea came from? I know it's the door to the outside world, and that it is significant that it keeps opening ...

SD: I can't remember now whether the idea for that big door came from Enda or from me but it doesn't really matter. What I know is that, yes, the door is massively important. In *The Walworth Farce*, it's that small door. And it was like everything in my design was pointing towards it, towards the possibility of escape, obviously. And in *The New Electric Ballroom*, it's different. The door is an intrusion—a masculine intrusion in that feminine world. And at the same time, it's very obvious—very in your face there in the centre—and very delicate. What I do remember about working with Enda on the design for *The New Electric Ballroom* is that there was something about the furniture—he wanted it to seem very *designed*. I think specifically for this play, I thought about the relationship between the costumes and the set. The costumes were also very precious. There are these women in their 70s who think they are seventeen. It's all about women—even though it's written by a man.

SO'G: I think all that plays into the way in which *The Walworth Farce* and *The New Electric Ballroom* are seen as sister works, and one play is viewed as the inversion of the other.

SD: Oh yes, and I just wanted to say, for me—I'm not sure if anybody noticed but—the designs were linked. In *The Walworth Farce*, the back wall was tilted very slightly towards the spectators, to try to give an impression of vertigo. And in *The New Electric Ballroom*, it was the opposite—because they had to be connected. And regarding *Penelope*, which is also great, it is a swimming pool, and it's a very striking set up. And that set up is so important to the play, in terms of the relations of power and all that ...

SO'G: Yeah, the physical layout of it.

SD: That's what I mean by the relations of power. There was something a bit funny about that show. I was looking for references. I was looking at modern architecture—forties architecture. Because, like *The New Electric Ballroom*, I wanted the world of *Penelope* to look quite designed.

SO'G: I noticed a correlation between *The New Electric Ballroom*, and the tiles, and those little tiles in the swimming pool in *Penelope*. I felt that there was a real sense of continuity there, in terms of the mid twentieth-century vibe.

SD: Yes. At some point when I was doing some research on modern architecture, I was trying to understand where that villa in *Penelope* would be. And I was kind of playing with the idea of where it would be. I imagined it might be somewhere in the Mediterranean. At the same time that I was doing the research, I discovered this house—I can't remember the architect—but when I saw it, I was like, this is where Enda's play happens. Then, a friend of mine came to see me in my studio and I was speaking to her. I said that I discovered this house—I didn't really speak about Enda's work—but I said that I discovered this house that is very beautiful. Then, after looking at this house I discovered that *Le Mépris*, which is a Godard movie, was shot there. So then I discovered afterwards that Godard's movie is also about

Penelope. It's about Ulysses. So it was funny because there was that link.

SO'G: So it was all interconnected.

SD: For *Penelope*, one of the first things I designed was the dress.

SO'G: I was going to ask you about costume in Penelope; that blue dress was very striking in the environment, I think.

SD: I was really trying to think about where it was taking place and because I had looked at this house, which was on a cliff, I decided that it really needed to be on a cliff. Because she's always watching the sea, you just needed to see her back which is really sexy. The dress had just a huge décolleté on the back. I just wanted the audience to see every muscle of her; I don't know, I think it's beautiful. Then there was the colour blue. That house in the film was red. It's not very visible in the design, but in my head I started thinking of the work of the artist Yves Klein from the middle of the twentieth century. There is a photo of Klein where he is jumping into the emptiness, which is a very beautiful photo. And that's one of the things I had in my mind. Yves Klein discovered a colour which is a really deep blue. For me, that is the colour that Penelope is looking at—that very specific and very intense blue. When she's looking at the sea, it's not really the sea in one sense: it's a print by Yves Klein.

SO'G: So it's reflected onto Penelope then, in the costume?

SD: On the dress? No, even though the dress was blue. I think I just wanted an all-blue environment. So it's all one—she is almost there with the sea. She is consumed by the sea so she is the same colour or something like that.

SO'G: To return then to *The New Electric Ballroom*. We talked about the doors. In the script, the characters often refer to this coffee cake. These are just minor details but I was wondering how it became a pink cake on stage?

SD: Ah, yeah, because there is lots of pink. It's a cliché but I think clichés usually work. It's a female world. Also some of the costumes are in pinks. I wanted to ostentatiously create a female-used world, to show how it is impossible for these characters to do things differently.

SO'G: Walsh's theatre necessitates many quick costume changes ...

SD: Oh yeah, I think he is just giving a challenge to everybody [giggles].

SO'G: In terms of these quick costume changes, I was wondering—on a very practical level—how this might have impacted on your design?

SD: I don't remember specific difficulties. In *The New Electric Ballroom*, the costumes were much more precious. Those were beautiful pieces in *The New Electric Ballroom*, I think. In *The Walworth Farce*, there were farce costumes. The quick changes are of that kind. All the plays offer completely different ways to approach costume, I think. The changes in *Penelope* are more magic. It's more poetic, I think. So, in one way, what was interesting about *The Walworth Farce* was to *see* the change, because it's funny and it shows their madness somehow. But I think it's a bit different in *Penelope*. It is more about trying to impress, but there is something magic about it. And it is done behind the screen; it's not visible. It was mad, technically it was completely insane. We went to see a magician and we learned some tricks that we were sworn to keep secret. But also, there was an absolutely fantastic dress-maker Doreen MacKenna working on the show. I mean, I designed, but the technicalities, the practicalities of it were handled by the dress-maker. Of course, it's important to consider these details in the design but it's also about the quality of the people making the costumes. The changes were crazy—really crazy. I loved it!

SO'G: These productions toured extensively. How did the changing spaces and contexts impact on your scenography in terms of how it was conceived and, perhaps, perceived?

SD: I didn't follow the shows everywhere, but I always think that this is fascinating to think about. In *Penelope*, there are the quick costume changes of the different lovers. And at the end, there is the image of Jackie, with JFK being killed, which must have resonated in the States. I'm also interested in how technically they rebuild the sets since I don't follow the tours everywhere. We rebuilt *The New Electric Ball Room* in Australia and we rebuilt *The Walworth Farce* in the States. And there was a version of *Penelope* in Washington. I know it's different but I find it hard to explain how it's different. And there is a lot of Irishness in the works. I know in places like the States you will have a lot of Irish people. But even so, it's not the same perception. I mean, some people abroad might have an idealized image of Ireland, which these plays challenge. But because they are strong plays, in a way, it doesn't really matter where they are staged.

SO'G: I read one review of a production of *Penelope* in the States in which the empty swimming pool is seen to represent post-Celtic Tiger Ireland. I wonder if you can see allusions like this in Walsh's plays and if it informs your approach to design? Did you see the swimming pool in this light for example?

SD: Specifically, to comment on the swimming pool and the Celtic Tiger, I don't know if I would have specifically thought about that. I guess on one level, of course, obviously these men are coming out of the

Celtic Tiger; all these men have lost out. So seeing the space as a physical representation of this, in one way this is accurate. But that would seem to me almost anecdotal. The design was my own story— with the blue of Yves Klein and all that. Maybe *I* told my story, but there are always different levels in a play. Is it a metaphor for Ireland? Probably, and a metaphor is there to be transcended. And I think—I hope—a good set is always a bit about that.

SO'G: I'm interested in how the theatre space impacts on reception. When I think of Walsh's work, I feel like there is a through-line, and that through-line is spatial. The characters are trapped; there's a sense of claustrophobia, of confinement—of stifling, contained spaces. How do you think this sense translates scenographically to larger theatre spaces? In terms of design, spatial organization and perhaps audience's perceptions?

SD: It seems to me the playing with perception in *Penelope* was about the immensity behind, the sea, the representation of wild nature. The outside versus inside again. Those men being stuck, alienated, and us as spectators facing the immensity. Having the option. Oh, it's fascinating to play with perception. Theatre is a lot about that—and it is fascinating. I think you can achieve confinement in a huge space. Absolutely. But you need to design *for* that space. *The Walworth Farce* was designed first for the Druid theatre. And Druid's space is a difficult space. It's a really charged space, and it's a beautiful space.

SO'G: Did the issues of dislocation and exile, so central to Walsh's drama, play into your approach to these works?

SD: There is a lot of stuff in Enda's work about inside and outside. And when we think about space what is really important is how we position the spectator—which position do you give to the spectator to listen to that story. I think it's the basis of theatre design. Then, the use of perception or not ...

SO'G: Playing with perception?

SD: If you need to. Actually, you always play with perception in scenography. Even if it is through very small gestures, the spatial, visual representation "manipulates" the spectator's mind.

SO'G: Going back to the published text of *Penelope*, the stage directions are very sensuous compared with the others. The opening details are: "After a little time, we realize that we're looking at a dilapidated swimming pool drained of water." Then we read, "the pool's been turned into a living space and it seems to have operated as such for years." And then when the lights come up fully, we have this still picture. Directions like these are all about cultivating a situation whereby a sense of the space and its function emerge very gradually. And I think they are also about playing with perception, which is something you already mentioned in relation to your approach to the design—and design in general. I was wondering how you negotiate stage directions like these scenographically?

SD: With the fact that you don't see straight away what the space is about?

SO'G: I feel like when Walsh wrote those directions, he was placing himself in the position of the spectator to a greater extent than in the other two. He's unpacking these details as an audience member might experience them in a very gradual way: you see this, you don't know what it is, then gradually it all begins to emerge. In the production, the audience starts to realize bit by bit what the significance of this space is. And we are given the time for this process to take place. In the play text, I think the stage directions are slightly different from the others, and I wonder how this informed your approach.

SD: Now I'm remembering. It *is* quite different. But *The Walworth Farce* and *The New Electric Ballroom* are together, and *Penelope* is a slight departure. I mean, it's a reinterpretation of a Greek story. The first thing that came to my mind when you said that is that it's the movement of a man that reveals what the space is. I guess if somebody writes in quite a visual way it's because it's a way to translate through words these things that you cannot see. And the fact that you don't see exactly what the space is straight away is quite important. At the beginning with *The Walworth Farce*, Enda wanted the set to be even closer to the audience. And we couldn't do it; we didn't have the space. I think for him it offered a possible way to get into that world. I think he approached this in a different way with *Penelope*. Here, you understand that world through the movement, through the way it comes to life. I mean, it's an appropriation of a foreign space; it's not a normal living space. Then again, in all three plays, the spaces end up not being used for what they were originally intended. The original look at the set is a punch, and then the spectator is pushed to observe details—here the fact the space has been inhabited for so long. What emerges is a sense of time, and the effects of time.

SO'G: I think that what happens at the beginning of *Penelope* is a stylized activation of the scenography, beginning with the still image in which we have the two performers on stage unmoving, and it's like looking at a picture, then the movement activates the scenography. The movement activates our understanding of the space and its function. I mean, scenography can't really be still; it has to be dynamic because it involves an engagement between live bodies and space.

SD: Absolutely. The space is only interesting when it's in use. That's why what is *essential* is the relationship between the designer and the director. This is massively important. Then you have, of course, the writer who is sometimes at the centre. Sometimes, I mean, it depends. One of the differences between the theatre here and in France is that writers are seen as more important here.

SO'G: In each play, there is a device through which the characters play music. Can you comment on the function of music in Walsh's work?

SD: Oh, it's really important. I mean, there are the central things, and the writing is important and all that. But the sound and the visuals are probably just as important. The sound is like a direct route to the heart. Enda is using the same kinds of objects; he's using food; lots of motifs are very similar.

SO'G: Tell me about the interaction between the choice of music and the direction and the design and the lighting, since all these are elements of scenography.

SD: Absolutely because it's all one. And that's why Enda's work is so interesting because it allows for bringing everything together. That is deep down what theatre is about. And scenography uses a variety of tools to converge as a body language for the production.

SO'G: Walsh talks about lighting in the stage directions too. I think he makes a lot of scenographic considerations.

SD: He's playing a lot with all these elements. He's kind of marking a difference between the moments where he is doing a production—a production in the sense of a magic effect—and the moments where it is realistic dialogue. Enda plays a lot with these because you have plays within plays and so on. The box in the box in the box ...

SO'G: Layers.

SD: Layers but also things you need to open. More than just layers.

SO'G: Okay, it looks like we will have to finish up here. Sabine Dargent thank you so much for this really illuminating discussion!

Performances and Bibliography

First Performances

Fishy Tales (1993)—Graffiti Theatre Company, Popes Quay, Cork.

A Christmas Carol (1994) Corcadorca Theatre Company, Granary Theatre, Cork.

The Ginger Ale Boy (1995)—Corcadorca Theatre Company, Granary Theatre, Cork.

Disco Pigs (1996)—Corcadorca Theatre Company, Triskel Arts Centre, Cork.

Sucking Dublin (1997)—Abbey Theatre Company, Samuel Becket Theatre, Dublin.

Misterman (1999)—Corcadorca Theatre Company, Granary Theatre, Cork.

Bedbound (2000)—Dublin Theatre Festival, New Theatre, Dublin.

Pondlife Angels (2005)—Cork Midsummer Festival, Granary Theatre, Cork.

Chatroom (2005)—Behind The Scenes Theatre Company, Buckhaven Theatre, Fife. National Theatre, London. & etc.

The New Electric Ballroom (2004)—Kammerspiele, Munich

The Small Things (2005)—Paines Plough Company, Menier Chocolate Factory, London.

The Walworth Farce (2006)—Druid Theatre Company, Town Hall Theatre, Galway.

How These Desperate Men Talk [under title of *Fraternity*] (2008)—Zurich Shauspielehaus, Switzerland.

Lynndie's Gotta Gun (2008)—Artistas Unidos, Lisbon. Druid Theatre Company, Galway.

Gentrification (2008)—Druid Theatre Company, Mick Lally Theatre, Galway

Delirium (2008)—An adaptation of Dostoevsky's *The Brothers Karamazov* for Theatre O, Abbey Theatre, Dublin. Barbican Theatre, London.

The Man in the Moon (2009)—co-written with Jack Healy, The Albany, Deptford, London.

My Friend Duplicity (2010)—short play—Traverse Theatre, Edinburgh Festival.

Penelope (2010)—Oberhausen Theater, Germany. Feb. 2010.

Room 303 as part of *Sixty Six Books: A Contemporary Response to the King James Bible* (2011) —Bush Theatre.

Once (2011)—Musical adaptation of the film *Once*, New York Theater Workshop (Off-Broadway: December 2011—January 2012)

Ballyturk (2014) 2014 Galway International Arts Festival at the Black Box Theatre.

Film

Not a Bad Christmas (1999)—Short

Disco Pigs (2001)–Vanguard Cinema, Temple, Film/Renaissance

Hunger (2008)–Blast!Films/Channel 4

Chatroom (2010)–Pathe, Ruby Films

Radio

Four Big Days in the Life of Dessie Banks, RTE Radio 1.

The Monotonous Life of Little Mr. P., BBC Radio Four

Published Plays and Screenplays

Disco Pigs and *Sucking Dublin*. London: Nick Hern, 1997.

"Disco Pigs" in *Far From the Land: Contemporary Irish Plays*. Ed. John Farleigh. London: Methuen (1998): 159-189.

bedbound & Misterman. London: Nick Hern, 2001.

The Small Things. London: Nick Hern, 2005.

Chatroom. New York: Samuel French, 2007.

The Walworth Farce. London: Nick Hern, 2007.

Delirium. London: Nick Hern, 2008.

The New Electric Ballroom. London: Nick Hern, 2008.

Penelope. London: Nick Hern, 2008.

The Walworth Farce and *The New Electric Ballroom*. New York: Theatre Communications Group, 2009.

Plays One. London: Nick Hern, 2011

Misterman. London: Nick Hern, 2012

Room 303 was published in Sixty Six Books: a Contemporary Response to the King James Bible. London: Oberon, 2012

Once. London: Nick Hern, 2013 and Glen Hansard

Ballyturk. London: Nick Hern, 2014

Plays Two. London: Nick Hern, 2014
The Walworth Farce. London: Nick Hern, 2014

Bibliography

Etienne, Anne, "Pond Life and Angels: Enda Walsh's adaptations to Cork" in *Drama Reinvented:Theatre Adaptations in Ireland 1970-2007.* London: Peter Lang, 2012.

Fitzpatrick, Lisa. "Enda Walsh." *The Methuen Drama Guide to Contemporary Irish Playwrights.* Ed. Martin Middeke and Peter Paul Schnierer. London: Bloomsbury, 2010.

Freshwater, Helen "*Delirium*: In rehearsal with Theatre O" in *Devising in Process* (ed) Alex Mermikides. Basingstoke: Palgrave Macmillan, 2010

Hanrahan, Johnny. "Theatre in Cork/Cork in Theatre, an Exercise in Perspective." *Druids, Dudes and Beauty Queens.* Ed. Dermot Bolger. Dublin: New Island, 2001. 92-103. Print.

Hynes, Garry, "From Galway to Broadway and Back Again", *American Journal of Irish Studies,* Vol. 9 (2012), pp. 79-96

Jordan, Eamonn, Dissident Dramturgies: Contemporary Irish Theatre. Dublin: IAP, 2011

Jordan, Eamonn, "It Would Never Happen On *The Waltons*: Enda Walsh's *The* Walworth Farce", *Staging Thought: Essays on Irish Theatre Practice and Scholarship,* Ed. Rhona Trench. Oxford: New York: Peter Lang, 2012. Print

Lonergan, Patrick, *Theatre and Globalization.* Basingstoke: Palgrave Macamillan, 2007

Lachman, Michal. "Zagracsiebie. Irlandczyk w teatrzezyciacodziennego" [Play Yourself: Theatricality in Frank McGuinness's and Enda Walsh's Drama]. *Dialog* 5 (2011): 62-73. [In Polish]

Llewellyn-Jones, Margaret. *Contemporary Irish Drama and Cultural Identity.* Bristol: Intellect, 2008.

O'Brien, Karen. "New Irelands: Enda Walsh Festival', *Theatre Journal* 63. 4 (2011): 646-49.

Ojrzynska, Katarzyna. "Dancing as If Language No Longer Existed": Dance in Contemporary Irish Drama. London: Peter Lang, 2014.

Pilny, Ondrej. "The Grotesque in the Plays of Enda Walsh" *Irish Studies Review,* 21:2, p 217-225 Published Online 25 June 2013.

Pine, Emilie. *The Politics of Irish Memory: Performing Remembrance in Contemporary Irish Culture.* Basingstoke: Palgrave Macmillan, 2010.

---. "Body of Evidence: Performing *Hunger"* in *Masculinity and Irish Popular Culture: Tiger's Tales,* eds Conn Holohan and Tony Tracy. Basingstoke: Palgrave Macmillan, 2014.

Roesner, David. *Musicality in Theatre: Music as Model, Method and Metaphor in Theatre-Making.* Surrey: Ashgate, 2014. Print.

Singleton, Brian. *Masculinities and The Contemporary Irish Theatre.* Basingstoke: Palgrave Macmillan, 2011.

Smart, Lauren, "Odysseus's New Address", *American Theatre* 30. 1 (2013): 28-28

Sternlicht , Sanford. Modern Irish Drama: W. B. Yeats to Marina Carr, Second Edition. New York: Syracuse, 2010.

Trotter, Mary, *Modern Irish Theatre.* Cambridge: Polity, 2008.

Wallace, Kevin "Fintan O'Toole: Power Plays" and the High Art/Low Art Discourse in the Narrative of Irish Theatre" in *Ireland and Popular Culture* ed. Sylvie Mikoski. Oxford: Peter Lang 2014. 115-28

Wallenberg, Christopher. "Small Rooms Full of Words", *American Theatre.* 27.3 (2010): 22-25.

Weaver, Jesse. "'The Words Look After Themselves": The Practice of Enda Walsh." *Irish Drama: Local and Global Perspectives.* Eds. Nicholas Grene and Patrick Lonergan. Dublin: Carysfort Press, 2012.

Newspaper Articles, Features and Interviews

Billington, Michael. "Enda Walsh: 'Pure theatre animal' explores solitude and the void below." *The Guardian* 18 Sept. 2014: n. pag. Web. 6 Dec. 2014.

Costa, Maddy. "One Man and His Monsters." *The Guardian.* 17 September 2008.Web. 26 November 2014. <http://www.theguardian.com/stage/2008/sep/18/theatre.drama>

"Enda Walsh in Conversation with Emelie FitzGibbon." *Theatre Talk.* Eds. Lilian Chambers, Ger FitzGibbon, and Eamonn Jordan. Dublin: Carysfort Press, 2001. 471-80. Print.

Fricker, Karen. "Pondlife Angels." *The Guardian.* N.p., 16 June 2005. Web. 29 Apr. 2015.

Patrick, Jon. "'Transformer'—Interview with Enda Walsh." *Film Ireland* 82 (2001): 17-18. Print.

Taylor, James C. "Irishman Enda Walsh doesn't let words get in the way." *Los Angeles Times* 8 Nov. 2009: n. pag. Web. 7 Dec. 2014.

"'Taking on *Once The Musical* Was Potentially Disastrous'—Enda Walsh Interview." *The Irish Post.* N.p., 10 Apr. 2013. Web. 02 May 2015.

Walsh, Enda. "Acceptance Speech: Enda Walsh." The Tony Awards. Beacon Theatre. 10 June 2012. Speech.

Walsh, Enda. "Femi Oyebode in conversation with Enda Walsh." Interview by Femi Oyebode. *Youtube.* The Art of Psychiatry Society, 27 July 2013. Web. 24 Feb. 2015. <https://www.youtube.com/watch?v=jPOnVlLlWzo>.

Walsh, Enda. "In conversation: Joe Dowling and Enda Walsh." Interview by Joe Dowling. *Youtube.* Walker Art Center, 25 May 2010. Web. 24 Feb. 2015. <https://www.youtube.com/watch?v=BCJdK-U1Q-4>.

Walsh, Enda Interview Recorded at the Steppenwolf Theatre Company 19 June 2012 YouTube Web.

Walsh, Enda. "Tony Nominee Enda Walsh on How Writing Once Lightened His Soul."*Broadway.com*. 22 May 2012. Web. 22 Jan. 2015. <http://www.broadway.com/buzz/162037/tony-nominee-enda-walsh-on-how-writing-once-lightened-his-soul/>.

Contributors

Nelson Barre is a PhD candidate at the National University of Ireland, Galway. He is the recipient of the Hardiman Research Scholarship for his doctoral research which examines ritual, memory, and performance in contemporary Irish theatre, specifically the works of Enda Walsh. His written work has appeared in *Comparative Drama* and *New Hibernia Review*, and another essay will appear in a forthcoming collection on the work of Mark O'Rowe.

Mary P. Caulfield is Assistant Professor of English and Humanities at the State University of New York at Farmingdale. She holds a PhD from Trinity College Dublin. Her current research combines the political and the performative, specifically with regards to contested figures in Ireland's past. Mary has published extensively on these topics and has just recently published a co-edited collection entitled, *Ireland, Memory and Performing the Historical Imagination* in the Autumn of 2014.

Sabine Dargent is the winner of two *Irish Times* Best Set Design Awards and has been nominated for two others. She works with a range of Irish directors and practitioners, designing sets, or sets and costumes. In addition, she designs street visuals (costumes, props and floats, for about 250 people performing each year) as part of the St. Patrick Festival: City Fusion and Brighter Future, a community project about inclusion and art. She has also worked on exhibitions, film and television. She trained in France, in conceptual art and physical theatre.

Tanya Dean is currently completing her Doctor of Fine Arts degree at Yale School of Drama, where she also received her Masters of Fine Arts in Dramaturgy and Dramatic Criticism. Her current research focuses on the role of fairy tales and folktales in European theater. Her recent publications include contributions to edited collections such as *The Routledge Companion to Dramaturgy*, *Radical Contemporary Theatre Practices by Women in Ireland*, *That Was Us: Contemporary Irish Theatre and Performance*, and *Interactions: Dublin Theatre Festival 1957–2007*; and journals such as *TDR*, *Theater*, and *Journal of the Fantastic in the Arts*. In 2013, she was awarded the Irish Society for Theatre Research New Scholars' Prize. Select credits as dramaturg include *The Yellow Wallpaper* by Charlotte Perkins Gilman, directed by Aoife Spillane-Hinks (Then This Theatre Company, Dublin); *The Glass Menagerie* by Tennessee Williams, directed by Gordon Edelstein (Long Wharf Theatre, New Haven; New York; Los Angeles); *Pilgrim* by Philip Doherty, directed by Aoife Spillane-Hinks (Gonzo Theatre Company, Dublin); and *Bones in the Basket: An Evening of Russian Fairy Tales* devised by Good Belly ensemble, directed by Devin Brain (Araca Theatre Project, New York).

Lisa Fitzpatrick is Senior Lecturer in the School of Creative Arts and Technologies, Ulster University. Her research is mainly engaged with issues of representing violence in performance and feminist practice in Ireland. She has published in *Performance Research*, *CTR*, *Modern Drama*, *Irish University Review* and *L'Annuaire Théâtral*.

Nursen Gömceli is Assistant Professor at the Department of English Language and Literature at Akdeniz University, Antalya. She has previously held positions at Hacettepe University, Ankara and Alpen-Adria University, Klagenfurt. Her PhD was on the work of the dramatist Timberlake Wertenbaker and she has published nationally and internationally on feminist drama, Wertenbaker and Harold Pinter. Her main research interests are in the area of contemporary British drama, feminist drama, feminist literary theory, the American short story, and Irish drama. Major publication: *Timberlake Wertenbaker and Contemporary British Feminist Drama*, Palo Alto, 2010.

Kay Martinovich is Assistant Professor in Acting at Northern Illinois University in DeKalb, Illinois. She also works as a professional theater director based in Chicago. From 1999-2006, she was Associate Artistic Director of Irish Repertory of Chicago, where she directed the American premieres of Marina Carr's *By the Bog of Cats...* and Brian Friel's *The Yalta Game*. Other Irish Rep credits include Tom Murphy's *Bailegangaire*, Stewart Parker's *Pentecost*, and Carr's *The Mai*. Kay holds a doctorate in Theatre Historiography from the

University of Minnesota and an M.Phil. in Irish Theatre and Film Studies from Trinity College, Dublin. Her work has been published in *New Hibernia Review* and she has essays in *Querying Difference in Theatre History* (2007) and *The Theatre of Marina Carr: "before rules was made"* (2003).

Kevin McCluskey is a PhD student in the School of Creative Arts at Queen's University Belfast. He has recently completed his doctoral thesis, entitled "Stage to Screen and Back Again: Film Adaptation and Irish Theatre".

Audrey McNamara holds a PhD in Drama and specializes on the work of Bernard Shaw. She is currently working on her monograph entitled *Bernard Shaw: From Womanhood to Nationhood* examining the period from 1890 to 1912 when the female suffrage movement and the Irish question were prominent issues. She is co-editor with Nelson O'Ceallaigh Ritschel on a Bernard Shaw Anthology *Shaw and the Making of Modern Ireland* and guest co-editor of the Shaw Annual 36.1 *Shaw and Money*. Audrey organized the hugely successful first Irish International Shaw Conference co-sponsored by University College Dublin and the International Shaw Society which was opened by the President of Ireland, Michael D Higgins in the National Gallery of Ireland May 2012. In August 2014 she wrote the programme note for the Abbey's production of *Heartbreak House* and interviewed the Director Roisin McBrinn on the Peacock Stage. In March 2015 she gave a plenary in the National Theatre in London as part of the theatre's *Man and Superman* program.

Mikel Murfi is a freelance actor, director and writer from Sligo. He has worked closely with Enda Walsh over many years. He has directed productions of *The Walworth Farce* and *Penelope*. He has Movement Directed Walsh's *Misterman* and has acted in *The New Electric Ballroom*, *Lynndie's Got A Gun* and *Ballyturk*. Summer 2015 sees him play the role of the Caretaker in Walsh's new opera *The Last Hotel*.

Katarzyna Ojrzyńska teaches British and Irish literature in the Department of Studies in Drama and Pre-1800 Literature, University of Łódź (Poland), where she earned her PhD. Her book *"Dancing as if language no longer existed:" Dance in Contemporary Irish Drama* was published in the Reimagining Ireland series (Peter Lang 2015).

Katarzyna's research interests include drama and performing arts, Irish studies, body culture studies, and disability studies.

Finian O'Gorman is a PhD candidate and IRC Government of Ireland Scholar in the Centre for Drama, Theatre and Performance in NUI Galway. His thesis topic is titled "Ireland's Theatre of Nation: The Amateur Theatre Movement, 1932-1980". His research interests are amateur theatre, theatre and cyberspace, postdramatic theatre, and the plays of Enda Walsh.

Siobhán O'Gorman is Government of Ireland Postdoctoral Fellow (2013-2015) at the School of Drama, Film and Music, Trinity College Dublin. There, she is working on her book project "A Stage of Re-Vision: Scenography in Irish Theatre 1950-1990." She taught at the English Department, NUI, Galway from 2008 to 2013, where she received a PhD for her thesis "Negotiating Genders from the Page to the Stage." She co-organized the Dublin Theatre Festival symposium "Performing Space" in 2014, and is also co-convenor of TaPRA's Scenography Working Group. Her research has appeared in a range of publications including *Irish Studies Review, Scene* and *Irish Theatre International*. She was a critic for *Irish Theatre Magazine* from 2008 to 2013 and is co-editor of Carysfort's forthcoming essay collection *Devised Performance in Irish Theatre: Histories and Contemporary Practices*.

Michelle Paull is Senior Lecturer in Theatre & Performance Studies at St Mary's University College, Strawberry Hill, Twickenham, London where she also teaches on the MA in Irish Studies and the MA International Ensemble. Her publications include Bernard Shaw in *Irish Writing London* ed. by Tom Herron (2013), Sean O'Casey for Irish Studies in Europe and Dermot Healy for Dalkey Archive Press in 2015. Michelle is the editor of *UpStage*, an online journal of fin de siècle theatre and her research interests include contemporary theatre & fiction, adaptation studies and Daphne Du Maurier. Michelle is currently writing a monograph entitled *Sean O'Casey: Critical Controversies about the later plays of Sean O'Casey*.

Kevin Wallace is a Lecturer in English at the Dun Laoghaire Institute of Art Design and Technology. He teaches Tragic Theatre, Twentieth Century Irish Literature & Drama, and American Literature & Drama, on the English, Media and Cultural Studies degree. His research interests include contemporary Anglophone theatre, semiotics, subjectivity, and gender studies. He has published variously on Marina Carr, Sarah Kane, Conor McPherson and Enda Walsh. He completed his PhD in 2011 at University College Dublin's school of English, Drama and Film.

Ian R. Walsh is a Lecturer in Drama, Theatre and Performance at the NUI Galway. He has a PhD from University College Dublin where he taught full time from 2010-2014. Ian has published widely on Irish theatre in peer-reviewed journals and edited collections. In 2012 his critically acclaimed monograph *Experimental Irish Theatre, After W.B Yeats* was published by Palgrave Macmillan. He has been a Theatre Reviewer for *Irish Theatre Magazine* and RTE Radio 1 and has also worked as a Director of Theatre and Opera.

Jesse Weaver is an American writer and researcher based in Dublin. He received his doctorate from University College Cork, where his research focused on the changing role of the playwright in Irish theatre production. He was a reviewer for *Irish Theatre Magazine* from 2008 to 2013 and wrote several features for the magazine focusing on new writing for the Irish stage. A playwright himself, Jesse's work has been seen in Chicago, New York, Dublin and the U.K.

Index

Carysfort Press was formed in the summer of 1998. It receives annual funding from the Arts Council.

The directors believe that drama is playing an ever-increasing role in today's society and that enjoyment of the theatre, both professional and amateur, currently plays a central part in Irish culture.

The Press aims to produce high quality publications which, though written and/or edited by academics, will be made accessible to a general readership. The organisation would also like to provide a forum for critical thinking in the Arts in Ireland, again keeping the needs and interests of the general public in view.

The company publishes contemporary Irish writing for and about the theatre.

Editorial and publishing inquiries to:
Carysfort Press Ltd.,
58 Woodfield,
Scholarstown Road,
Rathfarnham,
Dublin 16,
Republic of Ireland.

T (353 1) 493 7383
E: info@carysfortpress.com
www.carysfortpress.com

HOW TO ORDER

TRADE ORDERS DIRECTLY TO:
Irish Book Distribution
Unit 12, North Park, North Road,
Finglas, Dublin 11.

T: (353 1) 8239580
E: mary@argosybooks.ie
www.argosybooks.ie

INDIVIDUAL ORDERS DIRECTLY TO:
eprint Ltd.
35 Coolmine Industrial Estate,
Blanchardstown, Dublin 15.
T: (353 1) 827 8860
E: books@eprint.ie
www.eprint.ie

FOR SALES IN NORTH AMERICA AND CANADA:
Dufour Editions Inc.,
124 Byers Road,
PO Box 7,
Chester Springs,
PA 19425,
USA

T: 1-610-458-5005
F: 1-610-458-7103

Devised Performance in Irish Theatre

Edited by Siobhán O'Gorman and Charlotte McIvor

This important publication is the first collection of articles on the work of the internationally recognised award-winning theatre of Enda Walsh. In a wide range of essays, the book explores Walsh's radical theatrical imagination, its development, contexts and its ability to flourish across genres from theatre to film to musical. The volume aims to give a multitude of perspectives on Walsh's work with articles and interviews from leading theatre practitioners on the direction, production and designing of Walsh's theatre considered alongside critical essays by both emerging and established international scholars. Written in an accessible style, it will be of interest to all enthusiasts of contemporary theatre and performance.
Professor Brian Singleton, Trinity College, Dublin

ISBN 978-1-909325-78-4   €20 (Paperback)

Sullied Magnificence: The Theatre of Mark O'Rowe

Edited by Sara Keating and Emma Creedon

"Mark O'Rowe is one of contemporary theatre's great extremists -- vivid, violent, beautiful, grotesque, each play a savage war between form and content. It takes some daring to explore the minefields he creates and in this very welcome volume, the authors do so with an intelligence that matches their intrepidity. Anyone with an interest in Irish theatre now will want to read it."
(Fintan O'Toole)

ISBN 978-1-909325-66-1   €20 (Paperback)

Radical Contemporary Theatre Practices by Women in Ireland

Edited by Miriam Haughton and Mária Kurdi

Radical Contemporary Theatre Practices by Women in Ireland is an important contribution to the fields of Irish theatre and performance studies, and gender and performance in Ireland. The essays and interviews explore the work of women directors, designers, and playwrights on both sides of the Irish Border, who are currently shaping theatre practice on the island. By gathering such an impressive range of material, Mária Kurdi and Miriam Haughton have produced a collection that offers a snapshot of radical practice on the Irish stage in the early 21st century.

ISBN 978-1-909325-75-3   €20 (Paperback)

The Theatre of Marie Jones: Telling Stories from the Ground up

Edited by Eugene McNulty and Tom Maguire

Marie Jones is one of the most prolific and popular writers working in Northern Irish theatre today. Her work has achieved local relevance and international recognition. From her earliest work with Charabanc in the early 1980s to the present day, Jones's work has engaged with Irish (and, more often than not, specifically Northern Irish) experience in ways that reveal the extent to which the personal is political in a distinctive form of popular theatre. This volume of essays engages critically with Jones's oeuvre, her reception in Ireland and beyond, and her position in the canon of contemporary drama.

ISBN 78-1-909325-65-4   €20 (Paperback)

Blue Raincoat Theatre Company

By Rhona Trench

Since its foundation in 1991, Blue Raincoat Theatre Company is Ireland's only full-time venue-based professional theatre ensemble and has become renowned for its movement, visual and aural proficiencies and precision. This book explores those signatures from a number of vantage points, conveying the complex challenges faced by Blue Raincoat as they respond to changing aesthetic and economic circumstances. Particular consideration is given to set, costume, sound and lighting design.

ISBN 78-1-909325-67-8   €20 (Paperback)

Across the Boundaries: Talking about Thomas Kilroy

Edited by: Guy Woodward

Thomas Kilroy's long and distinguished career is celebrated in this volume by new essays, panel discussions and an interview, reconsidering the work of one of Ireland's most intellectually ambitious and technically imaginative playwrights. Contributors are drawn from both the academic and theatrical spheres, and include Nicholas Grene, Wayne Jordan, Patrick Mason, Christopher Murray and Lynne Parker.

ISBN 78-1-909325-51-7 €15.00 (Paperback)

Tradition and Craft in Piano-Paying,
by Tilly Fleischmann

Edited by Ruth Fleischmann and John Buckley
DVD Musical examples: Gabriela Mayer

This is a document of considerable historical importance, offering an authoritative account of Liszt's teaching methods as imparted by two of his former students to whom he was particularly close. It contains much valuable information of a kind that is unavailable elsewhere. It records a direct and authentic oral tradition of continental European pianism going back to the nineteenth century.

ISBN 78-1-909325-524 €30 (Paperback)

Wexfour: John Banville, Eoin Colfer, Billy Roche, Colm Toibin

Edited by Ben Barnes
A dedication of four short plays by Wexford writers to celebrate the 40th Anniversary of Wexford Arts Centre.

ISBN 78-1-909325-548 €10

For the Sake of Sanity: Doing things with humour in Irish performance

Edited by Eric Weitz

Humour claims no ideological affiliation – its workings merit inspection in any and every individual case, in light of the who, what, where and when of a joke, including the manner of performance, the socio-cultural context, the dynamic amongst participants, and who knows how many other factors particular to the instance. There as many insights to be gained from the deployment of humour in performance as people to think about it – so herein lie a healthy handful of responses from a variety of perspectives.

For the Sake of Sanity: *Doing things with humour in Irish performance* assembles a range of essays from practitioners, academics, and journalists, all of whom address the attempt to make an audience laugh in various Irish contexts over the past century. With a general emphasis on theatre, the collection also includes essays on film, television and stand-up comedy for those insights into practice, society and culture revealed uniquely through instances of humour in performance.

ISBN 78-1-909-325-56-2 €20

Stanislavski in Ireland: Focus at Fifty

Edited by Brian McAvera and Steven Dedalus Burch

Stanislavski in Ireland: Focus at Fifty is an insight into Ireland's only arthouse theatre from the people who were there. Through interviews, articles, short memoirs and photographs, the book tracks the theatre from its inception, detailing the period under its founder Deirdre O'Connell and then the period following Joe Devlin's arrival as its new artistic director. Many of Ireland's leading theatre and film artists trained and worked at Focus, including Gabriel Byrne, Joan Bergin, Olwen Fouèrè, Brendan Coyle, Rebecca Schull, Johnny Murphy, Sean Campion, Tom Hickey and Mary Elizabeth and Declan Burke-Kennedy. The book comes complete with a chronological list of productions.

ISBN 78-1-909325-43-2 €20

Breaking Boundaries. An Anthology of Original Plays from the Focus Theatre

Edited by Steven Dedalus Burch

Almost from the beginning, since 1970, new plays became part of the Focus's repertory. Of the seven plays in this anthology, all exhibit a range in styles from Lewis Carroll's fantastical world (*Alice in Wonderland* by Mary Elizabeth Burke-Kennedy), to a couple on the brink of a philandering weekend disaster (*The Day of the Mayfly* by Declan Burke-Kennedy), to a one-man show about Jonathan Swift (*Talking Through His Hat* by Michael Harding), an examination of two shoplifting thieves and the would-be writer who gets in their way (*Pinching For My Soul* by Elizabeth Moynihan), a battle royal between two sides of a world-famous painter (*Francis and Frances* by Brian McAvera), the reactions of multiple New Yorkers to that moment in September, 2011 (*New York Monologues* by Mike Poblete), to the final days of an iconic movie star (*Hollywood Valhalla* by Aidan Harney).

ISBN 78-1-909325-42-5 €20

The Art Of Billy Roche: Wexford As The World

Edited by Kevin Kerrane

Billy Roche – musician, actor, novelist, dramatist, screenwriter – is one of Ireland's most versatile talents. This anthology, the first comprehensive survey of Roche's work, focuses on his portrayal of one Irish town as a microcosm of human life itself, elemental and timeless. Among the contributors are fellow artists (Colm Tóibín, Conor McPherson, Belinda McKeon), theatre professionals (Benedict Nightingale, Dominic Dromgoole, Ingrid Craigie), and scholars on both sides of the Atlantic.

ISBN 78-1-904505-60-0 €20

The Theatre of Conor McPherson: 'Right beside the Beyond'

Edited by Lilian Chambers and Eamonn Jordan

Multiple productions and the international successes of plays like *The Weir* have led to Conor McPherson being regarded by many as one of the finest writers of his generation. McPherson has also been hugely prolific as a theatre director, as a screenwriter and film director, garnering many awards in these different roles. In this collection of essays, commentators from around the world address the substantial range of McPherson's output to date in theatre and film, a body of work written primarily during and in the aftermath of Ireland's Celtic Tiger period. These critics approach the work in challenging and dynamic ways, considering the crucial issues of morality, the rupturing of the real, storytelling, and the significance of space, violence and gender. Explicit considerations are given to comedy and humour, and to theatrical form, especially that of the monologue and to the ways that the otherworldly, the unconscious and supernatural are accommodated dramaturgically, with frequent emphasis placed on the specific aspects of performance in both theatre and film.

ISBN 78 1 904505 61 7 €20

The Story of Barabbas, The Company

Carmen Szabo

Acclaimed by audiences and critics alike for their highly innovative, adventurous and entertaining theatre, Barabbas The Company have created playful, intelligent and dynamic productions for over 17 years. Breaking the mould of Irish theatrical tradition and moving away from a text dominated theatre, Barabbas The Company's productions have established an instantly recognizable performance style influenced by the theatre of clown, circus, mime, puppetry, object manipulation and commedia dell'arte. This is the story of a unique company within the framework of Irish theatre, discussing the influences that shape their performances and establish their position within the history and development of contemporary Irish theatre. This book addresses the overwhelming necessity to reconsider Irish theatre history and to explore, in a language accessible to a wide range of readers, the issues of physicality and movement based theatre in Ireland.

ISBN 78-1-904505-59-4 €25

Irish Drama: Local and Global Perspectives

Edited by Nicholas Grene and Patrick Lonergan

Since the late 1970s there has been a marked internationalization of Irish drama, with individual plays, playwrights, and theatrical companies establishing newly global reputations. This book reflects upon these developments, drawing together leading scholars and playwrights to consider the consequences that arise when Irish theatre travels abroad.

Contributors: Chris Morash, Martine Pelletier, José Lanters, Richard Cave, James Moran, Werner Huber, Rhona Trench, Christopher Murray, Ursula Rani Sarma, Jesse Weaver, Enda Walsh, Elizabeth Kuti

ISBN 78-1-904505-63-1 €20

What Shakespeare Stole From Rome

Edited by Brian Arkins

What Shakespeare Stole From Rome analyses the multiple ways Shakespeare used material from Roman history and Latin poetry in his plays and poems. From the history of the Roman Republic to the tragedies of Seneca; from the Comedies of Platus to Ovid's poetry; this enlightening book examines the important influence of Rome and Greece on Shakespeare's work.

ISBN 78-1-904505-58-7 €20

Polite Forms

Harry White

Polite Forms is a sequence of poems that meditates on family life, remembering and reimagining scenes from childhood and adolescence through the formal composure of the sonnet, so that the uniformity of this framing device promotes a tension. Throughout the collection there is a constant preoccupation with the difference between actual remembrance and the illumination or meaning which poetry can afford. Some of the poems 'rewind the tapes of childhood' across two or three generations, and all of them are akin to pictures at an exhibition which survey individual impressions of childhood and parenthood in a thematically continuous series of portraits drawn from life. This is his first collection of poetry.

Harry White is Professor of Music at University College Dublin.

ISBN 78-1-904505-55-6 €10

Ibsen and Chekhov on the Irish Stage

Edited by Ros Dixon and Irina Ruppo Malone

Ibsen and Chekhov on the Irish Stage presents articles on the theories of translation and adaptation, new insights on the work of Brian Friel, Frank McGuinness, Thomas Kilroy, and Tom Murphy, historical analyses of theatrical productions during the Irish Revival, interviews with contemporary theatre directors, and a round-table discussion with the playwrights, Michael West and Thomas Kilroy.

Ibsen and Chekhov on the Irish Stage challenges the notion that a country's dramatic tradition develops in cultural isolation. It uncovers connections between past productions of plays by Ibsen and Chekhov and contemporary literary adaptations of their works by Irish playwrights, demonstrating the significance of international influence for the formation of national canon.

ISBN 78-1-904505-57-0 €20

Tom Swift Selected Plays

With an introduction by Peter Crawley.

The inaugural production of Performance Corporation in 2002 matched Voltaire's withering assault against the doctrine of optimism with a playful aesthetic and endlessly inventive stagecraft.

Each play in this collection was originally staged by the Performance Corporation and though Swift has explored different avenues ever since, such playfulness is a constant. The writing is precise, but leaves room for the discoveries of rehearsals, the flesh of the theatre. All plays are blueprints for performance, but several of these scripts – many of which are site-specific and all of them slyly topical – are documents for something unrepeatable.

ISBN 78-1-904505-56-3 €20

Synge and His Influences: Centenary Essays from the Synge Summer School

Edited by Patrick Lonergan

The year 2009 was the centenary of the death of John Millington Synge, one of the world's great dramatists. To mark the occasion, this book gathers essays by leading scholars of Irish drama, aiming to explore the writers and movements that shaped Synge, and to consider his enduring legacies. Essays discuss Synge's work in its Irish, European and world contexts – showing his engagement not just with the Irish literary revival but with European politics and culture too. The book also explores Synge's influence on later writers: Irish dramatists such as Brian Friel, Tom Murphy and Marina Carr, as well as international writers like Mustapha Matura and Erisa Kironde. It also considers Synge's place in Ireland today, revealing how *The Playboy of the Western World* has helped to shape Ireland's responses to globalisation and multiculturalism, in celebrated productions by the Abbey Theatre, Druid Theatre, and Pan Pan Theatre Company.

Contributors include Ann Saddlemyer, Ben Levitas, Mary Burke, Paige Reynolds, Eilís Ní Dhuibhne, Mark Phelan, Shaun Richards, Ondřej Pilný, Richard Pine, Alexandra Poulain, Emilie Pine, Melissa Sihra, Sara Keating, Bisi Adigun, Adrian Frazier and Anthony Roche.

ISBN 78-1-904505-50-1 €20.00

Constellations - The Life and Music of John Buckley

Benjamin Dwyer

Benjamin Dwyer provides a long overdue assessment of one of Ireland's most prolific composers of the last decades. He looks at John Buckley's music in the context of his biography and Irish cultural life. This is no hagiography but a critical assessment of Buckley's work, his roots and aesthetics. While looking closely at several of Buckley's compositions, the book is written in a comprehensible style that makes it easily accessible to anybody interested in Irish musical and cultural history.   *Wolfgang Marx*

As well as providing a very readable and comprehensive study of the life and music of John Buckley, Constellations also offers an up-to-date and informative catalogue of compositions, a complete discography, translations of set texts and the full libretto of his chamber opera, making this book an essential guide for both students and professional scholars alike.

ISBN 78-1-904505-52-5 €20.00

'Because We Are Poor': Irish Theatre in the 1990s

Victor Merriman

"Victor Merriman's work on Irish theatre is in the vanguard of a whole new paradigm in Irish theatre scholarship, one that is not content to contemplate monuments of past or present achievement, but for which the theatre is a lens that makes visible the hidden malaises in Irish society. That he has been able to do so by focusing on a period when so much else in Irish culture conspired to hide those problems is only testimony to the considerable power of his critical scrutiny." Chris Morash, NUI Maynooth.

ISBN 78-1-904505-51-8 €20.00

Buffoonery and Easy Sentiment':
Popular Irish Plays in the Decade Prior to the Opening of The Abbey Theatre

Christopher Fitz-Simon

In this fascinating reappraisal of the non-literary drama of the late 19th - early 20th century, Christopher Fitz-Simon discloses a unique world of plays, players and producers in metropolitan theatres in Ireland and other countries where Ireland was viewed as a source of extraordinary topics at once contemporary and comfortably remote: revolution, eviction, famine, agrarian agitation, political assassination.

The form was the fashionable one of melodrama, yet Irish melodrama was of a particular kind replete with hidden messages, and the language was far more allusive, colourful and entertaining than that of its English equivalent.

ISBN 78-1-9045505-49-5 €20.00

The Theatre of Tom Mac Intyre: 'Strays from the ether'

Eds. Bernadette Sweeney and Marie Kelly

This long overdue anthology captures the soul of Mac Intyre's dramatic canon – its ethereal qualities, its extraordinary diversity, its emphasis on the poetic and on performance – in an extensive range of visual, journalistic and scholarly contributions from writers, theatre practitioners.

ISBN 78-1-904505-46-4 €25

Irish Appropriation Of Greek Tragedy

Brian Arkins

This book presents an analysis of more than 30 plays written by Irish dramatists and poets that are based on the tragedies of Sophocles, Euripides and Aeschylus. These plays proceed from the time of Yeats and Synge through MacNeice and the Longfords on to many of today's leading writers.

ISBN 78-1-904505-47-1 €20

Alive in Time: The Enduring Drama of Tom Murphy

Ed. Christopher Murray

Almost 50 years after he first hit the headlines as Ireland's most challenging playwright, the 'angry young man' of those times Tom Murphy still commands his place at the pinnacle of Irish theatre. Here 17 new essays by prominent critics and academics, with an introduction by Christopher Murray, survey Murphy's dramatic oeuvre in a concerted attempt to define his greatness and enduring appeal, making this book a significant study of a unique genius.

ISBN 78-1-904505-45-7 €25

Performing Violence in Contemporary Ireland

Edited by Lisa Fitzpatrick

This interdisciplinary collection of fifteen new essays by scholars of theatre, Irish studies, music, design and politics explores aspects of the performance of violence in contemporary Ireland. With chapters on the work of playwrights Martin McDonagh, Martin Lynch, Conor McPherson and Gary Mitchell, on Republican commemorations and the 90th anniversary ceremonies for the Battle of the Somme and the Easter Rising, this book aims to contribute to the ongoing international debate on the performance of violence in contemporary societies.

ISBN 78-1-904505-44-0 €20

Deviant Acts: Essays on Queer Performance

Ed. David Cregan

This book contains an exciting collection of essays focusing on a variety of alternative performances happening in contemporary Ireland. While it highlights the particular representations of gay and lesbian identity it also brings to light how diversity has always been a part of Irish culture and is, in fact, shaping what it means to be Irish today.

ISBN 978-1-904505-42-6 €20

Plays and Controversies: Abbey Theatre Diaries 2000-2005

Ben Barnes

In diaries covering the period of his artistic directorship of the Abbey, Ben Barnes offers a frank, honest, and probing account of a much commented upon and controversial period in the history of the national theatre. These diaries also provide fascinating personal insights into the day-to-day pressures, joys, and frustrations of running one of Ireland's most iconic institutions.

ISBN 78-1-904505-38-9 €25

Interactions: Dublin Theatre Festival 1957-2007. Irish Theatrical Diaspora Series: 3

Eds. Nicholas Grene and Patrick Lonergan with Lilian Chambers

For over 50 years the Dublin Theatre Festival has been one of Ireland's most important cultural events, bringing countless new Irish plays to the world stage, while introducing Irish audiences to the most important international theatre companies and artists. Interactions explores and celebrates the achievements of the renowned Festival since 1957 and includes specially commissioned memoirs from past organizers, offering a unique perspective on the controversies and successes that have marked the event's history. An especially valuable feature of the volume, also, is a complete listing of the shows that have appeared at the Festival from 1957 to 2008.

ISBN 78-1-904505-36-5 €20

Synge: A Celebration

Edited by Colm Tóibín

A collection of essays by some of Ireland's most creative writers on the work of John Millington Synge, featuring Sebastian Barry, Marina Carr, Anthony Cronin, Roddy Doyle, Anne Enright, Hugo Hamilton, Joseph O'Connor, Mary O'Malley, Fintan O'Toole, Colm Toibin, Vincent Woods.

ISBN 978-1-904505-14-3 €15